Mr. Mark V. Hildebrand
852 Alderbrook Lane
Cupertino, CA 95014

D0435713

talking right

Talking Right

How Conservatives Turned Liberalism Into
a Tax-Raising, Latte-Drinking, Sushi-Eating,
Volvo-Driving, *New York Times*-Reading,
Body-Piercing, Hollywood-Loving,
Left-Wing Freak Show

Geoffrey Nunberg

PublicAffairs
new york

Published in the United States by PublicAffairs™,
a member of the Perseus Books Group.

Library of Congress Cataloging-in-Publication Data

Nunberg, Geoffrey, 1945-

Talking right: how conservatives turned liberalism into a tax-raising, latte-drinking,
sushi-eating, Volvo-driving, New York Times-reading, body-piercing,
Hollywood-loving, left-wing freak show / Geoffrey Nunberg.

cm.

Includes index.

ISBN–13: 978-1-58648-386-9

ISBN–10: 1-58648-386-2

1. English-language—Political aspects—United States. 2. English-language—Social
aspects—United States. 3. English-language—United States—Semantics. 4. English
language—United States—Usage. 5. Political science—Terminology. I. Title.

PE2809.N87 2006

306.440973—dc22

2006043788

First Edition

10 9 8 7 6 5 4 3 2 1

Contents

Contents

Introduction

Signs and symbols, language, are the means of
communication by which a fraternally shared experience is
ushered in and sustained. But conversation has a vital import
lacking in the fixed and frozen words of written speech. . . .
That and only that gives reality to public opinion.
—*John Dewey, The Public and Its Problems, 1927*

a re the Democrats simply tone deaf? That impression was hard to escape when the party floated a new slogan in the fall of 2005 that was aimed at the 2006 midterm elections: "Together, America can do better." Or more accurately, a newly augmented slogan—in 2004, John Kerry had used "America can do better," without the "together" part. According to the congressional newspaper *The Hill*, Democrats had chosen the slogan to address the party's "messaging problems" after testing it in focus groups along with a number of alternatives. "We know the majority of people agree with us on the issues," one Democrat was quoted as saying, "but this effort is an acknowledgment that we need to communicate better."

The response to the slogan was, to put it mildly, tepid. The *Washington Post* reported that Democratic governors were scoffing at it, and the liberal commentators excoriated it. "Pathetic," said Hendrik Hertzberg in the *New Yorker*. And the *Los Angeles Times*'s Rosa Brooks concurred: "'You can do better' is what you say to a dim child whose grades were even worse than expected. Is this really the Democrats' message to the nation: that we don't need to be quite as pathetic as we now are?" The blogger Wonkette was characteristically caustic: "Now we know where the Democrats stand," she said. "They stand for betterness." And indeed, the slogan seemed to epitomize Democrats' inability to come up with an overarching theme other than "Listen, anybody would be an improvement over this bunch of bozos." (Wonkette mused that the rejected slogans probably included "You Could Do Worse," "It's Not Like There's a Third Party," and "Sorry About That Kerry Thing.")

Given the slogan's resounding vacuity, it might seem like piling on to point out that it's ungrammatical in the bargain, with the *together* sitting uncomfortably with the singular *America*. Saying "Together, America can do better" is a bit like saying "Together, the North won the Civil War"— you know what it's supposed to mean, but you have to do a little mental stutter-step to get there. It's clearly a sentence written by a committee: you can tell that one faction wanted to go with "America can do better" while another favored "Together, we can do better" to get the unity theme in there, so they decided to split the difference. Of course, faulty syntax by itself has never been an impediment to successful advertising. But the slogan could stand in, only a little unfairly, for the Democrats' general failure to get their communicative act together, right down to an inability to get their adverbs and subjects to agree.

What makes the party's choice of slogan ironic—or not to mince words, downright depressing—is that the Democrats have been struggling with their "messaging problem" for some time now. I first became involved in those efforts in the spring of 2003, when Senator Byron Dorgan invited three linguists, George Lakoff, Deborah Tannen, and me, to make a panel presentation to the Democratic Senate caucus on "Framing Policy Issues to Enhance Public Understanding," with the aim of helping the Democrats counter the Republicans' success in using language to advance and often obscure their agenda. We talked about "issue framing" and linguistic stereotyping, and the senators seemed receptive and clearly concerned about the problems. And despite that lame slogan, it's clear the Democrats have been trying in their hugger-mugger fashion to respond to Republican rhetoric more assertively.

But as I was reflecting afterward on those discussions, it struck me that the Democrats haven't fully grasped how deep their linguistic problems go, or how they directly reflect the Democrats' inability to tell a coherent story about themselves (I mean over and above observing tautologically that they aren't Republicans). This book shows how that failure has had consequences that go beyond anything that improved framing or better slogans could remedy. The right's most notable linguistic achievement isn't its skill in coining distracting catchphrases, but its success in capturing the language of everyday political discussion.

talk to most people about "political language" and they're likely to think of the language that politicians and pundits use when they're trying to rouse public support for particular candidates and policies. Most of the books and articles on political rhetoric concentrate on the language of speeches and public pronouncements, rather than the language that ordinary people use when they are talking about political topics—not surprising, since until recently those were the only records of political language available, and scholars naturally congregate where the light is. But while the language of politicians and pundits is ultimately aimed at persuading people to act in certain ways, it can only get there by first persuading them to talk in certain ways. As John Dewey observed, it's only in private conversation that political opinion crystallizes, as people absorb the words they read or hear from on high and incorporate the ideas they stand for into the stories they tell about politics and their lives. Language is a kind of informal plebiscite: when we adopt a new word or alter the usage of an old one, we're casting a voice vote for a particular point of view.

Until a few years ago, you could only observe those shifts in language use in an anecdotal, Andy Rooney sort of way—"Have you noticed how everybody seems to be talking about *values* these days?" Or what's only slightly better, you could listen to the way a handful of people talked about politics in focus groups, without any real sense of how typical their language was. Now it's possible to date and measure those shifts in language, thanks to the Web, the online discussion groups, and all the databases of press stories and broadcast transcripts. It's true that those tools weren't designed with the aim of gauging public opinion, the way political polls and surveys are. As scientific instruments go, they're highly imperfect: they ignore distinctions of meaning, their counts can be inaccurate, and they're not necessarily representative of the language that people use when they're kicking around political issues with their co-workers or at the breakfast table.

But whatever their limitations, the tools allow us to examine how words are being used by both the press and the general population, and to measure changes in their popularity and shifts in their meaning. Needless to say, these methods have transformed the way we word wonks come at our subject. In the Victorian age, it took a small army of volunteer readers twenty years to amass the 3.5 million citation slips illustrating the usage of all the words in the English vocabulary that were used to prepare the first edition of the *Oxford English Dictionary*. These days it takes Google just half a second to report that it gets 6.8 million hits for the single phrase *liberal media* (though you're best off taking the exact figure a bit cautiously).* And it doesn't take much longer than that to track the way *class warfare* waxes and wanes in the press and the online discussion groups according to the political climate, or to determine whether conservative or liberal writers are more likely to use the word *redneck*.

As a window on public opinion, language can hardly take the place of polls and surveys. Language comes at the world from a different angle, more oblique but in its own way just as telling, if you read it right. The appearance of new phrases like "the liberal mindset" and "hidden agenda"; the shifting meanings of *elite, liberal, government,* or *patriot*; or even the fact that conservatives tend to say "you liberals" a lot more than liberals say "you conservatives"—all these things testify to the way political attitudes are embedded in the words that people use to express them.

It's only when you look at those patterns of usage that you discover how deep the Democrats' linguistic problems go. Over recent decades, the left has lost the battle for the language itself. When we talk about

---

* In a note at the end of this book, I discuss some of the complications and problems in using search engines and press databases to measure word frequencies.

politics nowadays—and by "we" I mean progressives and liberals as well as conservatives and people in the center—we can't help using language that embodies the worldview of the right.

The challenge facing liberals and Democrats is to recapture that ordinary language. That's what this book is about.

chapter one

A Loss for Words

I'm a Democrat man, I'm a Democrat man.
Please, please don't be no fool no more.
—*John Lee Hooker, "Democrat Man"*

every time the right makes new political gains—which is to say, pretty regularly over the past quarter century—Democrats repeat the need to find "fresh language" to make their case. So there was nothing novel in the reactions to the Democrats' presidential and congressional setbacks in 2004, particularly when exit polls seemed to suggest that the Republicans' victory was due to their strength among voters concerned about "moral values." "We've got to start talking to those people in red states with a language that resonates with them," said the Democratic National Committee chairman, Terry McAuliffe. The *Washington Post*'s E. J. Dionne pointed to the Democrats' need "to restore the language of values to the party's rhetoric." The syndicated columnist Ellen Goodman complained that "the entire moral vocabulary is now a wholly owned language of the religious right" and charged progressives with being "tongue-tied in talking about values"—like others, she cited the linguist George Lakoff's *Moral Politics* as a blueprint for progressive linguistic renewal.

You can see why Democrats would look to language to explain their electoral failures. Ever since the Republicans first began to woo Southern and working-class voters during the Nixon years, the decisive factor in American politics has been voters' apparent willingness to subordinate substantive interests to symbolic ones. In poll after poll, a majority of middle-class voters acknowledge that the Democrats would do a better job on most of the issues that affect their daily lives, from Social Security and taxes to the environment and education. But when it comes to the crunch, a significant number of voters seem to ignore their own best interests and make their choices on the basis of patriotic appeals and cultural issues, only to be rewarded with policies that favor the rich and powerful at their expense. How could the right get away with that, Democrats ask, unless the Republicans have been turning voters' heads with a snappy line of patter? If voters can't see where their interests lie, it must be because the Democrats aren't telling their story well enough.

The question is, what exactly does "fresh language" entail? For a lot of people on the left, it's a question of better "issue framing," usually just a dignified-sounding name for spin. As the story goes, the Democrats have to coin more evocative metaphors, catchphrases, and taglines to drive home the parties' differences on domestic issues and neutralize the right's advantages on "moral values." And there's no question Democrats could use help in this area. When you listen to the language of modern politics, the right seems to have all the best lines—"compassionate conservatism," "the culture of life," "Clear Skies," "Healthy Forests," "No Child Left Behind," "the ownership society," "partial birth abortion," "the death tax." Meanwhile, the best the Democrats can come up with is wonky mouthfuls like "Social Security lockbox" and "single-payer." As Joe Klein has said, lousy bumper stickers are a chronic Democratic woe.

The tendency to think of the left's linguistic problems in terms of catchphrases and slogans reflects a widespread understanding of how language shapes public opinion—the idea that the right choice of words can trigger associations at a deep, subconscious level that will winningly frame a policy or a brand in the public's mind. It's the assumption that has built a cottage industry of corporate language consultants who offer to contrive strings of syllables that will make for instant brand identification or a successful IPO. In a sense, this is just a reprise of an antique faith in the magical power of words, except that nowadays the magic is mediated by the scientific apparatus of focus groups, handheld instant-response dials, computer-generated word lists and frequent invocations of words like *linguistic* and *neuro-*.

That picture of the workings of political language has made a media darling of the pudgy, boyish Republican wordsmith Frank Luntz, who's credited with getting the Republicans to adopt phrases like "opportunity scholarships" for vouchers and "climate change" for global warming. Luntz's achievements have become so legendary that he's often given credit for introducing turns of phrase that have actually been part of the political lexicon for decades, in something like the way every political witticism is sooner or later attributed to Will Rogers or Winston Churchill.*

Luntz's influence became particularly evident in 2003, when the Environmental Working Group provided the press with a confidential memo he'd written after George W. Bush's "arsenic in the water" gaffe early in his first term. (Or, probably more accurately, a "confidential" memo—Luntz's advisories wind up in the press with such regularity that there's little doubt he is his own mole.) The memo offered suggestions for ameliorating the negative perception of Republicans' environmental policies—use "common-sense solutions" or "balanced approaches" in place of "rollbacks" and "deregulation," talk about "climate change" rather than "global warming," stress the need for "sound science," and make frequent use of words like *cleaner*, *safer*, and *healthier*. By the time the memo was made public, a lot of that language had already worked its way into Republican speeches, paving the way for Bush administration initiatives with names like Clear Skies and Healthy Forests.

Luntz has an undeniable gift for concocting phrases and a genius for self-promotion, and he has managed to persuade a lot of people that he has reduced the art of sloganeering to a science, often suggesting that his choice of words is governed by arcane linguistic rules. In 2000, the *New*

* Luntz is also given credit for coming up with the term *death tax* for the estate tax, but that was coined in the Gingrich period by Jack Faris of the National Federation of Independent Business ("In Two Parties' War of Words, Shibboleths Emerge as a Clear Winner," *New York Times*, April 27, 2001).

Yorker ran a flattering profile of Luntz by Nicholas Lemann that was called "The Word Lab," and subtitled "The Mad Science Behind What the Candidates Say." Lemann quoted Luntz as saying that "words starting with an 'r' or ending with an '-ity' are good—hence 'reform' and 'accountability' work and 'responsibility' really works." (You think of Walter Matthau playing the vaudeville comedian Willie Clark in Neil Simon's *The Sunshine Boys:* "You want to know what's funny? Words that begin with 'k' are funny.") It sounds impressive, until you realize that according to that principle, a successful slogan for the Republicans would be "Rapacity, Rascality, and Rigidity."

In fact, saying that what Luntz does is not exactly science gives "not exactly" a bad name. But then, Luntz certainly isn't the only language guru who steeps his spiel in snake oil. And in any case, what matters is whether the language they come up with is effective, not whether there's any real science behind it. After all, the Republicans didn't need focus groups to come up with "a chicken in every pot, a car in every garage" back in 1928—or for that matter, with the less successful "Prosperity is just around the corner" in 1932.

Still, it's Luntz's work that Democrats usually have in mind when they talk about the need to "reframe the issues"—why shouldn't the Democrats have a word lab of their own? Shortly after the election, the Third Way organization, formed by centrist Senate Democrats such as Evan Bayh, Thomas Carper, and Blanche Lincoln, announced plans to sponsor polling that would help Democrats find more effective political language to advertise their policies, citing the Republicans' apparent success in using "death tax" to describe the estate tax.

It's not surprising that Democrats tend to wax apoplectic over the blatant deceptiveness of some Republican phraseology. "The Clear Skies bill is one of those Orwellian names you pull out of the sky, slap it onto something," John Kerry charged during the second 2004 presidential debate, and *Orwellian* seems to be always in the air when Democrats talk about Luntz—Google turns up over four thousand Web pages that pair the word with Luntz's name. But that in itself suggests the limitations of this language. To describe a phrase as Orwellian implies that it wears its misdirection on its sleeve. When people hear a phrase like "No Child

10

Left Behind" or "the ownership society," they usually have a pretty good sense that somebody's trying to put the best face on something.

True, sometimes a bit of linguistic sleight of hand can pass under the radar, particularly when the public is hazy on the details of the program it's attached to. Republicans had success in talking about "the marriage penalty," for example. And *death tax* sounds a lot more ominous than *estate tax*, not just because it links the two awful certainties of existence but because the tax applies to so few estates that most people had no idea it existed before the Republicans raised the issue. The irony of *death tax* is that a duty that affects a handful of Americans has the potential of scaring everyone. Yet even then, the use of that phrase in the wording of questions in the 2002 National Election Survey increased support for estate tax repeal by only a few percentage points.

Indeed, the language that Luntz and the other wordsmiths of the right have contrived hasn't actually brought many voters over to the Republicans' positions on issues like education, the environment, and the economy. But that doesn't mean the language serves no purpose—it can help the Republicans merely by allaying public concerns about their insensitivity to those issues, so that people can go ahead and vote for them on grounds like national security or moral values. In his memo on the environment, in fact, Luntz himself admits that his linguistic suggestions are aimed as much at deflecting criticism as at winning supporters: "The first (and most important) step to neutralizing the problem and eventually bringing the public around to your point of view on the environment is to convince them of your *sincerity* and *concern*. Any discussion of the environment has to be grounded in an effort to reassure a skeptical public that you care about the environment for its own sake—that your intentions are strictly honorable."

That's what "compassionate conservatism" comes down to, in the end—paying lip service where lip service is due. We've come a long way since the time when Spiro Agnew could dismiss environmental concerns by saying, "If you've seen one tree, you've seen them all." And after the public rejected the militant conservative rhetoric of Newt Gingrich's Contract with America in the early 1990s, Republicans came to the realization that the public was suspicious of confrontational language, a point that the sociologist Alan Wolfe documented in *One Nation, After All*, a far-reaching survey of middle-class American moral attitudes. By the 1990s, many of the values that had been liberal rallying cries of the 1960s and 1970s—equal opportunity, tolerance for diversity, and concern for the environment, for example—had become part of the fabric of received American morality. So Republicans began to use expressions like *inclusive, color-blind, hate speech,* and *environmental sensitivity,* though often in ways that altered—or sometimes, contradicted—their original meanings.* Used defensively, those phrases blur the image of the party as "in the pockets of corporate fat cats who rub their hands together and chuckle as they plot to pollute America for fun and profit," as Luntz put it.

But names and slogans can be overrated as tools for building popular support for a policy or program, particularly when the public already has some familiarity with the issues. Despite Bush's incessant invocations of "the ownership society," the public has been distinctly cool to his proposals for privatizing Social Security, and those opinions didn't change when the Republicans substituted "personal accounts" for "private accounts" after the latter turned out not to poll well. It's true that the public's reaction was sharpened by the Democrats' insistent use of "private" and "privatization," but those labels worked because they squared with the public's perception of the issue. People may not have had a clear understanding of the president's proposals, but they knew that the Republicans and the Wall Street money managers weren't the ones they trusted to look after their retirement funds.

a fair number of Democrats see the surge of interest in reframing, messaging, and rebranding as a blind alley. The dissatisfaction began to bubble to the surface in the spring of 2004 in a number of critiques directed at George Lakoff's growing influence. What reframing comes down to, said the political analyst Ruy Teixeira, is merely "a

* "The President believes the senator is an inclusive man," Bush's press secretary Ari Fleischer said after Senator Rick Santorum made remarks that seemed to equate homosexuality with incest and polygamy.

reshuffling of tired old rhetorical clichés [which] shows no signs of being any more politically effective than the Democrats' previous unframed appeals." In a May 2005 piece in the *Atlantic* called "It Isn't the Message, Stupid," Josh Green ridiculed the idea that the Democratic Party could be revived "with snazzier packaging and a new sales pitch." And in another *Atlantic* article, Marc Cooper dismissed Lakoff's work as "neuroscientific hooey," which amounted to assuming that "reframing American politics according to liberal values—in essence rewiring our collective circuitry—is but a matter of simple wordplay."

Lakoff is fair game for some of these criticisms. His brand of linguistics is far from hooey, but it doesn't offer any magical insights into crafting effective political language. When it comes to the crunch, in fact, Lakoff is not in Luntz's class as a phrase-maker. His rewording proposals can sound like send-ups of PC euphemisms. Recasting trial lawyers as "public protection attorneys" and taxes as "membership fees" isn't likely to assuage the public's aversion to either. And more seriously still, his analysis of the liberal-conservative division tends to reinforce the political stereotypes of a nation riven by deep cultural differences, which plays nicely into the right's hands.

But Lakoff also has a lot of shrewd things to say about the use of political language. The real problem here is the wishfulness with which a lot of liberals have taken to "reframing" as an easy palliative for the Democrats' problems. Too many Democrats are smitten with what William Galston and Elaine C. Kamarck have called the Myth of Language—"the thesis that the problem with the Democratic Party is not what it believes, but rather how it speaks." As Marc Cooper puts it, that's the delusion of "a stratum of despairing liberals who just can't believe how their commonsense message has been misunderstood by the eternally deceived masses." If people perceive that the Democrats are philosophically adrift, it isn't simply because the party hasn't found the right sales pitch: what we have here is more than just a failure to communicate. In the Democrats' "Olympian state of denial," as Josh Green observes, they've been diverted "from a truth that ought to be perfectly clear: rather than being misunderstood, they were understood all too well."

There's no question that the Democrats' problems go beyond the words they use. As advertisers know, names and slogans can't transform public perceptions if they don't evoke a compelling story. Listening to some of the talk about reframing and rebranding, you might recall General Motors' efforts to rescue the moribund Oldsmobile line in the 1990s, as the company desperately launched new models with names like the Alero, Achieva, and Ciera. In the end, it came to nothing, and GM ultimately had to retire the line. They kept saying, "This is not your father's Oldsmobile," but everybody could see that's exactly what it was.

What the Democrats need, a lot of people say, is not new language but new ideas, on the theory that if you build it, they will come. That's the perception that has led to the recent vogue for explaining the Republicans' success by pointing to their ability to spin "better narratives" than the Democrats. Democratic pollster Stanley Greenberg says that the Republicans had "a narrative that motivated their voters," and Senator Barack Obama is calling for a "new narrative" for the Democrats. Thomas Frank, the author of *What's the Matter with Kansas?* says that "Conservatives have captured the narrative of social class." And in an April 2005 piece in the *New Republic* called "Story Time," Robert Reich argues that "Republicans have mastered the art of political narrative and, in doing so, exiled Democrats from politics itself."

Like "framing," "narrative" manages to be evocative without being specific. At the most basic level, it implies that the Democrats need to weave their positions together in a more coherent story, rather than simply enumerating a bunch of policy positions. As Bill Clinton's adviser James Carville put it: "They produce a narrative, we produce a litany." There's an undeniable truth to this observation. People may be sympathetic to the Democrats' positions on particular issues like ANWAR drilling or Social Security privatization, but those don't add up to a coherent brand image.

But people have different ideas about what it means for the Democrats to have a "narrative." For Robert Reich, it implies the need to evoke basic American myths and archetypes, according to a kind of political *Golden Bough*. Reich argues that the Democrats have to anchor their appeal in what he identifies as four "essential American stories": The Triumphant

Individual, The Benevolent Community (neighbors rolling up their sleeves for the common good), The Mob at the Gates (the United States as "a beacon light of virtue" in a world threatened by barbarian forces), and The Rot at the Top ("the malevolence of powerful elites"). For the *American Prospect*'s Robert Kuttner, it's a question of rediscovering the Democrats' populist roots: as Robert Kuttner says, "It's still a tale of two Americas, and Democrats need to tell it more convincingly."

For centrists, on the other hand, "having a narrative" tends to be a matter of making an accommodation, real or rhetorical, to some of the concerns of middle-American voters. According to Brad Carson, the Democratic representative who ran a surprisingly strong Senate race in Oklahoma in 2004, Democrats can win votes in red states only if they position themselves as a party of reform and "move away from any hope of bringing peace to irreconcilable moral disputes. Instead, Democrats should create a meta-message, one based on hope, values, and strength, that can be offered to voters everywhere." And Will Marshall, of the centrist Progressive Policy Institute, insists that Democrats must be "comfortable using the language of faith" with heartland voters, so as to dispel the idea that "bicoastal elites look down on them as Bible-thumping primitives."

As varied as they are, those proposals all have the virtue of acknowledging that the Democrats' communication problems go deeper than anything that can be implemented simply by doing a global search-and-replace to substitute new phraseology for old. But while a lot of people recognize that the party needs more than a mere shift in vocabulary, few have understood how deep and pervasive the problem is. The fact is that "having a narrative" involves something more than fashioning new campaign themes, even broadly coordinated ones—it means making that story part of the fabric of American political discourse. And while this isn't chiefly a matter of words, words matter to it. A large part of the Republicans' successes over the past thirty years or so is attributable to their ability to change the political subject—diverting resentments that have their roots in economic inequalities to debates over "values," making programs that chiefly benefit the wealthy sound like they're aimed at benefiting the middle class, turning *government* into a term of abuse, and making reservations about the direction of American foreign policy sound like signs of weakness of purpose or questionable loyalty. The right couldn't have achieved all of that except by bending the meanings of words to their purposes and by getting Americans to accept those new meanings.

That achievement isn't merely a question of coining effective slogans and catchphrases. It reaches deep into the language itself, coloring the meanings of the ordinary words that people invoke when they're chewing over political questions. In fact, the best way to get a real sense of the displacement of the linguistic center of gravity is to listen not to Fox News, Rush Limbaugh, or White House speeches, but to the so-called liberal media (the SCLM, as Eric Alterman conveniently abbreviates the phrase). Look at the way words like *values*, *elite*, and *liberal* are used in the *New York Times*, the *Washington Post* or on CNN—or for that matter, in the discussion groups on the Web—and you can see how far political attitudes have shifted to the right over the past thirty years.

a conservative reader might ask why I've concentrated here on the language of the right. Don't liberals color their language in tendentious or misleading ways as well? You bet they do, and I'll occasionally remark on this, particularly when it's too irresistible to ignore. But I'm interested here not so much in the ways liberals and conservatives talk as in the marks that they leave on the core vocabulary of American political discourse. People are always using words in ways that presuppose a certain point of view, but the vast majority of those usages fade away as soon as they're uttered, and of the remainder, few of them circulate outside the partisan circle that the speaker belongs to. Republicans have been referring to "the Democrat Party" for around eighty years, but that name has never been adopted by the media or entered the ordinary language, whereas *reverse discrimination* was first used in the early 1960s by opponents of affirmative hiring and housing programs and was very rapidly drawn into the language.

Up to a generation ago, liberalism had a huge effect on the language. But the great shifts in usage that it brought about—most importantly in the language of race and gender—were largely accomplished in the 1960s and 1970s. By now, for example, there aren't a lot of businessmen in any part of the country who will unselfconsciously use "my girl" to refer to their female secretaries (not many still call them secretaries, either). And the language of race has been transformed to the point where remarks made just a few decades ago seem unimaginably condescending now. In a speech at Berkeley in 1966, Robert Kennedy said, "Some of us say the Negro has made great progress—which is true—and that he should be satisfied and patient—which is neither true nor realistic." These days, no public figure would use *Negro,* or prefix any racial or ethnic term with that reductive *the*, which turns a group into an anthropological specimen. And most would try to find a way around that awkward generic *he* in the bargain.

One indication of liberals' success in embedding their language in the American lexicon is that conservatives have not only adopted it, but have tried to turn some of it against liberals—for example, by invoking *colorblind* as a slogan in their efforts to do away with affirmative action. Still, it's hard to think of many terms that liberals have contributed over the past twenty-five years or so that have made their way into the vocabulary of American politics the way those earlier ones did. I'm not thinking of the odd slogan or catchphrase that has enjoyed a vogue, like "patient's bill of rights" or "It's the economy, stupid." I mean words that do the kind of work that *values* and *elite* have done for the right. Academic journals and conferences may still be bristling with the rebarbative political jargon of the left, but the only time you're likely to encounter it in the general media these days is when some conservative is poking fun at it.

Of course conservative media watchdogs are always pointing to this or that usage to prove the existence of liberal media bias. They hear it when a network refers to Bush's "domestic wiretapping" or when someone says that gas prices have reached a "record high" without noting that the figure has not been adjusted for inflation. And their hackles rise when they hear a report on Israel that mentions "cycle of violence," "peace process," or "occupied territories."* Well, there's no pleasing some people, but

---

* Those criticisms don't extend to Fox News, where those phrases have been uttered 799 times over the past five years.

even if you did believe that those expressions betray liberal bias, they don't reflect shifts in the language itself—the fact that a reporter says that gas prices are at "record high" doesn't mean that *record high* has been assigned a new, "liberal" meaning. And when critics of media bias do try to point to deeper linguistic regularities, like the media's alleged tendency to label conservatives more often than liberals, they invariably turn out to be dead wrong. Nowadays, it's the right that controls the basic language of politics.

In that sense, the challenge that Democrats and liberals face really is in part linguistic: they can't regain their political ascendancy except by either reclaiming the basic political vocabulary or replacing it with a new one. Whatever they come up with in the way of new and compelling ideas and a new sense of political purpose, they'll have a hard time packaging them so long as the right has its name all over the wrapping paper. That's not something that can be accomplished by speechwriters, press releases, or advertisements alone, particularly in a single election cycle or two. It took the right twenty-five years to achieve its control of American political discourse and it will take a while to win it back. But for starters, let me try to set aside some familiar but distracting assumptions about political language.

chapter two

The Shadow of Language

One notices, if one will trust one's eyes,
The shadow cast by language upon truth.
—*W. H. Auden, "Kairos and Logos"*

a s I drove around San Francisco during the 2004 election campaign, I kept seeing a bumper sticker that read "Orwell and Bush in 2004." It always struck me as a little unfair to Orwell—he has been turned into a writer like Horatio Alger, whose name is a synonym for the themes he wrote about. In the half century since Orwell's death, *Orwellian* has become the most widely used adjective derived from the name of a modern writer. It's more common than *Kafkaesque*, *Hemingwayesque*, and *Dickensian* put together; it even noses out the rival political reproach *Machiavellian*, which had a five-hundred-year head start. Along with the popularity of Orwell's other creation, *Newspeak*, it points to the chronic suspicion of language that has become a pervasive motif in American political life.

It's fair to say that there has never been an age that was so wary of the mischief and deception that political language can work. We've made the subject a part of the required curriculum—not many students manage to get through their educational careers without being assigned *1984* at some point. (The novel shows up every fall and spring in the Amazon.com list of fiction bestsellers, as high-school and college students

19

order the books on their English class reading lists.)* And "Politics and the English Language" has become not just the most widely read essay *about* the English language, but most likely *in* it as well.

Most people wouldn't see anything odd in that: the growing mistrust of political language seems a natural reaction to the growth of political double-talk and mendacity. After all, the greater the danger, the greater the vigilance: you expect people to become more alert to the dangers of burglary when the crime rate goes up. It isn't surprising that warnings about the treacherousness of political rhetoric have grown more insistent as governments have made more strenuous efforts to control public opinion. The complaints were already audible in the eighteenth century. When the Girondin minister Jean-Marie Roland tried to extenuate the murders of priests committed by revolutionary mobs in Paris in September 1792, Edmund Burke denounced him with words that could have been the model for Orwell's "Politics and the English Language":

> The whole compass of the language is tried to find sinonimies and circumlocutions for massacre and murder. Things are never called by their common names. Massacre is sometimes *agitation*, sometimes *effervescence*, sometimes *excess*; sometimes *too continued an exercise of a revolutionary power*.

Complaints like Burke's were heard throughout the nineteenth century, though they really didn't become a persistent political concern until World War I, when governments learned to exploit the full resources of the state to mobilize public opinion and the art of political and military euphemism came into its full modern flower. The mutinies among French troops in 1917 were described in dispatches as "acts of collective indiscipline," and the writers of the daily communiqués from the Western Front were instructed to use the phrase "brisk fighting" to describe any action in which more than 50 percent of a company was killed or wounded. That was when *propaganda* entered the everyday vocabulary.

---

* When I looked in February 2006, *1984* was at Amazon ranking 51 and *Animal Farm* was at 84. Orwell's *The Road to Wigan Pier* was at 24,579.

As one journalist who had been active in the American morale efforts noted: "Before 1914, 'propaganda' belonged only to literate vocabularies and possessed a reputable, dignified meaning. . . . Two years later the word had come into the vocabulary of peasants and ditchdiggers and had begun to acquire its miasmic aura."

Still, Orwell deserves credit for giving these complaints their modern form by evoking the specter of totalitarian states that used language not just to mask atrocities, but to make dissenting ideas literally unthinkable. In "Politics and the English Language," he wrote: "Political language— and with variations this is true of all political parties, from Conservatives to Anarchists—is designed to make lies sound truthful and murder respectable, and to give an appearance of solidity to pure wind." And as antifascism and anticommunism became prevailing themes in American politics, it was a natural step to put *1984* in the lesson plan as a warning that the abuse of language can lead ultimately to gulags and death camps.

What's curious is that Orwell's ideas about language have survived the regimes that originally inspired them. Newspeak may have been a plausible-sounding development in 1948, when totalitarian thought control seemed a real and even imminent possibility. But the collapse of communism revealed the bankruptcy not just of the Stalinist social experiment, but of its linguistic experiments as well. After seventy-five years of incessant propaganda, "socialist man" turned out to be a cynic who didn't even believe the train schedules.

Yet the terms *Newspeak* and *Orwellian* are as widely used today as they were twenty years ago. In fact, the words have become more powerful as their historical background has faded (nowadays, students tend to think of *1984*'s Oceania as just another fantastic dystopia like the worlds of *The Matrix* and *Blade Runner*). And whatever ideological significance Orwell's ideas about language may once have had, they're now accepted unquestionably by all sides, if rarely in the spirit of self-criticism that Orwell himself encouraged. People on the left hear Orwellian resonances in names like the USA PATRIOT Act or the Department of Homeland Security's Operation Liberty Shield, which authorized indefinite detention of asylum seekers from certain nations. People on the right hear them in "reproductive health services," "Office of Equality

Assurance," and "English Plus" for bilingual education. And just about everyone discerned an Orwellian note in the name of the Pentagon's Total Information Awareness project, which was aimed at mining a vast centralized database of personal information or patterns that might reveal terrorist activities.* It may be a matter of debate as to which of those terms are actually deceptive packaging and which are merely effective branding, but they share the picture of the way political language can deceive. And in our time people don't restrict their warnings about "Orwellian Newspeak" and the like to political language—you hear the same charges about advertising language, academic jargon, and corporate euphemisms like *head-count reduction* and *rightsizing*.

Whenever a belief about language is widely and uncritically accepted, from the condemnation of the double negative to the claims that Eskimo has hundreds of words for snow or that women talk more than men, it's a good bet it's doing some ideological work on the side. And there's surely something paradoxical in the very universality of those ideas about political language. When people describe language as Orwellian, it's usually with the implication that it's designed to mislead a credulous or uncritical public. In "Politics and the English Language," Orwell wrote that a "reduced state of consciousness [is] favorable to political conformity." And in 1944, he wondered at the Italians' apparent willingness to accept the absurdities broadcast on Mussolini's Fascist radio, like the claim that Britain was on the edge of collapse: "For quite long periods . . . people can remain undisturbed by obvious lies, either because they simply forget what is said from day to day or because they are under such a constant propaganda bombardment that they become anaesthetized to the whole business."

But on the face of things, the very prominence of Orwell's ideas about language seems to belie the idea of a public that's passive, gullible, or anaesthetized to propaganda and political euphemism. These days, even that elusive character "the man in the street" is likely to be skeptical of what he hears from politicians, whichever side they're on. The deceptiveness of political language is standard fare on talk radio and cable news,

---

* The name was ultimately changed to the Terrorist Information Awareness program, in an effort to reassure Americans who had nothing to hide.

not to mention the late-night talk-show monologues, *The Daily Show,* and the 650,000 Web sites that contain the term *Newspeak.* In our own time there are no proles, only consumers who are as adept at evaluating a political ad or a debate performance as a tire commercial. There may still be some people in America who take everything they hear from politicians and corporate spokespersons at face value, but it's doubtful whether they could field a basketball team.

That's the paradox of our attitudes about political language: each of us believes that we're inured to manipulation, but that everyone else in the room is susceptible to it. There's always an undercurrent of condescension when people describe some bit of language as Orwellian: "Mind you, I'm not fooled for an instant, but Joe Sixpack is likely to fall for it." When we picture the prison house of language, it's always from the outside looking in.

But as advertisers know well, no audience is easier to beguile than one that's smugly confident of its own sophistication. Officially, we like to pretend that we're a people who prize simplicity and directness and don't have the time or patience to bandy words. That's why we're always following *semantic* with words like *nit-picking* and *quibble,* with the implication that an excessive concern about language is merely a distraction from the things that really matter. Unfairly or no, the sentence that Bill Clinton will probably be most remembered for is the hairsplitting "It depends on what the meaning of 'is' is" that he delivered in answer to a grand jury question about his relations with Monica Lewinsky, which earned him derisory (if high-concept) epithets like "Deconstructionist-in-Chief" and "Existential Willie."

But we're also obsessed with the power of words. Not even the medievals of Pierre Abelard's age spent as much time as we do disputing and litigating meanings or chewing over the implications of symbols, labels, epithets, and titles. Do Web searches on "the A-word," "the B-word," and so on, and you'll come up with hundreds of terms, from atheism, AIDS, and abortion to Zionism and zoning, each standing in for a controversy that has been framed around some charged expression. And the same politicians who pooh-pooh "mere semantics" are ready to go to the mattresses over the difference between *insurgents* and *terrorists.*

In their own ways, though, both our skepticism about language and our faith in it are overdrawn. The euphemisms, misnomers, and obfuscations that fill political speech—call them "Orwellisms"—can be accomplices to deception, but they depend on our own willing complicity. One notable feature of Orwellisms is how transparently evasive they tend to be. *Ethnic cleansing, revenue enhancement, voluntary regulation, tree-density reduction, extra affirmative action*—phrases like those are up front about having something to hide. It may not be clear at first exactly what they're supposed to refer to, but you can tell right off that somebody's trying to put one by you—nobody is about to assume that those names were picked because they were the plainest and more direct ways of describing something. When we describe a phrase as Orwellian, we're usually making an aesthetic judgment as much as a moral one: it implies not that it's deceptive but that it's crudely or blatantly deceptive.

But even when we recognize those descriptions as misleading, we're willing to buy into them when it suits our purposes. In private, people ridicule the inanity of the corporate buzzwords they're required to parrot. Yet when they use those words, it isn't usually just a cynical accommodation of corporate management, but a sign of their willingness to be a team player. (If school songs weren't always a little stupid, singing along with them wouldn't convey the same sense of uncritical loyalty.) Or often a euphemism is a convenient way of holding an unpleasant reality at arm's length. People know perfectly well that expressions like *friendly fire, headcount reduction,* and *senior citizen* are just substitutes for more direct expressions, but even so, the names seem to keep the unpalatable facts of death and age at bay. As Orwell put it in condemning the use of the phrase *elimination of unreliable elements,* "Such phraseology is needed if one wants to name things without calling up mental pictures of them." That's why it's so important for us to believe that there really are people out there who hear this language with naive credulity. Imagining how our own language sounds in their ears, we can persuade ourselves to half believe it.

Yet even people who welcome the psychic cover that Orwellisms provide find it hard to sustain the cognitive dissonance that they require. That's why it's in the nature of expressions like those to lose their euphemistic character over time, like drapery that takes the form of the objects it was meant to cover. *Final solution* and *ethnic cleansing* began their lives as circumlocutions, but by now they're stamped with all the horror of the events they were supposed to palliate, and made all the more chilling by their pathetic failure to veil reality. And *collateral damage* may still be a deplorable circumlocution for civilian casualties, but no one is still likely to be misled into thinking it refers to damage to airstrips or fuel depots. (For that matter, *casualty* itself started out as a euphemism for the dead and wounded when it was first introduced around the time of the Crimean War—before that, the word referred simply to an accidental loss, the way it still does in the names of insurance companies.) And for the same reason, corporate buzzwords and political slogans and euphemisms tend to have a brief half-life. Not many politicians would try to get away with "revenue enhancement" as a name for tax increases anymore. And for every "Tippecanoe and Tyler too" and "A chicken in every pot," there are a dozen slogans like "Making Us Proud Again," "America Needs a Change," and "Prosperity for America's Families" that become Trivial Pursuit items before the next election cycle rolls around.*

e dmund Burke's complaint about the language of the French revolutionaries—"Massacre is sometimes *agitation*, sometimes *effervescence*, sometimes *excess* . . ."—was the first modern use of the formula that George Orwell later popularized as a way of objecting to political euphemism: "an X is called a Y." An ordinary, everyday term X is contrasted with its euphemistic equivalent "Y," which is always written in quotes or italics. The most famous modern examples are from Orwell's "Politics and the English Language": "Millions of peasants are robbed of their farms and sent trudging along the roads with no more than they can carry: this is called *transfer of population* or *rectification of frontiers*." But you can pull sentences like that one from any column or book objecting to the misleading uses of political or corporate language: "Layoffs

---

* Those were the slogans of Gerald Ford in 1976, Walter Mondale in 1984, and Al Gore in 2000.

are called *head-count reductions*"; "The aged are described as *senior citizens*"; "Outsourcing torture is 'extraordinary rendition.'"

The ostensible point of that formula is to suggest that the italicized or quoted expressions on the right-hand side are deceptive or illegitimate. But the formula also tends to legitimize the expression on the left-hand side of the equation, so that phrases like *massacre* or even *outsourcing torture* come to seem transparent names for things, which stand in a direct relation to reality. The idea here—and this is true not just of Orwell but of the way most people think about political language—is that things really have two kinds of names: true names that correspond to their true natures, and false names that obscure or misrepresent their natures. The true names are the words which everybody uses in everyday conversation and which come immediately to mind when we first perceive or think of something. In fact, Orwell talks about these words as arising from the nature of things themselves:

> When you think of a concrete object, you think wordlessly, and then, if you want to describe the thing you have been visualising you probably hunt about until you find the exact words that seem to fit it. When you think of something abstract you are more inclined to use words from the start, and unless you make a conscious effort to prevent it, the existing dialect will come rushing in and do the job for you, at the expense of blurring or even changing your meaning.

If you're giving Advice to Writers, you can't go wrong recommending language that seems to correspond to concrete perception. As Orwell noted, the statement "the race is not to the swift, nor the battle to the strong" has a lot more going for it than "success or failure in competitive activities exhibits no tendency to be commensurate with innate capacity."

But that picture of language can lead us badly astray when we apply it to what Burke called the "common words" of political discussion, the ones that appear on the left side of Orwell's formula "an X is called a Y." When you look at the way people deploy that formula, the X-word is almost never a genuinely concrete word like *ball* or *sneeze*—those words

26

rarely have any political significance. (Somebody might ridicule you for calling a ball a spheroid or a sneeze a sternutation, but the objection to the fancier words is simply that they're pretentious, not that they're deceptive.) Sometimes, in fact, the word on the left of that equation is one that would have appeared on the right just a generation earlier. Some years ago, a writer in *Commentary* complained about the language of the juvenile justice system by saying:

> . . . the label *juvenile delinquent*, though legally applicable to any child who commits a crime, is now only applied to the multiple hard-core offender who defies the best intentions of various probation officers, lawyers, law guardians, social workers, fact-finding hearings, investigations, reports, and judges to divert, minimize his penetration, and adjust him out of the system altogether. In short, he is what the layman would call a sociopath.

Of course *Commentary* probably gets a better class of layman than the average magazine, but even for them, *sociopath* is a long way from a concrete word like *sneeze*.

Objections to jargon and euphemism are well taken, but they tend to leave you with the impression that the "plain" or "common" words that people defend are unproblematic. Yet in political language, it's the common words that work the most mischief, precisely because they're the ones that people are unlikely to examine for their hidden assumptions. They may not be "concrete" in the way that words like *ball* and *apple* are, but they can be equally hard to see through—they seem to be opaque when we hold them up to the light.

Those "plain words" work on us far more deeply and unconsciously than any others, and they can persist for long periods of time without becoming frayed or yellowed the way euphemisms tend to do. I'm thinking of the simple, everyday words that the philosopher Richard Rorty calls our "final vocabulary"—"final" because these words are "as far as we can go with language." As he puts it: "All human beings carry about a set of words which they employ to justify their actions, their beliefs, and their lives. These are the words in which we formulate praise of our friends and contempt for our enemies, our long-term projects, our deepest self-doubts and our highest hopes . . . ." As Rorty observes, these can sometimes be abstract words like *right* and *beautiful*, but the ones that do most of the work are the "thicker, more rigid, and more parochial terms" like *professional standards*, *creative*, and *decency*.

American politics has its final vocabulary too, words like *conservative* and *liberal*, *choice* and *freedom*, *values* and *tradition*, *bias* and *elite*, *diversity* and *discrimination*—and for that matter, *Newspeak*, *propaganda*, and *Orwellian*. Words like these can be defined and analyzed at endless length, of course; they are not basic terms like *brown* or *pain*, which can't really be explained in other words without circularity. But when we use the words in our ordinary conversation, they're usually not up for discussion, no more than *acceptable* is when a mother tells her child, "That's not acceptable behavior." They're used to put a claim beyond the reach of argument: *The employees freely chose to work there*, or *What do you expect from a liberal?* and the like. In that sense, they're like proverbs; the only way to answer them is with other words of the same kind. When someone says "absence makes the heart grow fonder," you don't pick nits with the proverb; you counter by saying, "Out of sight, out of mind."

The words of our final vocabularies don't mean; they evoke. Like proverbs, they draw their power from their ability to call up scenarios, images, or moral tales. How do you teach someone the meaning of *appeasement*? You could read her the dictionary definition: "The policy of granting concessions to potential enemies to maintain peace," as the *American Heritage* puts it. That would be a reasonable thing to do if the word in question were *palliate* or *placate*, say. But if that definition were all there is to the meaning of *appeasement*, you could use it as a fair description of the Bush administration's policies toward North Korea or Iran—literally speaking, after all, appeasement is just a matter of trying to cut a deal to avoid a destructive confrontation. That's how people used to use the word, often in an approving way—Churchill himself advocated a policy of "prudence and appeasement" toward the Turks when they went to war with the Greeks in 1919.

But after Munich in 1938, *appeasement* could only stand in for pusillanimous capitulation to the insatiable demands of a tyrant. The word comes with a series of stills attached to it: Neville Chamberlain with his silly high collar, striped pants, and drooping mustache; Hitler's face superimposed over goose-stepping German troops; Churchill glaring defiantly over his cigar. When Condoleezza Rice used the word on *Meet the Press* to describe the French and German reluctance to go to war over Saddam Hussein's alleged weapons of mass destruction, it wasn't a charge anyone could answer by arguing that the historical analogy wasn't really very apt (Churchill didn't actually advocate going to war with Hitler in 1938, for one thing). It was simply part of a semantic blitzkrieg aimed at seizing the moral high ground for the administration, and there was no way to counter it except with an equally potent symbol that connoted rash bellicosity.

It's easy to see how that works with *appeasement*, which conjures up a specific story and which isn't used much anymore in a literal way—it's one of those words that seem to have grown capital letters, like *stonewalling* and *isolationism*. But the principle is the same for most other words that play the most important part in political life—not just the obvious symbol-words like *freedom* or manufactured tags like "the war on terror," but most of the ordinary words that people use when they're making political judgments, like *liberal, values, bias, government,* and *traditional*. It's as misleading to look for the political meaning of *liberal* in the dictionary as it is for *appeasement*. "An advocate or adherent of liberalism" doesn't begin to account for the Volvo-driving, latte-sipping stereotypes that the word trails behind it.

When the words of our final vocabularies enter the public realm, we think of them as a kind of political symbol. As Walter Lippmann explained the notion eighty years ago, symbols are essential to political life. The process of building consensus out of the "vague and confusing medley" of individual opinions, he said, requires reducing complex issues to a few simple alternatives that can be represented by "symbols which assemble emotions after they have been detached from their ideas." For Lippmann, symbols might be objects like the flag or the White House, a name like Lincoln or Flanders Fields, a rallying cry like "make the world safe for Democracy," or a word or phrase like *Americanism, justice,* or *law and order.* What these all had in common was that they obviated the need to consider policies and issues in all their complex details by reducing them to emotionally charged words or icons:

> The question of a proper fare on a municipal subway is symbolized as an issue between the People and the Interests, and then the People is inserted in the symbol American, so that finally in the heat of a campaign, an eight cent fare becomes un-American. The Revolutionary fathers died to prevent it. Lincoln suffered that it might not come to pass, resistance to it was implied in the death of those who sleep in France.

Some people use *symbol* very elastically to refer to any specific anecdote or trait that stands in voters' minds for some broader characteristic: a $600 ashtray becomes a symbol of government waste; a candidate's hedges and qualifications become a symbol of his indecisiveness; the plight of Terri Schiavo becomes a symbol of either disrespect for the sanctity of human life or political meddling in people's private decisions, depending on who you listen to. Our reliance on cues like these isn't necessarily irrational. Whether we're evaluating a candidate, a new air purifier, or a potential date, it's usually impractical or too much trouble to assemble and assess all the information we would need to make a fully informed decision—as Lippmann put it, "The facts exceed our curiosity." In most cases we're forced to fall back on rules of thumb or cognitive shortcuts. We make our decision on the basis of a familiar brand name, a celebrity endorsement, the professionalism of a Web page design, or a person's haircut. (You think of Nelson Algren's three rules for a happy life: "Never sit down to play poker with anybody called Doc, never eat at a place called Mom's, and never sleep with a woman who has more problems that you do.") As the political scientist Samuel Popkin suggests, you can think of voters' reliance on political symbols as "just another form of information cost-saving."

But the symbol-words of political discourse are different from specific symbols and cues. Unlike an anecdote about a $600 ashtray, they don't simply encapsulate a particular issue, candidate, or trend. They tell us *how* those specific symbols signify, so that we can group them as episodes in a grander political narrative that we evoke over and over again. *Values* stands in for an assortment of news items and running stories—the "War on Christmas," right-to-die laws, the Ten Commandments monument, that lenient judge in Vermont—and connects them all to an overarching narrative about the slights and insults that out-of-touch liberals are visiting on traditional American standards of morality and patriotism. And for that reason, it's far more important to control the notion expressed by *values* than to control the more transitory symbols or catchphrases that stand in for a specific issue.

But precisely because they're so vague and general, those basic symbol-words are particularly subject to manipulation. As Lippmann noted in his satirical remark on the politics of subway fares, it's in the nature of political discourse to draw those words as expansively as possible, so as to reduce the details of an issue to the purely emotional response that items like *freedom* or *values* can evoke. As the writers of a recent book on political language put it: "Words like *patriotism* and *terrorism* do not let us breathe. They exhaust the air around us. We reason less well in their presence . . . ." And when words become purely connotative or evocative, it can be easy to extend their auras by multiplying their meanings or applying them to things they didn't originally refer to.

O ver recent decades, conservatives have taken control of most of these symbol-words, and with them the basic vocabularies that most Americans rely on to form their political judgments. Their success here isn't like their success in popularizing their slogans and catchphrases. For one thing, the right has achieved its control of the everyday political vocabulary through a process that doesn't call much explicit attention to itself, which makes these words very different from the obvious euphemisms and catchwords that tend to put people on their guard. When Fox News decides to start using "homicide bombing" in place of "suicide bombing," everybody recognizes it as a pointed gesture (one aimed more at the other media who keep using "suicide bomber" than at the Palestinians or the Iraqi insurgents). And its an equally pointed gesture when Republicans insist on referring to "the Democrat Party," which was originally coined to suggest that there was nothing particularly democratic about their opponents. The usage may irritate some Democrats—that's what it's supposed to do. But nobody really expects it to catch on generally, and indeed if it did, it would lose its partisan significance, the same way the originally disparaging connotations of *Whig* and *Tory* (originally "rebel" and "bandit," respectively) were lost when they became the standard names of the British parties.

But the right's new uses of words like *values, liberal, bias,* and the rest aren't the sort of things that the media and the public are apt to mark as blatantly partisan in the way "the Democrat Party" is. Conservatives have been able to establish the meanings of these words in everyday usage without setting off many alarm bells. That's why the most telling evidence for the right's linguistic dominance comes not from looking at the way people talk at *National Review* or Fox News but from the language of the mainstream media and the Web.

Take the way the right has narrowed the meaning of *elite,* so that it's more likely to be used to describe "liberal" sectors like the entertainment industry, the media, and the academy than leaders of business or the military. It isn't surprising that on Fox News, references to the business elite are outnumbered by almost 50-to-1 by references to the media elite. But even on "liberal" CNN and in the daily press, *media elite* outnumbers *business elite* by 2- or 3-to-1. Yet when you look at British papers, whether the left-wing *Guardian* or the right-wing *Telegraph,* those proportions are reversed. British papers refer to the business elite about three times as often as to the media elite, which is pretty much the same thing you saw in American papers in the 1970s and 1980s, before the right's campaign against the "elite liberal media" went into high gear.

The same patterns emerge when you look at media's use of words like *liberal, values, bias,* and so on. Even in the mainstream media, those words tend to be used in ways that presume the point of view of the right. In fact, there's usually not that much difference between the way these words are used by the "liberal" press and in conservative papers like the *Washington Times* and the *Wall Street Journal.* In the *Washington Times,* for example, references to conservative values outnumber references to liberal values by almost 7-to-1. In the *Washington Post,* the ratio is 4-to-1—a bit less skewed, but still dramatically favoring the conservative view of things. Or take *economic freedom*. In their ordinary conversation, people still tend to use that phrase in something like the way Franklin Roosevelt did, to refer to personal economic security ("The inheritance gave me the economic freedom I needed to become a painter"). But when you look at editorials and op-eds in either the *Wall Street Journal* or the *New York Times*, you only see the phrase used in a Reaganesque sense, to refer to freedom from government intervention in the markets.

It may be tempting to explain this by pointing to the pressure that conservatives have put on the media through their incessant complaints about liberal media bias. As critics like Eric Alterman, Trudy Lieberman, and David Brock have pointed out, one function of those attacks is to "work the refs," intimidating the media into spiking stories unfavorable to the administration and dutifully passing along conservative talking points. And there's no question the right has been successful in this campaign, as you can tell when you look at the language of the media. For example, a number of newspapers have substituted the Republicans' *death tax* for *estate tax* without qualifying the phrase with quotation marks or hedges like "so-called." ("House Would End Death Tax," read a headline in the *Pittsburgh Post-Gazette* on April 14, 2005, as if the tax had never gone by any other name.) When the Republicans leaned on the media in late 2004 to replace "private accounts" with "personal accounts" in coverage of the administration's Social Security proposals, a lot of editors and journalists promptly fell into line: between November 2004 and March 2005, the proportion of press and broadcast references to "personal accounts" rather than "private accounts" roughly doubled. And when the administration began to shift from "the war against terrorism" to "the war on terror" in early 2002, the media promptly followed suit: when you plot the changing frequency of the phrases in White House speeches and press stories, the curves track each other perfectly.

But this doesn't really explain the media's adoption of the right's senses of words like *values* or *elite*. When a newspaper decides to use *death tax* or *personal account*, it's usually the result of a deliberate editorial decision. But the skewings in the usage of words like *values* and *elite* don't grow out of any explicit or momentary policy. The media almost never use phrases like *working-class liberals*, *Hispanic liberals*, or *black liberals*, though they'll use those words to modify *conservatives*. That isn't something that journalists do deliberately or that editors keep their eye on, nor would a journalist who spoke of *working-class liberals* attract the critical attention of one of the right-wing media watchdog groups like the Media Research Center. It's simply that whatever their own personal political views, journalists have unconsciously accepted the right's depiction of liberalism as a middle-class lifestyle choice, so that even those working-class people or blacks who enthusiastically endorse the whole roster of "liberal" issue positions are more apt to be described simply as Democrats.

The media don't adopt those patterns of usage merely in a conscious effort to "balance" their coverage—really, it isn't a conscious effort to do anything at all. Nowadays, that's just the way most people talk when you wake them up in the middle of the night, and journalists are no exception: the patterns in the way the media uses these words are usually reproduced pretty closely on the Web or in online newsgroups. It's true that the media play an important role in diffusing that language. But these aren't the sort of language patterns that conservatives could have imposed through deliberate pressure on the media. And as it turns out, they didn't have to.

how have conservatives been able to pull off their linguistic coup? First and foremost, they've told the right stories. Unlike tags such as *death tax* and *personal account*, a word like *values* acquires its significance from its continued association with stories that dramatize the same underlying theme of liberal arrogance and moral decay. At a certain point, the word comes to stand in for those stories even for people who don't find the larger narrative credible. They may be unhappy about the way the right has co-opted *values*, but they interpret the word that way themselves. To the best of my knowledge nobody has done the experiment, but it's a safe bet that if you pulled fifty people off a bus and gave them a word-association test, even in San Francisco or on Manhattan's Upper West Side, you'd find that *values* evoked *conservative* a lot more often than it did *liberal*.

Since the late 1960s, the right's appeals have rested on a collection of overlapping stories about the currents of contemporary American life—stories that illustrate declining patriotism and moral standards, the out-of-touch media and the self-righteous liberal elite, the feminization of public life, minorities demanding special privileges and unwilling to assimilate to American culture and language, growing crime and lenient judges, ludicrous restrictions on permissible speech, disrespect for religious faith, a swollen government that intrudes officiously in private life, and arching over all of them, an America divided into two nations by differences in values, culture, and lifestyle. With occasional exceptions like Bill Clinton's 1992 campaign, Democrats and liberals have not offered compelling narratives that could compete with those. And to the extent that our basic political vocabulary is fleshed out by narratives, it's no wonder that the right has been able to dominate it.

But as the saying goes, it's not just the story, it's the way you tell it. The most successful national politicians on the right have been those who could tell its narratives with conviction. The modern model is Ronald Reagan, not just because of his ease in spinning anecdotes and homilies, but because he conveyed a faith in plain words and simple truths. People often describe his style as conversational, but it was far from the language that people actually use around the breakfast table.* Really, it was what you could think of as stage colloquial—the contrived naturalness that "plain folks" used in populist movies from the 1930s and 1940s—but Reagan brought to that an actor's gift for believing whatever he happened to be saying at the time. There's something of that in George W. Bush, too, though he comes by his artlessness as a birthright. Nobody's likely to describe him as a raconteur, though like Reagan, he has had eloquent writers. And also like Reagan, he has a talent for conveying plainspoken directness, and his nonchalant ungrammaticality inures him against any charges of slickness. (As James Carville and Paul

---

* For example: "Here in Wyoming, back where your farmers and ranchers and workers and small-business people dream big and toil hard to make dreams come true"; "The ideas, the muscle, the moral courage and, yes, the spiritual strength that built the greatest, freest nation the world has ever known." That isn't the way anybody actually talks at the breakfast table: "Pass me the cream cheese and, yes, another bagel."

Begala observe, his message comes down to: "I must be telling the truth. I'm too inarticulate to lie.") And also like Reagan, he comes off as someone with no patience for contrivance or nuance. Listening to Reagan or Bush pronounce *freedom,* you have the sense that nothing could be more simple, except to the clever people who make everything seem more complicated than it is.

Of course the Democrats have had good storytellers, too, like Bill Clinton and John Edwards. But the stories they told—Clinton's populist appeals in 1992, Edwards's tale of "Two Americas" in 2004—were always seen as individual election pitches rather than as themes that defined the party's point of view. Not Reagan or FDR, not even Lincoln could single-handedly transform the language of politics. An influential leader can leave some memorable words and phrases behind him, but the narratives that shape the core vocabulary of politics have to seem to be ubiquitous and persistent—they have to suggest a movement, rather than just a campaign.

And the right does have a movement, built around the network of well-funded foundations, think tanks, and policy institutes that conservatives have established over recent decades. Those groups have been enormously successful in shaping the issues and terms of political debate and disseminating conservative views in the media, and they can take direct credit for coining or diffusing a number of the catchphrases that conservatives use to frame their positions. And they've played a big role in fostering the ideological discipline that the conservative movement has managed to impose on its troops. As Michael Tomasky showed in a study of newspaper editorials published by Harvard's Shorenstein Center, for example, conservative papers are far less likely to break with "their" administrations and far more likely to criticize the other side than liberal papers are.

All of this has contributed to the right's famous ability to keep its troops on message, as they hit on the same phrases over and over again. I happened on a striking demonstration of the right's linguistic consistency back in 1996, when I was playing around with one of those programs that produces an automatic summary of texts by analyzing their word frequency and recurrent syntactic patterns. Out of curiosity, I ran it on a collection of all the speeches that had been given over the first two nights of the Republican National Convention in San Diego, and it promptly distilled them into five key sentences:

> We are the Republican Party—a big, broad, diverse and inclusive party, with a commonsense agenda and a better man for a better America, Bob Dole. We need a leader we can trust. Thank you, ladies and gentlemen, for being part of this quest in working with us to restore the American dream. The commonsense Republican proposals are the first step in restoring the American dream because Republicans care about America. But there is no greater dream than the dreams parents have for their children to be happy and to share God's blessings.

Those sentences neatly encapsulate just about every Republican address given over the course of the last few decades—leave out Dole's name and you could post it tomorrow on the site of the Republican National Committee. But when I tried the same experiment a month later on the combined texts of the speeches from the first two nights of the Democratic National Convention in Chicago, the software returned pure word salad. Because Democrats are chronically incapable of staying on message, no single group of phrases rose to the statistical surface. That by itself goes some way toward explaining conservatives' success in establishing their language in the media and the public mind. As psychologists have shown—not that we needed them to—merely repeating a word serves to drive it into memory.

The right's stories are echoed and amplified by the broadcast commentators who fill the airwaves with right-wing chatter, often piped in directly from Republican sources. Political speechifying and partisan harangues have always been a form of popular entertainment in America, from the torchlight rallies of Jackson's age to the parades, barbecues, and pole-raisings of the late nineteenth century to the WASPish columnists and radio pontificators of FDR's time. But people have never before had access to a 24/7 stream of the stuff: right-wing talk radio and Fox News are the first media in American history to turn political indignation into a successful business model. If you care to, you can hear more political talk in a single week than anyone in the nineteenth century could experience in an entire lifetime. And the new formats are made for storytelling, with an endless stream of liberal outrages to report: every day a new, more ridiculous item about a school in Texas that prohibited students from wearing red and green during the Christmas season or a British woman who married a dolphin, a portent of what gay marriage will bring.

The new broadcast formats blur the line between public and private language as never before. Unlike even FDR's Fireside Chats (which were actually rather formal by modern standards), the language of the political talk media is invariably conversational. Whether you're listening to the monologues of Limbaugh and his ilk or the Crips-vs.-Bloods melees on the cable news networks, you have the sense that what you're hearing is pretty much the language that people would use if they were talking over a beer. (You see a similar contrast when you compare the high, neutral style of editorials and op-ed commentaries with the informal chatter of the political blogs, which can often have the same familiar tone as personal e-mails.) More than any earlier media format, that is, the talk shows can offer people scripted models for their own barbershop arguments—for a lot of people, in fact, they probably take the place of them. John Dewey pointed out in 1927 in *The Public and Its Problems* that the ability to make that connection between public and private discourse is crucial to controlling public opinion: "Publication is partial and the public which results is partially informed and formed until the means it purveys pass from mouth to mouth . . . That and only that gives reality to public opinion." The exchanges between the hosts and callers on talk shows offer a kind of conversational apprenticeship, in the same way modern sports-talk radio teaches fans how to talk to one another about football. Those broadcasts don't simply shape the everyday vocabulary of politics; they also shape the tone of discussion and the sense of what political divisions are really about. They have a lot to do, for example, with the fact that Americans perceive the country as having become more polarized even though there is actually more popular agreement on most major issues than there was a generation ago. And despite the modest recent successes of liberal counterprogramming, the left hasn't really found a broadcast format that's equally effective in conveying its narratives and helping to recapture the degree-zero language of political life.

In the rest of this book, I'll be drawing out those connections between words and stories, looking at both how the right has commandeered the core political vocabulary and how liberals might take it back. For now, though, let me make a point about how *not* to go about this. "In thinking about symbols it is tempting to treat them as if they possessed independent energy," Walter Lippmann wrote, and Democrats and liberals are particularly susceptible to that temptation. Seeing the success that the right has had with *values*, for example, they've persistently tried to reclaim the word, as if it had a talismanic power of its own. *Values* does have a certain ambiguity that has made it useful to conservatives. But the word isn't terribly important for its own sake. It's simply a convenient label for a file of press clippings that support a larger theme, and if it hadn't been available, the right could have used some other word in its place with pretty much the same effect (we might have been talking about "standards issues," for example). And by the same token, liberals could develop a successful counternarrative to the right's "values" story without having to hitch it to the V-word.

I don't mean to suggest that liberals shouldn't continue to stake their claim to *values*, which at least calls attention to the way the right has usurped the word. But one way or another, this isn't really about a word. And by the same token, I'll show in the next chapter why liberals can't escape the stereotypes that attach to their own name simply by running from the label or rebaptizing themselves as progressives—that problem goes deeper than a single word, too. A well-crafted slogan or catchphrase can work its magic on its own. But the words of the deep vocabulary of politics are inseparable from the stories that give them their meanings.

chapter three

Trashing the L-word

Given the aversion this word inspires in Democratic
candidates, future civilizations sifting through the rubble
may well conclude that "liberal" was a euphemism
for "pederast" or "serial killer."
—*Timothy Noah, 1986*

In 1960, the *New York Times Sunday Magazine* published an article by
the philosopher Charles Frankel called "A Liberal Is a Liberal Is a . . . ."
Frankel observed that it was hard to find a major figure in American politics who had not had a kind word to say about liberalism, from Hoover
to Truman or Taft to Eisenhower. Indeed, he said, "anyone who today
identifies himself as an unmitigated opponent of liberalism . . . cannot
aspire to influence on the national political scene."

Frankel noted that even politicians who indulged in attacks on "liberals" were always careful to qualify the word. Southern conservatives complained about "Northern liberals," and usually added that they
themselves were liberals in matters of social welfare. Even Senator Mc-
Carthy usually restricted himself to attacking "phony liberals," leaving
open the inference, as Frankel put it, "that he had nothing against genuine liberals, if only he could find one."

Frankel's article was accompanied by a cartoon that showed a group of
politicians labeled "Left-Wing Democrat," "Middle-Wing Democrat,"

"Right-Wing Republican," and so forth, all sitting at a table in front of a TV camera and applying makeup from jars bearing labels like "Liberal Cream," "Liberal #7," and "Do-It-Yourself Liberal Kit."

If that cartoon were run again today, the jars would all contain vanishing cream. Nowadays not even most politicians on the left wing of the Democratic party are willing to own up to being liberals. When someone presses them, they either dismiss the significance of labels in general or acknowledge the label defensively, the way Howard Dean did during the 2003 primary season: "If being a liberal means a balanced budget, I'm a liberal." (As Ann Coulter observes, for once accurately: "The surest sign one is dealing with a liberal is his refusal to grant meaning to the word 'liberal.'") And ordinary voters are equally wary of the label. Over recent decades, the number of Americans willing to describe themselves as liberals has been hovering around 20 percent, with around 35 percent describing themselves as conservatives, and the rest opting for "moderate" or "middle of the road."

i t's tempting to see the declining fortunes of the liberal label simply as a sign of the shift to the right among the American electorate: if people have rejected *liberal*, it must be because they've rejected liberalism. Granted, liberalism was never a precise doctrine, particularly in the postwar decades, when its tent was spread so wide. But however liberalism was defined, there's no question that its appeal began to diminish shortly after its high-water mark in the Kennedy years. It was partly the victim of a complacency born of its own successes. Already in 1955, Richard Hofstadter was writing that "the dominant force in our political life no longer comes from the liberals who made the New Deal possible." But it was also challenged by the white backlash to civil rights legislation, the perceived failure of Great Society social programs, and the bitter divisions over the Vietnam War. Before long, liberalism was under assault from both the New Right and the New Left—it was just a few years after the Frankel article appeared that the folksinger Phil Ochs released "Love Me, I'm a Liberal," a sardonic catalog of liberal hypocrisies ("I love Puerto Ricans and Negroes /as long as they don't move next door").

By the late 1970s, liberalism was already associated with "profligacy, spinelessness, malevolence, masochism, elitism, fantasy, anarchy, idealism, softness, irresponsibility, and sanctimoniousness." And then on August 14, 1988, Ronald Reagan made the stigma quasi-official when he told the 1988 Republican National Convention, "The masquerade is over. It's time to . . . say the dreaded L-word; to say the policies of our opposition are liberal, liberal, liberal."

Rather than owning up to the label, the Democratic candidate Michael Dukakis tried to change the subject, responding that "the L-word of this campaign is 'leadership.'" That strategy suited the purposes of his opponent, George H.W. Bush, who made a running gag out of Dukakis's coyness about acknowledging the label. Dukakis, he said, had avoided appearing on *Wheel of Fortune* because "[h]e was afraid that Vanna might turn over the L-word." It wasn't until a few days before the election that Dukakis finally got around to saying, a little defensively, "Yes, I'm a liberal, in the tradition of Franklin Roosevelt and Harry Truman and John Kennedy." The declaration was treated as major news ("Dukakis Uses L-Word" was the page-one headline in the *Boston Globe*). But the damage was done by then, not just to the Dukakis campaign but to the liberal label, which would be branded from then on as "the L-word," according to the familiar formula we use when we want to pretend a word is unspeakable. By now, it's considered noteworthy when a politician admits to being a liberal. Even in supposedly "liberal" papers like the *New York Times* and the *Washington Post,* liberals are four times as likely as conservatives to be described as "unapologetic" or "unabashed." In this day and age, it's assumed that liberalism is something most people would have qualms about owning up to.

But if voters are reluctant to declare themselves liberals nowadays, they haven't bailed out on most of the views that defined liberalism in the past. By substantial margins, Americans feel that the Democrats would do a better job than the Republicans at taking care of the environment, making the tax system fair, safeguarding Social Security, and improving the health care system. In a 2003 CBS–New York Times poll, only 11 percent of respondents believed the president's tax cuts were very likely to create new jobs, which a lot of people would take as a central tenet of conservative faith. And the overwhelmingly negative response to the Bush administration's efforts to privatize Social Security in 2005 made it clear that Americans were not prepared to throw the most important achievements of the New Deal aside in the name of "the ownership society." In short, Americans seem to have a lot more misgivings about the liberal label than about liberal ideas. The real shift to the right has been among the Republican leadership and party activists, who have moved much farther to the right of the American mainstream than the Democrats have moved left. And they've dragged political discourse along with them.

In fact, the whole idea of liberalism as a political doctrine sometimes seems to be beside the point these days. The word itself isn't used nearly as much as it used to be—today, the media talk about liberals a great deal more than they talk about liberalism. And when *liberalism* comes up, it's usually in phrases like "West Side liberalism" or "Hollywood liberalism," where it suggests a social clique rather than a philosophical school— "Hollywood liberalism" isn't the same sort of thing as "Chicago economics." These days, it's as if being a liberal has less to do with a commitment to a particular -ism than with being a political fashion victim. What were once regarded as political ideals have become merely the ancillary signs of a decadent lifestyle.

t he trashing of the liberal label is one of the most significant changes in the language of American politics in recent times. By now, most of the politicians who would have proudly called themselves liberals forty years ago have abandoned the name, if not the liberal worldview. Even those who identify with liberal principles are more likely to describe themselves as "progressives"—something like what the Ford Motor Company did in 1960 when it discontinued the Edsel line but continued to market the same car with a different grille and trim under the name of Galaxie. The fact is, the progressive label has been on something of a tear. It's used not just by activists who inherited the New Left's disdain for liberals, but by centrists and old-fashioned pols. It figures in the name of the Progressive Policy Institute of the centrist Democratic Leadership

Council. And during the 2003 gubernatorial recall election, California governor Gray Davis said that he was confident he would prevail because "I don't think they're going to replace my progressive agenda with a conservative agenda"—this from a Democrat who was not exactly known for cruising in the party's left lane.

Progressive has its advantages: it conveys the right message to *Nation*-reading, Pacifica-listening voters without connoting anything negative to the majority of the electorate—to most, in fact, it doesn't connote much of anything at all. And the word clearly irks the right, as you can tell from the way conservative publications like *National Review* tend to set it in quotation marks, the form of passive resistance that's used by those who have allowed the other side to stake out the linguistic territory. Some conservatives have even tried to usurp the word. Shortly after the 2004 election, the Seattle *Post-Intelligencer's* Julia Youngs wrote that "George W. Bush kept the presidency because he was the more progressive candidate." Bush's victory, she said, was a sign that voters repudiated the left's resistance to "progressive ideas" like proactive pursuit of terrorists, limitations on abortion, privatization of Social Security, and the flat tax. If actual progressives could get past the butter-wouldn't-melt effrontery of that statement, they might find the appropriation of their label flattering.

Has *liberal* had its day? Seventy years is a pretty good run for a political label, and perhaps some day *liberal* will be replaced by *progressive* or some other term, particularly if the nation has to undergo an upheaval comparable to the Great Depression. But labels have returned from near-oblivion before. Fifty years ago, *conservative* was on the ropes; in a 1949 editorial, the *Wall Street Journal* said:

> If a man eschews extreme fads in clothing himself, we say he is a conservative dresser and we are more inclined to employ him in our business or be seen in his company. If a banker is described as conservative most people are more inclined to trust their money to his care. But if a man is described as a "conservative" in politics then the reaction to him is very likely to be altogether different. He is likely to be suspected of wanting to

cheat widows and orphans and generally to be a bad fellow who associates with a lot of other bad fellows. Consequently very few people will admit they are conservatives and if they are accused they will go to great lengths to prove otherwise . . . [Conservatives] have been propagandized and bullied into believing that they must shun a word and the word is the very one that describes their attitude.

You could write the same article today substituting *liberal* for *conservative* (though you might have trouble getting the *Journal* to print it). "Everyone has a good word for liberal benefactors and liberal helpings of potatoes . . . ."

Still, the liberal label still has its defenders, not just because of the tradition of thought it stands for, but because it would be a strategic error to abandon it. For the present, the opposition between liberals and conservatives is too deeply etched in the language and on the media's split screens to be dropped anytime soon, particularly with the right hammering incessantly on the "elite liberals" theme. *Liberal* is the word that ordinary people use when they're talking about political polarities, and Democrats who avoid it in favor of *progressive* seem to confirm the widespread suspicion that liberals aren't talking the same language as other Americans, even when it comes to pronouncing their own name right.*

For as long as the Democrats refuse to come to terms with the liberal label, it will continue to dog them. As Dukakis learned, a candidate's reluctance to acknowledge the label may often strike voters as a sign of unwillingness to own up to his principles. And it's a fair bet that John Kerry's refusal to call himself a liberal helped him less among centrists than it hurt him among voters of all stripes who already had doubts about his constancy of principle.

What's worse, the Democrats' phobia about the liberal label has given the right free rein to define the word in its own terms, pushing the meaning of *liberal* to the political margins. There was a time when *liberal* and

---

* Some on the right have taken to using *progressive* as a disparaging term—Bill O'Reilly likes to rail at "secular progressives." That might ultimately help to establish the label in general usage, but not exactly as a neutral replacement for *liberal*.

leftist were contrasting terms; now the right tends to use them inter-changeably.* Not long ago, in fact, the Republican minority leader of the South Carolina Senate described a Democratic legislator as "one of the most liberal leftists that we have in the House"—not an uncommon wording these days, which implies that *liberal* has actually outflanked *leftist* as a term for extreme political views. It's a vicious circle: the more Democrats shun the liberal label, the easier it is for the right to demonize it, making Democrats even more reluctant to wear it than before. If the flight from the liberal label continues, self-avowed liberals may wind up like the Celts of medieval Europe, driven to the peripheries of the conti-nent by invading tribes.

This isn't a problem only for the left and center-left of the Democratic party. True, there are plenty of individual Democrats who see no need for the liberal label, and even some centrists who rejoice in its imminent passing. But in the end, the eclipse of the label has left the party groping for a unifying philosophical center to fill the role that the broad-tent conception of liberalism did from the time of FDR to the Kennedy era. Mid-twentieth-century liberalism may not have been a very precise or stirring philosophy, or even a philosophy at all. Lionel Trilling described it back in 1951 as "a large tendency rather than a concise body of doc-trine." But it did give Democrats a common touch point in a line of po-litical tradition, just as conservatism does for today's Republicans.

"In a representative government," Franklin Roosevelt said in 1941, "there are usually two general schools of political belief—liberal and con-servative. . . . Since at least since 1932, the Democratic Party has been the liberal party." Nowadays, to all but the right, the Democrats are merely the party formerly known as liberal. The absence of an ideological center haunts the party. Slogans like Clinton's "Opportunity, Responsibility, Community" may make for good photo backdrops, but they're too vague to provide the sense of party identity and tradition that a commitment to liberalism did in the past. A 2005 Democracy Corps survey found that 55

* On the Web, Martin Sheen and Susan Sarandon are more likely to be labeled left-ists than Fidel Castro is.

percent of voters said the Republicans know what they stand for, as opposed to only 27 percent who said the same thing of the Democrats.

You can see the problem reflected in the media, where Republicans are identified in terms of an ideological reference point far more often than Democrats are. Middle-of-the-road Republicans like George Pataki or Rudy Giuliani are usually described as "moderates," which locates them relative to the party's mainstream, but middle-of-the-road Democrats like Evan Bayh and Max Baucus tend to be called "centrists," which locates them relative to the broader political horizon. In fact, the press identifies politicians as "mainstream Republicans" four times as often as it identifies them as "mainstream Democrats," and it is almost five times as likely to speak of Republicans as "true believers." In the public mind, *Republican* names a movement, whereas *Democrat* is only a ZIP code.

There's a certain self-delusion in Democrats' avoidance of the L-word; it suggests that they really haven't understood the magnitude of the linguistic shift that has taken place. Liberalism isn't like a brand of automobile that has fallen out of favor—it can't be reinvigorated simply by marketing it under a new name with a NASCAR-approved grille. The trashing of the liberal label is only the most obvious sign of a process that has rewritten whole pages of the American political dictionary, as familiar words have acquired new meanings that reflect a changed conception of what politics is about. Even if you could magically eradicate *liberal* from the collective consciousness, you wouldn't dispel all the fatuous stereotypes that have accumulated around the word or reverse the broader shifts of political meaning that they stand in for. In the end, this really isn't so much about reclaiming *liberal* as about redressing the shift in political language that the stigmatization of the liberal label stands in for. To understand what has happened to *liberal*, you have to understand how the right has rewritten the language of class.

chapter four

Class Dismissed

I wanna be a lawyer
Doctor or professor
A member of the UMC
I'll pretend to be liberal
But I'll still support the GOP,
As part of the UMC.
        —*Bob Seger, "Upper Middle Class"*

like much of the new language of the right, the redefinition of *liberal* goes back to the Nixon years, as liberalism was coming under attack, and Vietnam and the fallout of the civil rights movement were opening new fissures in American society. Or I should really say the Agnew years, since it was Nixon's vice president Spiro Agnew who pioneered the new populist tone of Republican rhetoric. Agnew's phraseology was impishly sui generis—it's hard to imagine Ronald Reagan or either of the Bushes describing his press critics as the "nattering nabobs of negativism" or "pusillanimous pussyfooters." But with his coded appeals to "law and or-der" and his attacks on the "liberal intellectuals" who were destroying the country's strength, the student radicals and hippies, and the "effete corps of impudent snobs" of the media, he became the Mrs. O'Leary's cow of the culture wars.

49

The new language borrowed something from the populist rhetoric George Wallace had used in the 1960s and 1970s to win support among white backlash voters in the South and working-class voters who would later be described as Reagan Democrats. But for Republican purposes, Wallace's rhetoric was too stridently racist (too stridently everything, really), and his language still appealed too directly to working-class interests and resentments. He supported welfare entitlements and was more or less friendly to unions, and he claimed to speak, a bit too specifically, for "the bus driver, the truck driver, the beautician, the fireman, the policeman, and the steelworker, the plumber, and the communications worker, and the oil worker, and the little businessman."

The Republicans realized, though, that they could harness the same resentments that Wallace had spoken for, turning themselves into what the historian Michael Kazin has described as "a counter-elite, a welcome home for white refugees from the liberal crackup." To accomplish this, however, they had to blur and broaden Wallace's target audience, transforming it into the "silent majority" of whites who were frustrated by what they took to be liberal indifference to their anger about crime, race, and the counterculture. In Kazin's words: "As liberalism crumbled, astute minds in the party recognized that the defense of middle-class values— diligent toil, moral piety, self-governing communities—could now bridge gaps of income and occupation that the GOP had been unable to cross since the Great Depression."

That shift was announced with the appearance of the new label "Middle Americans." The phrase had been coined by the mildly liberal columnist Joseph Kraft in 1967 to refer specifically to "the low and middle income whites of this country." But it soon acquired an ideological cast that Kraft himself described as a "vulgarization," as Middle Americans were "tricked out as sure guides to wise policy." The *Wall Street Journal* described them as "the 'conservative' elements of American society . . . who don't speak out much but are every day frustrated by rising prices and taxes, afraid of crime, inconvenienced by a declining pattern of life in rural towns, as well as cities, worried about what might happen to their children in college or in Vietnam, and in general troubled by the feeling that the whole nation is gradually beginning to fall apart." In

1970, *Time* magazine anointed Middle Americans "Man and Woman of the Year," pointing to their role in electing Richard Nixon president two years earlier. And anticipating the later use of the phrase, *Time* boosted the number of Middle Americans to 100 million by adding white-collar workers to the group.

To build a coalition across the disparities of income and occupation among their new base, though, the Republicans had to find new language. They needed ways of downplaying the differences in economic interests between the working-class white voters they were courting and their traditional constituencies in business and the upper middle class. They had to unify their appeal to those groups by rewriting the old language of populism in ways that diverted the traditional conflicts between "the people" and "the powerful" into "cultural" resentments over differences in lifestyle and social values. And in the course of things, they managed to redefine the distinction between conservatives and liberals, so as to depict liberals as the enemies of the values of "ordinary Americans."

the language of conservatives has always been aimed at blurring or extenuating the harsher facts of economic class or at excluding the subject from political discussion entirely. Since the days of the New Deal, in fact, Republicans have realized that they could get political mileage simply by accusing the other side of raising the issue of class. Whenever Democrats criticize Republican programs that benefit the wealthy, they can count on being charged with engaging in "class warfare." The phrase spiked in the press at the height of the Gingrich revolution in 1995, when Al Gore started talking about "the people versus the powerful" in the summer of 2000, and then again when Republicans were pushing through their tax cuts for the rich at the beginning of 2003. The proposed reduction in the marginal income tax rate, Bush said in 2001, "ignites the great outcry of class warfare." And the media often play along with the pretense that "class warfare" is a "Democratic mantra," as Bob Schieffer described it on a 2003 *Face the Nation* broadcast.

"Class warfare" is a phrase that puts Americans in mind of cloth caps and barricades—you think of *Les Miz*, not *Mr. Smith Goes to Washington*. The problem isn't so much *warfare* as *class* itself. Republicans never extol the virtues of "class cooperation," or "class alliances"—those phrases would be the logical opposites of "class warfare," but they'd imply that America does have economically based social classes. The charge that Democrats are engaging in class warfare really means only that they're guilty of the unseemly lapse of bringing up the subject of class at all.*

As it happens, though, Democrats almost never raise charges of "class warfare," much less "ignite" it as a cry, as Bush put it, and only a handful of them are willing to throw the phrase back at the Republicans who accuse them of engaging in it. When House Ways and Means Chairman Bill Thomas dismissed Democrats' objections to the unfairness of the administration's 2003 tax proposals as "playing the class warfare card," New York representative Charles Rangel responded: "Is it class warfare? You bet your life. But you declared it against the working people of America." But the vast majority of Democrats would have ducked the subject even then, out of a circumspection about talking about class that Republicans count as among their strongest political assets. The Republican strategist Lee Atwater observed just after George H.W. Bush's 1988 victory over Michael Dukakis that "[t]he way to win a presidential race against the Republicans is to develop the class warfare issue . . . to divide up the haves and have-nots and to try and reinvigorate the New Deal coalition and to attack." Fortunately for the Republicans, Democrats have rarely been willing to test that thesis, partly out of timidity and partly because they've had trouble finding language that allows them to "smoke out the almost un-American issue of class," as Robert Kuttner puts it.

Conservatives offer several reasons why class should be excluded from political discussion. On the one hand, they argue that to point out the existence of disparities of income and privilege is divisive—as Bush has put it, it's "an attitude that tends to pit groups of people against each other." To dwell on class differences, conservatives say, is to deny the

---

*In the United Kingdom, right-wing Conservatives never charge the left with engaging in "class warfare," precisely because nobody would have the cheek to claim that class is a "foreign" idea that has no place in British politics. You can't imagine a British politician of any stripe maintaining that the British "do not see society as a layer cake," as David Brooks says of Americans—of course they do, and they know their place in it to the nearest crumb.

fundamental openness of American society, where anyone can rise as high as he or she desires through pluck and industry. From that point of view, policies that favor the rich give the rest of us a motivation for working harder. In the words of Larry Kudlow, CNBC's supply-side enthusiast, to penalize the rich through high taxes would "blunt incentives for the non-rich who are working hard to climb the American ladder of prosperity." And in a 2003 *New York Times* op-ed entitled "The Triumph of Hope over Self-Interest," David Brooks argues that "income resentment is not a strong emotion in much of America," since Americans "have always had a sense that great opportunities lie just over the horizon, in the next valley, with the next job or the next big thing. None of us is really poor; we're just pre-rich . . . ." Brooks went on: "Americans read magazines for people more affluent than they are *(W, Cigar Aficionado, The New Yorker, Robb Report, Town and Country)* because they think that someday they could be that guy with the tastefully appointed horse farm. Democratic politicians proposing to take from the rich are just bashing the dreams of our imminent selves."

That's a popular argument in the corridors of Washington's right-wing think tanks, but you have to be pretty remote from Main Street to take it seriously. True, there are some working Americans who intend to wind up rich some day and who have already packed the appropriate political attitudes into their hope chests. But for the majority, wealth is a fantasy, not a hope. To suppose that all those ordinary readers of the ads in the *New Yorker* believe they'll have their own horse farms some day is like supposing that the average middle-aged male who reads *Playboy* actually expects to wake up some morning to find a twenty-year-old centerfold sharing his pillow. And you have to be in a near-pathological state of denial about working Americans' circumstances to imagine that their principal incentive for working hard is the hope of becoming rich, or that increasing taxes on the wealthy is liable to "blunt incentives" to work hard—that the moment you add a couple of points to the marginal tax rate for families making more than $339,000 a year, all those folks holding down two jobs to put Hamburger Helper on the table are going to start slacking off on the job.

The fact is, it's hard to believe that many conservatives actually buy any of these arguments about the popular appeal of tax cuts that benefit the rich. If they did, after all, they'd be a lot more forthcoming about the real nature of those programs ("You'll all thank us when your ship comes in"), rather than always claiming they're aimed at providing relief for middle-class taxpayers and small businesses. And while they invariably describe the programs as aimed at providing "Jobs and Growth," the perennial backdrop logo for presidential speeches about the economy, they refrain from spelling out the exact mechanism involved: "Here's the deal: we give a bunch of money back to the rich and then they'll hire more of you to work for them."

When it comes to the crunch, the right's success in selling its economic programs to the public is more a triumph of misinformation than of dreams. There are various reasons why working Americans hold so many mistaken and often self-defeating notions about the effects of Republican economic policies—their own lack of interest and economic sophistication contributes a lot, and so do the statistical misrepresentations and accounting tricks that minimize the benefits to the rich and exaggerate the advantages to "middle-class taxpayers." But a lot of this has to do with the right's use of language that is calculated to blur the distinctions between economic classes.

he sleight of hand starts with the way the right talks about class itself. Or rather, doesn't talk about it, except when it's preceded by *middle*. The press may have no reservations about describing people as working class, but that phrase never appears in the speeches at whitehouse.gov, whereas *middle class* appears more than three hundred times. In those contexts, the phrase sounds reassuringly inclusive. Saying that the administration's tax program provides "middle-class tax relief" doesn't seem to be singling out any particular group for special attention. When you ask Americans to volunteer a description of themselves, after all, anywhere from 75 to 90 percent of them will opt for *middle-class*, whether their annual incomes are below $25,000 or more than $125,000 (nine out of ten of the latter choose the middle-class label, and it isn't until you get to around $500,000 that people begin to opt for other words like "affluent").

But *middle-class* has both social and economic meanings. In the social sense, *middle-class* is opposed to *lower-class* and *upper-class*. In the economic sense, it's opposed to "the wealthy" or "the affluent" on one side and *working-class* on the other. (There's "the underclass," too, but that word doesn't figure much in Americans' ordinary conversation.)

When we talk about *middle-class voters* or *middle-class tax cuts*, we're using *middle-class* in an economic sense; those phrases are opposed to

Social Class	Economic Class
Upper	The Wealthy etc.
Middle	Middle
Lower	Working
(The Underclass)	

phrases like *working-class voters* or *tax cut for the wealthy*. When we talk about a *middle-class lifestyle* or *middle-class speech*, we're using it in a social sense. And it's in the social sense that *middle-class* is closely associated with words like *respectability*, *morality*, and *values*.

When Americans report their social class, the vast majority opt for "middle." Think "upper-class," after all, and what comes to mind is dissolute socialites like Paris Hilton or Katherine Hepburn's character in *The Philadelphia Story*. Those connotations make even most wealthy Americans feel uneasy, particularly in these ostentatiously egalitarian times. As *Forbes* magazine observed in an article called "The Billionaire Next Door," nowadays even the very rich "seem fanatically determined to appear middle class. Bill Gates likes to be seen in his oversize sweater, Jeffrey Bezos sits at a ramshackle desk he made from an old door, and Warren Buffett always reminds us about his modest Omaha house." And at the other end, "lower-class" carries intimations of trailer-trash shiftlessness and inner-city family breakdown that make even relatively low-income workers reluctant to assume the label.

But a much smaller proportion of Americans consider themselves as middle-class in the economic sense of the term. When people are asked to pick a class description from a list rather than simply to volunteer one, the proportion describing themselves as middle-class drops to around 45 percent, with another 45 percent describing themselves as working-class. Those differences are effaced in political rhetoric, where "middle-class" does duty for everyone—it substitutes values and lifestyle aspirations for more unforgiving realities of income and educational level.

That ambiguity has permitted conservatives to play a version of what the grammarian H. W. Fowler described as "legerdemain with two senses": they take Americans' widespread self-identifications as middle-class in the *social* sense of the term as evidence for saying that class in the *economic* sense is irrelevant in American politics. As the conservative writer Bruce Bartlett puts it, "The border between wealth and middle class is so fluid that there is almost no meaningful distinction. Many of those [whom] liberals see as poor actually think of themselves as middle class . . . ." Abigail Thernstrom of the conservative Manhattan Institute writes that since "the overwhelming majority of people, when asked by pollsters, identify themselves as middle class, political campaigns based on class warfare predictably crash." Indeed, that sort of language by itself goes a long way toward explaining why the right has done better than the left in using class solidarity to its advantage. If we are all middle-class to-gether—the $27,000-a-year schoolteacher, the $450,000-a-year CFO—then the only class difference worth talking about is the one that separates us both from the guy cadging change by the freeway ramp. It's no wonder that "class warfare" is an expression that sets Americans to looking over their shoulders.

That blurring of class lines is a ubiquitous theme in the language of the right. According to the White House, for example, the estate tax falls most heavily on small businesses and family farms. But when Republicans talk about "small business owners," the term includes not just the proprietor of a dairy farm or a family hardware store, but anybody who has any income at all from a sole proprietorship or partnership. By that standard, "small business owners" include a corporate CEO who rents out his ski condo for a couple of weeks a year or a million-dollar-a-year network anchor who earns a few thousand dollars in speaking fees, not to mention a U.S. president who earns a few hundred dollars in income from an oil and gas company he has a small interest in.

At the same time, other words that used to be restricted to the rich have been redefined to include ordinary workers. Take *entrepreneur*, a word that George Bush loves to wrap his mouth around: "*Entrepreneur*," he said in a speech in 2004, "Isn't that a lovely word? You know, entrepreneur—we want entrepreneurs." Those words would have sounded uncomfortably candid in the mouth of a Republican like Taft or Eisenhower, back in the day when *entrepreneur* referred to people who provided the capital to launch major business enterprises. (*Entrepreneur* was pressed into service in the late nineteenth century to replace *capitalist*, which had been tainted by its association with silk-hatted predators.)

But these days, conservatives use the word to refer to anybody who goes into business for himself. During the 2004 election, for example, Commerce Secretary Don Evans complained to Wolf Blitzer on CNN that the Democrats had been citing unemployment figures drawn from the payroll survey, rather than the household survey that counts Americans who are self-employed: "Senator Kerry . . . wants to ignore the some ten million workers in that survey that are the entrepreneurs who are self-employed like truck drivers, like painters, like child-care workers, like hairdressers, like auto mechanics."

It's true that many of the people that conservatives celebrate as entrepreneurs have opted go into business for themselves, assuming not just the financial risks but the absence of health insurance and other benefits that the American system is unable to provide them. But a great many are also "involuntary entrepreneurs," in the tart phrase of Jared Bernstein of the Economic Policy Institute. By the right's definition, in fact, there's an upsurge in entrepreneurship whenever the economy heads south, as people are forced to take on piecework and odd jobs to make ends meet. (During the recent recession a report from the pro-entrepreneurial Kauffman Foundation applauded the sharp rise in self-employment among blacks and Hispanics as a sign that those groups have a higher rate of entrepreneurship than whites and Asians. Well, they'd better.)

It's a perfect example of the modern penchant for inflating people's job titles in lieu of raising their salaries—the same process that has elevated Wal-Mart's salespeople into "associates" and made "customer service executives" of the people who answer the phone when you call the cable company to complain about your bill. In the right's new language, the guy who does dump runs in his pickup truck and the manicurist working out of her home stand shoulder to shoulder with Bill Gates and Warren Buffett.

There's a parallel ambiguity in the way Republicans use the word *ownership*. "In a new term," Bush said during the 2004 campaign, "we'll continue to spread ownership to every corner of America." On its face, that sounds a lot like Oprah's "Everybody gets a car!" But Bush's "ownership" is a lot broader and vaguer than that—it covers tax incentives for establishing health savings accounts, reduced taxes on investment income, and Social Security privatization. More legerdemain with two senses: *ownership* blends the original sense of the word that we use to talk about actually having title to something with the new sense that business consultants are getting at when they talk about giving employees "a sense of ownership," not by giving them an equity stake but by encouraging them to "celebrate the company's vision." (Nowadays, pride of ownership doesn't always require a deed.) It's notable that Europeans find Bush's "ownership society" untranslatable—usually a sign that there's nothing "natural" about the concept behind a word. In fact, many of the Bush proposals would actually increase disparities in wealth, by displacing the tax burden from investment income to wages and by favoring those in the top brackets who naturally benefit most from tax incentives. "Spreading ownership," in this sense, is just another way of saying "concentrating wealth"—what *owners* comes down to is just another word for "haves."

Semantic ploys like these help to conceal the effects of Republican economic policies from ordinary voters, not to mention allowing conservatives to go to bed with a clear conscience. And the maneuvers are understandably infuriating to liberals, who see them as so much flim-flam aimed at deluding working Americans into buying into programs that harm their own economic interests. But while those devices may neutralize or modulate working people's mistrust of Republicans' economic policies, they can't by themselves bring ordinary voters on board with the broad political and economic programs of the right. And the sleight of hand that Republicans have practiced with items like *small business* and *entrepreneur* hasn't persuaded ordinary voters to identify their interests with those of the wealthy. In surveys, the vast majority of Americans say that the rich do not pay their fair share of taxes (only 15 percent believe that the rich are asked to pay too much). Linguistic legerdemain or no, if Republicans had to rely exclusively on winning support for their economic policies among working Americans, they'd be permanently out of power.

These days, conservatives dismiss the importance of economic class with another argument, which is almost the opposite of the first. As this story goes, the reason Americans don't mind programs that benefit the rich is not that they expect to be rich some day themselves, but that they care less about crassly economic divisions than about cultural ones. As David Brooks puts this argument just a few paragraphs after his assurance that Americans think of themselves as "pre-rich":

> Americans do not see society as a layer cake, with the rich on top, the middle class beneath them and the working class and underclass at the bottom. They see society as a high school cafeteria, with their community at one table and other communities at other tables. They are pretty sure that their community is the nicest, and filled with the best people, and they have a vague pity for all those poor souls who live in New York City or California and have a lot of money but no true neighbors and no free time. All of this adds up to a terrain incredibly inhospitable to class-based politics.

It isn't clear how Brooks would square that picture of I'm-glad-I'm-not-an-alpha Americans who are indifferent to the great wealth at the next table with the passage that precedes it, where the same people are depicted as poring over the *New Yorker* and *Town and Country* and rapt in their reveries of the horse farms they'll own someday. But that contradiction is implicit in virtually everything conservatives have to say about why Americans are unresponsive to class-based politics: Americans all expect to be rich some day, and anyway, they don't care about having a lot of money.

It was only in the late 1970s, though, that the right found a way to convert the old populist language of class resentments into a new idiom that stripped it of any real economic content and turned America into a vast version of Brooks's high-school cafeteria, divided only by values and fashions. As Thomas Frank puts it, it was based on "a way of thinking about class that both encourages class hostility and simultaneously denies the economic basis of the grievance":

> Class, conservatives insist, is not really about money or birth or even occupation. It is primarily a matter of authenticity, that most valuable cultural commodity. Class is about what one drives and where one shops and how one prays, and only secondarily about the work one does or the income one makes. What makes one a member of the noble proletariat is not work per se, but unpretentiousness, humility, and the rest of the qualities that our punditry claims to spy in the red states that voted for George W. Bush.

But class is a notion that pervades the English vocabulary, and to suppress its economic realities, the right had to rewrite a large chunk of the American lexicon in "cultural" terms, and redefine the liberal-conservative distinction in the process.

One impetus for that shift was the emergence of "values issues," a catchall that could include both symbolic issues like school prayer and the inclusion of "under God" in the Pledge of Allegiance and more substantive ones like abortion and crime. In earlier eras, issues like those had played almost no role in distinguishing conservatism and liberalism. Most people would have accepted Roosevelt's description of the two sides as "two general schools of political belief," which chiefly differed on how active a role the government should take in regulating the markets. In fact, New Deal–era liberals had very little interest in the moral issues that had burned so hot in the heart of the Progressives who preceded them— making civil servants honest, redeeming the unfortunate from drink, inculcating immigrants with American ideals. As the historian Gary Gerstle has said, the New Dealers "reserved their moral passion for economic reform; their moral compass pointed to such words as 'security,' 'opportunity,' and 'industrial democracy.'" Nor did moral issues figure very prominently in Republicans' attacks on the New Deal—they had their hands full fighting market regulation and Social Security.

By the 1970s, though, values issues had moved to center stage in American political life, and by now the values tail is wagging the economic dog. A 2005 Harris poll showed that Americans were more likely to identify people as being liberals or conservatives according to their views on issues like abortion and gay rights than their views on taxes. It's true that being pro-choice or pro-gay marriage won't by itself qualify you as a liberal nowadays, but it may very well disqualify you from being a conservative, whatever your views on taxes, deregulation, or the war on terror. But to accomplish that shift, the right had to suppress the political connotations of liberalism and turn it into a lifestyle brand.

chapter five

The Volvo Dodge

He's silent majority . . . but he keeps making noise.
—*John Updike,* Rabbit Redux, *1971*

from a linguistic point of view, branding is simply the process that turns the associations or overtones of a word into part of its meaning. That's what marketers and advertisers are paid to accomplish, but it can happen without their efforts, in either a positive or negative way. Rolls-Royce comes to stand in for opulent luxury; the DeLorean becomes a synonym for a commercial flop; the favorite prefix of McDonald's becomes a sign of cheapness in words like *McMansion* and *McJobs*.

With political labels, branding involves coloring the purely descriptive meaning of a label with the stereotypical traits of the people who wear it. In extreme cases, the original meaning of the term may be obscured as its connotations are made the basis for a new meaning. That can happen to a label anywhere on the political spectrum: over the years it has been the fate of words like *tory, bolshevik, populist,* and *fascist*. But the Democratic left has always been susceptible to a particular kind of stereotyping by its opponents. People don't usually require a convoluted story to explain the political views of bourgeois conservatives or proletarian radicals. But it takes more ingenuity to discredit the motives of people who don't seem to be motivated by obvious self-interest. So conservatives have always tried to dismiss those concerns as the signs of baser motivations like social pretension, dilettantism, or effete sentimentality.

In one form or another, that maneuver has been a staple of the pseudo-populism of the American right since the 1840 "cider election." The intellectually challenged William Henry Harrison was an Ohioan from an aristocratic Virginia background whom the Whigs successfully repackaged as a cider-sipping frontiersman in the Jacksonian mode, sending him out on the campaign trail in a wagon topped by a log cabin and attacking his Democratic opponent Martin Van Buren as an effete Easterner who ate off gold plates, put cologne on his whiskers, and was "laced up in corsets such as women in town wear"—an effete snob *avant la lettre*.

Attacks like those have left their mark on the language in a long line of disparagements for people who seem to subordinate their own class interests to the cause of social justice. In the 1920s, a *Wall Street Journal* editorial described supporters of the progressive Robert La Follette as "visionaries, ne'er do wells, parlor pinks, reds, hyphenates [foreign-born Americans], soft handed agriculturalists and working men who have never seen a shovel." *Parlor pink* was a particularly deft touch, which managed to convey bourgeois affectation, ideological timidity, and effeminacy at the same time. (*Time* magazine coined the variant *pinko* in 1926.) A few decades later, the acerbic right-wing columnist Westbrook Pegler contributed the adjective *bleeding-heart*, a durable phrase that reduces all altruism to girlish sentimentality. And in the 1950s, *egghead* evoked Adlai Stevenson's minimalist tonsure by way of adding an anti-intellectual note to the mix. (It was around then that William F. Buckley famously quipped that he would rather be governed by the first two thousand names in the Boston phone book than the entire Harvard faculty.)

Most of those disparagements echoed antique class resentments—as the conservative writer Peter Viereck put it, they were allegations that had been "made for centuries by pseudo-wholesome, 'pious' peasants against 'effete' noblemen." Until recent times, the right dismissed liberals as an influential but relatively small group of intellectuals, bohemians, and bourgeois fellow-travelers who were motivated by infantile rebelliousness or misplaced sympathy for the downtrodden. But in the late

1960s, the tenor of antiliberal rhetoric began to change. Now the right cast the net much more widely, to include a wide swath of middle-class American society that was defined more by its tastes than its political convictions.

t he moment was propitious for that shift. The Nixon years may have been a troubled time politically, but they were also the high-water moment of postwar prosperity. Wages hadn't yet begun to stagnate, inflation was at reasonable levels, and consumer goods were becoming ever more accessible. To many, it looked as if America was becoming a consumerist monoculture, and it was natural that consumerism began to leave its mark on the way people talked about social groups. In the 1950s and 1960s, Americans had taken their social vocabulary from sociologists and social psychologists, as they adopted expressions like *status symbol, peer group, organization man,* and *the power elite.* In the 1970s, though, marketers became the new cartographers of the American social landscape. People turned to advertisers for words like *lifestyle* and *yuppie,* and marketing terms like *upscale* and *demographics* became part of everyday conversation. In the public's mind, if not in reality, consumption patterns were trumping the old economic and social indicators of class. The entry requirements for becoming a preppie were relaxed from four years at Choate to an afternoon at Abercrombie and Fitch, *Ivy League* came to denote a style of dress, and *blue-collar* became a name for a dogged style of basketball or a bare-brick decor.*

There were echoes of that new language in the way people were characterizing the newly discovered "Middle Americans" in terms of their cultural tastes and consumer preferences. Kevin Phillips described the group in his influential 1969 book *The Emerging Republican Majority* as "the great, ordinary, Lawrence Welkish mass of Americans from Maine to Hawaii." And *Time* magazine described them as people whose car windows were plastered with patriotic decals, who learned baton twirling

---

* "Head for the heart of Emeryville's manufacturing district, specifically, Semifreddi's Bakery, where you can lunch blue-collar style on upscale sandwiches, salads, focaccia and soups (tomato rice with Swiss chard and lots of freshly shaved Parmesan the other day) in a warehouse-type setting." (*San Francisco Chronicle,* December 4, 1991).

rather than reading Hermann Hesse, who skipped *Midnight Cowboy* but went back several times to see John Wayne in *The Green Berets*, and who stood in line to see the Rockettes at Radio City Music Hall rather than *Oh, Calcutta!*—all of these, presumably, choices that had political significance. From there, it was only a short stretch to turn to consumer categories to redraw the conservative-liberal distinction.

against that background, the right began to brand liberals in a literal way, according to the products they consumed. There was a telling sign of the shift in the replacement of "limousine liberal" by "Volvo liberal." "Limousine liberal" first surfaced during John Lindsay's 1969 New York mayoral campaign against Mario Procaccino, which was cast as a clash between working stiffs from the outer boroughs and wealthy Manhattan liberals who could champion programs like busing because they had no personal stake in public education. But when "Volvo liberal" first appeared about a decade later, it carved the social pie very differently. It didn't simply depict the prototypical liberal as middle-class rather than wealthy (a Volvo doesn't cost any more than a Buick, after all). It also signaled a view of political affiliation as merely another lifestyle choice. At its inception, "Volvo liberal" was just another one of those pop marketing descriptions like "baby boomer" and "soccer mom," but it rapidly became a disparagement. By 1981, Pat Buchanan was accusing his radio sparring partner Tom Braden of being a member of the "the Volvo, white wine and cheese set."

The brand image of the Volvo was ideal for this sort of stereotyping: not only was it an unglamorous car from socialist Sweden that people bought simply because they thought it was safe, but its name had a serendipitous gynecological resonance—probably the main reason Volvos rather than Saabs were singled out for political stereotyping. And other products associated with an upscale urban lifestyle were accorded the same treatment, particularly those that were soft or light enough to convey effeteness, like white wine, Brie, and caffè latte. (Port and Stilton might be equally upmarket, but they don't connote effete self-indulgence the way brie and caffè latte do, and anyway, British products don't figure in these stereotypes now that Anglophilia has yielded to Francophilia in the catalog of liberal vices.)

The modern stereotype of liberals was succinctly summarized in a television ad that the arch-conservative Club for Growth ran during the 2004 Iowa presidential primary, back when Howard Dean was still the leading Democratic contender. An announcer asks a middle-aged couple leaving a barbershop what they think of Dean's plan to raise taxes on families by $1,900 a year. The man responds: "I think Howard Dean should take his tax-hiking, government-expanding, latte-drinking, sushi-eating, Volvo-driving, *New York Times*-reading . . . "—and then his wife picks up the litany: ". . . body-piercing, Hollywood-loving, left-wing freak show back to Vermont, where it belongs." That was a demographic pastiche, of course: you have an image of Marilyn Manson on the porch of his house on Lake Champlain TiVo-ing "Curb Your Enthusiasm" and laughing so hard at Maureen Dowd's column that he chokes on his unagi cone. But it neatly encapsulated the nosegay of political, social, sexual, and geographical attributes that had piled up around the liberal stereotype over the preceding decades, as if there were obvious connections among people's place of residence, their fiscal views, and their inclinations in seafood and body ornament.

Some people have tried to take these connections seriously, as if liberals could be reduced to a marketing category whose brand preferences were revealing indicators of their ideological identifications. David Brooks has tried to connect urban liberals' fondness for expensive coffee drinks and bottled water to their predilection for inconspicuous consumption:

> You'll have noticed already that you just spent nearly $3 for a cup of coffee; you're going to have to get into the overpriced coffee habit. That's because this is the land of the Latte Liberals. People around here are disturbed by the widening gulf between rich and poor, and are therefore somewhat uncomfortable that their own family incomes tend to come in comfortably above the $100,000 level. So their dilemma is how to spend money in a way that won't make them look like vulgar Republicans. One

way is to spend extravagantly on things that used to be cheap, like coffee, bread, water and casual clothes. That way they don't look like Donald Trump, just upscale grad students.

Brooks writes entertainingly and caustically of the lifestyle of the inhabitants of urban liberal enclaves whom he calls Bobos ("Bourgeois Bohemians"), and others have savaged the political posturing of Hollywood and the academy, though it's fair to say that liberal America is still waiting for its Evelyn Waugh. But a deft satirist would find equally easy pickings in the political and cultural pretensions of any number of conservative sets: the shallow upper-class WASPs that William Hamilton routinely skewers in his *New Yorker* cartoons, the preternaturally clean-cut summer interns at right-wing think tanks who could teach Upper West Side liberals a thing or two about smug, or the bow-tied Ivy Leaguers at *National Review* and the *Weekly Standard* composing panegyrics to Merle Haggard and Wal-Mart. Any philosophy that can command the loyalty of many dedicated people is bound to attract its share of ideological groupies. Almost seventy years ago, George Orwell skewered the affectations of middle-class socialists of his day in *The Road to Wigan Pier*: "One sometimes gets the impression that the mere words 'Socialism' and 'Communism' draw towards them with magnetic force every fruit-juice drinker, nudist, sandal-wearer, sex-maniac, Quaker, 'Nature Cure' quack, pacifist, and feminist in England." Making appropriate adjustments for changing fads and fashions, that would do for the pretensions of some left-wing circles today. But Orwell would have bristled at the idea that the fatuity of some of socialism's fellow-travelers discredited its lofty goals: "The only thing for which we can combine is the underlying ideal of Socialism; justice and liberty. . . . Justice and liberty! Those are the words that have got to ring like a bugle across the world." Sex maniacs, fruit-juice drinkers, or no.

In fact, lifestyle and consumer preferences aren't nearly as good a predictor of political preferences as the right likes to pretend. It's true that Volvo owners skew Democratic, but only by about 4-to-3, not a very big difference when other factors like geography are added to the mix, and one that has been shrinking as Volvos become more expensive and luxurious—

among buyers of new Volvos, Democrats have only a slight edge. As indicators of partisan affiliations go, owning a Volvo is somewhat less reliable than rooting for a baseball team that wears a blue uniform.* And it turns out that the majority of Brie consumers are Republicans. That's actually not surprising, given that Brie is a lot easier to find in the gourmet shops in upscale suburbs than in supermarkets in working-class neighborhoods. But whoever actually buys the stuff, it stands in perfectly for the right's stereotype of liberals—soft, pale, runny, and French.

That's the real point of the right's branding exercises. They're basically just a kind of product placement: the right puts liberals in Volvos and conservatives in Ford pickups for the same reason advertisers put their own beer in the hands of a bunch of regular guys and Brand X in the hands of snooty poseurs.

A few years ago, for example, *National Review*'s Rich Lowry wrote an appreciation of motorcycling, applauding its "quintessentially American qualities" of individualism, risk-taking, and the sense of freedom and possibility of the open road. While admitting that he himself had had very little personal experience with the sport, Lowry applauded bikers for their "love-it-or-leave-it patriotism" and the "free spirit" of those who refuse (unwisely, to be sure) to wear helmets. Motorcyclists, he said, "tap into a spirit that is more robust, rugged and masculine than the 'tall-skim-double-mocha latte, please' culture of contemporary America." Lowry proceeded to recast William F. Buckley's famous aphorism about the first two hundred names in the Boston phone book and the Harvard faculty as "I would rather be governed by two thousand motorcycle riders than all the Volvo drivers in the United States." Leaving aside whatever that might reveal about Lowry's inner life, his rewriting of the quip says a lot about what has happened to American conservatism. Whether or not you agree with Buckley about the role of intellectuals in American public life, his remark was an incisive bit of political commentary, whereas Lowry's remark has no real political content at all. It's merely an attempt to appropriate a romantic aura of "freedom and possibility"

* The colors of Major League Baseball home uniforms coincided with the 2004 presidential vote of their states 65 percent of the time.

that has never had any particular connection to political conservatism. (Think of motorcycling, after all, and the names that come to mind include Marlon Brando, Peter Fonda, and Bruce Springsteen, not to mention Che Guevara, none of them likely to appear in the subscription rolls of *National Review*.)

The right has been remarkably successful in pigeonholing liberalism as a white upper-middle-class affectation. Just look, for example, at the way liberals are referred to in the media, even in the *New York Times* and the *Los Angeles Times*. Wherever you look, the liberal label is almost exclusively reserved for middle-class whites. Phrases like *working-class liberals*, *Hispanic liberals*, and *black liberals* are virtually nonexistent, though *conservative* is frequently used to describe members of all those groups. When the media are referring to members of the working class or minority groups who vote left-of-center, they invariably describe them as Democrats, with the implication that their political choices are shaped by economic self-interest or traditional party loyalty, rather than by any deep commitment to liberal ideals. It's as if you can't count as a liberal unless you can afford the lifestyle. Liberalism is treated less as a political credo than as the outward expression of a particular social identity, like a predilection for granite countertops and bottled water.

The right's brand-war rhetoric has become so familiar to Americans by now that we can lose sight of how very odd it all is. The whole business is puzzling to Europeans—even in the United Kingdom, despite the close ties between the modern conservative movements in Britain and the United States. During the 2004 Democratic primary season, the London *Daily Telegraph*'s Alec Russell lamented the "Tough Times for the Innocent Volvo," wondering, "Could this be the first election swung by the Volvo, or rather anti-Volvo, vote? You may think of the Swedish car as a symbol of county tranquility, but in America it is a raging term of abuse." But then, like other Europeans, the British aren't about to be deluded into rewriting their class system as a battle of the brands, not when genuine class distinctions are still a pervasive presence in their national life.

For that matter, the right's brand warfare is weird even by American standards. However brand-conscious we may actually be, we profess to believe that consumer preferences are a superficial basis for judging people. Most Americans past adolescence will tell you it's the height of shallowness to admit that you pick your friends or your dates according to the cars they drive or the clothes they wear. Yet the right cites those same consumer choices in all seriousness as if they were reliable signs of the deep differences in character and values that shape two distinct political cultures. Aren't people supposed to get over that stuff in high school?

In fact, the right's stereotypes are as reductive and condescending for conservatives as they are for liberals. Can't conservatives drive a Volvo or a Prius, eat organic vegetables, prepare and can their own apple butter, and listen to bluegrass and jazz on NPR? Of course they can, says *National Review*'s Rod Dreher, in a piece on what he calls "crunchy" (as in Granola) conservatives, provided they don't let labels frame their experience. Accepting the right's stereotypes of liberal and conservative consumer habits, Dreher writes, "means accepting bad beer, lousy coffee, Top-40 radio, strip malls, and all popular manifestations of cheapness and ugliness as proof that One Is Not an Effete Liberal." Fair enough, as long as you make a place for the liberals who are fine with being NASCAR dads and love George Jones.

chapter six

Color Wars

One fish two fish red fish blue fish.

—*Dr. Seuss*

t he very superficiality of conservatives' incessant references to brands and lifestyle is crucial to the way they've delineated the adversaries in the "culture war." As it happens, that phrase appeared around the same time that "Volvo liberal" did, exploiting some of the ambiguities that had crept into the word *culture* over the preceding decades. When people first started to talk about "culture wars" around 1980, they were referring to the controversies over PBS, the National Endowment for the Arts, the "Great Books" requirements at universities, and the multicultural curriculum—that is, battles over "culture" in the sense that the *Oxford English Dictionary* defines as "the intellectual side of civilization." But before long the phrase was being used to refer to a war *between* cultures in the anthropologists' sense, which was being fought over issues like abortion, gun control, and the teaching of "creation science" in the schools. That was what Pat Buchanan was getting at when he spoke of a "cultural war" in a famously provocative speech at the 1988 Republican National Convention:

My friends, this election is about much more than who gets what. It is about who we are. It is about what we believe. It is about what we stand

73

for as Americans. There is a religious war going on in our country for the soul of America. It is a cultural war, as critical to the kind of nation we will one day be as was the Cold War itself.

There's no question that the kind of "cultural war" that Buchanan was referring to was and remains a very real feature of American public life. But Republicans realized that the armed conflict that Buchanan was talking about wasn't a struggle they could build broad middle-class coalitions around. Indeed, Buchanan's speech was widely regarded as undercutting George H.W. Bush's "kinder, gentler nation" message, hurting him with voters who were made uneasy by Buchanan's confrontational tone. (Buchanan was denied the opportunity to address the convention four years later.)

That picture of a divided nation was obviously congenial to the Republicans' strategy of recasting economic divisions as cultural ones. The trick was to formulate it in ways that didn't alarm voters who might be troubled about the way things were going in America, but weren't ready to take to the trenches over the issue. So the right adopted the rhetoric of cultural division while avoiding the millenarian pronouncements of the likes of Buchanan or Jerry Falwell. Conservatives talk about a culturally divided nation, now conveniently color-coded as "blue" and "red" America, as if the country were embroiled in a grim game of capture the flag.* "You've got 80 percent to 90 percent of the country that look at each other as if they were on separate planets," said Matthew Dowd, a Republican strategist, in 2001. Writing in the *New York Post* in the same year, John Podhoretz described the country as "devolving into two nations" separated by a "head-spinning" difference of affect. And the conservative commentator Michael Barone made the "two nations" allusion more explicitly when he cited Benjamin Disraeli's famous description of Victorian England as divided into

two nations between whom there is no intercourse and no sympathy; who

* The red-blue distinction was a fortuitous side effect of the way the networks reported the election results in 2000, but it conjures up the stark and irreconcilable divisions that color labels have always suggested in the past—the blue and gray of the American Civil War or the whites and reds of the War of the Roses and the Russian Revolution.

are as ignorant of each other's habits, thoughts, and feelings, as if they were dwellers in different zones or inhabitants of different planets; who are formed by a different breeding, are fed by a different food, are ordered by different manners, and are not governed by the same laws.

But where Disraeli's two nations were the rich and the poor, now, says Barone, "the divide is not economic, but cultural. . . . They are as different as Bill Clinton's preferred vacation spot, Martha's Vineyard, and George W. Bush's ranch in Crawford, Texas. . . we are, in important ways, two separate nations who live uncomfortably together."

Only someone with a willful disregard for history would compare the difference between Bush and Clinton voters to the disparities between the rich and poor of Disraeli's England, who were as different from one another—in living conditions, attitudes, education, life expectancy, even height and weight—as the Elves and Orks of Tolkein's Middle Earth. And for that matter, it takes another kind of willful disregard to imagine that the cultural differences between upper-middle-class Texans and New Englanders are more dramatic than the economic differences between the inhabitants of Beverly Hills and Watts, or that Americans are unaware of their differences in attitude (that's pretty much all anybody talks about nowadays). But the media have been quick to pick up on the idea of a nation riven by "a values chasm," "parallel universes," or "a clash of cultures." "The divide went deeper than politics," wrote the *Washington Post*'s David Broder; "it reached into the nation's psyche." "Not since the Civil War has the country been so divided," said the political scientist John Kenneth White, the author of *The Values Divide*. And the Discovery Channel broadcast a special called "Red and Blue," in which a family of Louisiana tomato farmers switched places with a family of educators from Topanga Canyon in Los Angeles, with predictably risible results. So it's no wonder that most Americans accept the picture of a culturally polarized nation: a large majority believe by a very wide margin that they have fewer shared values than they used to.

As it happens, though, all the research shows that that picture is wrong. In *One Nation, After All*, Alan Wolfe reported on hundreds of interviews conducted in a number of communities. He concluded that the majority of Americans have roughly similar opinions on most of the important cultural issues facing the nation; Americans, he said, "long for a sensible center and distrust ideological thinking." Those conclusions are supported by survey data that show that Americans have actually become more unified in their attitudes about issues like racial integration, crime, and especially women's roles. In his recent book *Culture War? The Myth of a Polarized America,* the political scientist Morris Fiorina of Stanford and the Hoover Institution pointed out that polls show substantial agreement between the inhabitants of red states and blue states on issues like gun control, women's rights, equality of opportunity, and capital punishment, not to mention on whether large companies have too much power. "The simple truth," he says, "is that there is no culture war in the United States. No battle for the soul of America rages." And in the *Atlantic Monthly,* Jonathan Rauch made the same point anecdotally but tellingly when he cited a Gallup survey performed for the online dating service match.com, which showed that 57 percent of unmarried Americans would be open to marrying someone who held significantly different political views. As Rauch noted, "Just how deep can our political disagreements be, I wonder, if most of us are willing to wake up next to them every morning?"

Hence the challenge facing the right: how do you promote the notion of a red-blue "cultural divide" that preempts the divisions of class without actually making it sound so deep or consequential that you risk alienating a large group of cultural noncombatants or excluding a large part of your constituency? The fact is, after all, that the coalition that the right has built cuts sweepingly across the traditional cultural differences between religious, regional, ethnic, and class-based communities that have long histories of common experience. It joins country-club Republicans and working-class anti-abortion activists, and people from Biloxi, Salt Lake City, and Sun City, Arizona. It joins Pentecostals and evangelicals, conservative Catholics, and Orthodox Jews (hence the need for the new term "people of faith," which the right uses as a flag of convenience for people who support its policies on religious grounds). Within the conservative elite, it joins the largely Jewish neocon intellectuals who went to Ivy League schools and live in New York and Washington with Catholic conservatives and the capital-C Christian leadership of groups like the Family Research Council and the Christian Coalition. And when you zero in on the county-by-county and town-by-town election maps, you see the red-blue line separating people from identical educational and social backgrounds, depending on whether they went into fields like banking and industry or architecture and teaching.

The solution was to give "culture" a new and diluted definition, which had also become conveniently available around the time "Volvo liberal" first appeared in the late 1970s. That was when people began talk about the "cultures" of groups like sorority girls, low riders, corporations, or video gamers—virtually any group that could lay claim to its own mores, modes, or magazines, whether or not its members had any deeper traits in common.

So when it comes to delineating the cultural features that define America's "two nations," conservatives assiduously hug the surface, drawing the distinctive character traits of red- and blue-state inhabitants in vague and sweeping generalities. In red-state America, David Brooks says, "the self is small," whereas in blue-state America, "the self is uncommonly large." Red-staters are tradition-minded, says Michael Barone, whereas blue-staters are liberation-minded. Writing in April 2003, shortly after the initial military successes in Iraq, the *Wall Street Journal's* Peggy Noonan described the qualities of the "big and real America" to which George W. Bush belongs:

> But there was always another America, and boy has it endured. It just won a war. Its newest generation is rising, and its members are impressive. They came from a bigger America and a realer one—a healthy and vibrant place full of religious feeling and cultural energy and Bible study and garage bands and sports-love and mom-love and sophistication and normality.

Sports-love, mom-love, sophistication, and normality—that would seem to make red Americans of us all, apart from the city dwellers who don't have garages, skipped the Super Bowl, and feel ambivalent about their mothers.

The *New York Post*'s John Podhoretz produces similar platitudes when he reports on his ethnographic fieldwork over "two successive weekends in Las Vegas" and concludes that the two nations are divided, not by class, race, or even style, but rather by affect:

> The distinction between Las Vegas and New York—between Bush Red and Gore Blue—is head-spinning. Those of us who reside in Gore Blue-land cannot live without irony, which is to say, we cannot live without a filter of distance. We see the absurdity in everything, and we struggle to believe. . . . Bush Red is a simpler place.

No one seems to mind if these generalizations embrace contradictory stereotypes—what about all those humorless PC types conservatives love to make fun of? And if Podhoretz believes that red-staters are incapable of irony, he has clearly never listened to a Jeff Foxworthy routine or to George Jones singing "She Thinks I Still Care." (Country music battens on irony, not surprising for a genre that's always dwelling on the fragility of happiness.) But the point of the exercise is simply to spin time-honored bromides about the homespun virtues of Republican voters into pseudo-ethnography. As Thomas Frank puts it, "Reading through the 'two Americas' literature is a little like watching a series of Frank Capra one-reelers explaining the principles of some turbo-charged Boy Scout law." What it comes down to, as Frank observes, is merely saying that red-state inhabitants are unpretentious, humble, courteous, reverent, loyal, and above all more authentic than their blue-state counterparts.

When it comes to the crunch, in fact, what Podhoretz describes as a "head-spinning" cultural division between "two nations" is really no more than another of those parlor games that capture the American fancy every so often, as people set about pigeonholing everything according to its place in some simplistic scheme of classification: highbrow, middlebrow, and lowbrow; U and non-U; camp and kitsch; modern and postmodern; wired and tired. By now, there's no aspect of American life that someone hasn't tried to place on the national color wheel. The Cincinnati Reds' pitcher Joe Valentine, who was raised by lesbian parents, describes himself as a "blue state guy playing in a red state sport."

An article in *Brandweek* reports that Scotts is introducing a new fertilizer aimed at the blue-state market, and *Advertising Age* describes Maxwell House's efforts to "make the blue can a badge of the red states, to make coffee selection a battlefront in the culture wars." Tina Brown writes in the *Washington Post* about Paula Zahn's "swingy new red-state hair." And the *New York Times* quotes the program director of a Los Angeles radio station disparaging competitors who play "red-state rock." That phrase pretty much sums up the entirety of the sociopolitical theory behind the blue-red cultural distinction: if you like Lynyrd Skynyrd, you'll love George Bush.

The charm of those pigeonholing exercises always has a lot to do with their absurd reductiveness—the object is to group the most unlike things into a single hopper (Middlebrow: Walter Lippmann, Edna Ferber, and Walt Disney). But when marketers do their demography in detail, America turns out to be an increasingly heterogeneous place. As Michael J. Weiss puts it in *The Clustered World,* "the mass market of the post–World War II area didn't just fade away, it shattered into niche markets." The marketing information company Claritas divides the nation into sixty-two distinct segments, with names like "pools and patios," "kids and cul-de-sacs," and "rural industrial," which differ from each other not just in product choices but political views as well. (Hence the vogue for buzz-words like "narrowcasting" and "particle marketing.") And the sweeping treatises on the red-blue divide invariably run roughshod over the nu-anced demographic analyses which entered the political literature in 1969 with Kevin Phillips's *The Emerging Republican Majority* (which the polit-ical journalist George Packer has described as the book that invented the 1970s) and which have shaped the political analyses of Stanley Greenberg and John Judis and Ruy Teixeira, among many others.

But even if the consumerist take on the red-blue divide doesn't square with market realities (think of all those Brie-slurping Republicans), it provides the right with a clutch of "cultural" distinctions that cut across all its new constituencies. The curious thing about the right's strategy of guilt-by-brand-association, in fact, is that it coincided with the diminish-ing importance of regional differences in consumption: nowadays, peo-ple in every part of the country order their lifestyles from the same menus. There are Restoration Hardware stores in Metairie, Louisiana, and Tulsa, and Godiva chocolate boutiques in Shreveport and Spokane. And however Volvo selects its dealer locations, it isn't by looking for concentrations of liberal guilt. Lubbock, Texas, boasts a dealership (as well as several Starbucks locations), and so do other red-state bastions like Cheyenne, Wyoming, and Murfreesboro, Tennessee. For that matter, there are two Harley-Davidson dealerships in San Francisco and another in Corte Madera just across the Golden Gate Bridge in Marin County. Or drive a few miles further to Infineon Raceway in Sonoma, the site of the Dodge 350 on the NASCAR circuit. The last time I was there, in 2005, my daughter and I stood outside the pit area next to a group of people who were holding plastic cups of Napa Valley Chardonnay and peering for a glimpse of Jeff Gordon or Dale Earnhardt Jr. But then the NASCAR organization realizes that even those of us who live in places like Northern California, Delaware, Chicago, and the Boston area may find it thrilling to watch a string of 750-horsepower cars roar by at 140 miles an hour, whatever our views on Social Security privatization.

The same holds wherever you look. Country music and hip-hop have expanded far beyond their original regional or race-based markets, even as they're facing stiffer competition on their own turfs—the top-rated radio station in Nashville in 2005 was the adult contemporary WJXA, with the nearest country station down at number four. In 2004, the *New York Times* reported that *Will and Grace,* a sitcom about gay life in New York, is one of the most popular shows among younger Republican women (setting aside any reservations they may have had about its content, Republicans promptly bought time on the show).

Whether you examine political attitudes, social values, or lifestyle, in short, it's simply hallucinatory to believe that there's a "cultural divide" in America that bears comparison with the economic divisions between rich and poor in Victorian England or the political divisions of the Civil War—or for that matter with the cultural division between the North and South of fifty years ago. But it's precisely the vagueness and superficiality of the right's cultural stereotypes that make them so useful: they create an illusion of shared experience among people whose actual commonalities don't extend to much more than the products on their shelves and a general sense of grievance. You get a sense of just how blurry and expansive the boundaries of "red-state culture" are when you hear right-wing writers proclaiming their identification with middle-American voters, even if they actually have no more in common with the longneck-drinking, pickup-driving classes than Paris Hilton does. Take the way radio talk-show host Laura Ingraham begins her book *Shut Up and Sing* by castigating "elite Americans":

> They think we're stupid. They think our patriotism is stupid. They think our churchgoing is stupid. They think having more than two children is stupid. They think where we live—anywhere but near or in a few major cities—is stupid. They think our SUVs are stupid. They think owning a gun is stupid. They think our abiding belief in the goodness of America and its founding principles is stupid.

The most significant word in those passages is *we*. How abstract must the notion of "red-state culture" be if it entitles Ingraham—who is the daughter of a Connecticut lawyer, and who went to Dartmouth and the University of Virginia Law School and now lives in Washington, D.C.—to claim the right to share a first-person plural pronoun with a Pentecostal deer hunter from Oklahoma? And Ann Coulter, another Ivy-educated second-generation lawyer from Connecticut (and with the vowels to prove it), goes on about red-state denizens with the effusiveness of a fifth-grader reporting on a zoo visit. "I loved Kansas City! It's my favorite place in the world . . . It's the opposite of this town. They're Americans, they're so great, they're rooting for America!" "I love Texas Republicans! . . . Americans are so cool!" "Queens, baseball games—those are my people. American people." It's as if all differences of class and background have been swept aside, leaving Coulter, Ted Nugent, and Johnny Ramone to swill in a communion of Clinton-hating ectomorphy.

American political discourse doesn't provide many spectacles as improbable as those right-wing fanfares to the common man. But modern conservatives never tire of contrasting their own solidarity with Southerners and rural Americans with the disdain that liberals have for them. In fact, the word *redneck* is about twenty times more likely to appear in the pages of conservative publications like *National Review* than in the *Nation* or the *American Prospect*, chiefly because conservatives are fond of setting the word in the mouths of imaginary left-wing elitists in the course of reminding the good people of the heartland how much contempt liberals have for them.* Liberals, writes Mackubin Thomas Owens, "yammer on ceaselessly about 'tolerance' and 'diversity' [but] don't seem inclined to extend those concepts to many of their fellow citizens, whom they portray as religious bigots, racist rednecks, and generally stupid people." Laura Ingraham writes that "mocking the pickup-driving, tobacco-chewing, shotgun-owning South is one of the elite rites of passage." And the *Washington Times*'s Greg Pierce writes of the supporters of Howard Dean: "To them, America's red states are populated by ignorant cowboys, unwashed swampies, hellfire preachers, beauty parlor bimbos, redneck sheriffs, Confederate flag wavers and retarded hillbilly kids sitting in trees playing the banjo."

Not that you don't hear liberals saying just this sort of thing. Writing in the *Chicago Sun-Times* just after the 2000 election, William O'Rourke described Bush's America as "Yahoo Nation":

> It is a large, lopsided horseshoe, a twisted W, made up of primarily the Deep South and the vast, lowly populated upper-far-west states that are filled with vestiges of gun-loving, Ku-Klux-Klan sponsoring, formerly lynching-happy, survivalist-minded, hate-crime perpetrating, non-blue-blooded, rugged individualists . . . which contains not one primary center of intellectual or creative density.

That passage owes a debt to conservative rhetoric; it has exactly the same structure and cadence as that Club for Growth ad about the latte-drinking, sushi-eating liberals. And both descriptions have their roots in the conservatives' earlier culture-war attacks on flag-burning, bra-burning, pot-smoking, draft-dodging, America-hating, lip-curling, card-carrying

---

* The same ratio applies to the dismissive "flyover country," which is ten times as likely to appear in *National Review* as in the *Nation* or the *American Prospect*.

do-gooders. It's syntax that turns what people do into what they are, and it's as arrogant and reductive coming from one side as from the other.

But those Tobacco Road stereotypes of the South and rural America are the same disparagements that the Republicans hurled at the Populists a century ago and that both Northerners and "genteel" Southerners have always trotted out when they wanted to ridicule poor Southern whites. Indeed, Southern politicians have been exploiting that "redneck and proud of it" rhetoric for more than a century to stir up resentments against Northerners and the rich. What's new is that now Eastern establishment conservatives are trying their hands at the same game, confident that the right-mindedness of their political views will exempt them from any suspicion of condescension. In this they're no different from the middle-class socialists of Orwell's time, who invariably claimed to be above class snobbishness—a vice, as Orwell put it, "which we can discern in everyone else but never in ourselves." Yet these same people aren't above pulling out some "not-our-class-dear" stereotypes of their own when it's convenient. Coulter, David Limbaugh, Jonah Goldberg, Tony Snow, and Oliver North are only a few of the conservatives who have referred to the Clintons or their staff as "white trash," the gentility's time-honored rebuke for members of the lower orders who get ideas above their station.

chapter seven

I Married an Elite

It's a funny world, that world they're sketching—
a world in which Big Bird is an elitist and
right-wing media magnates are populists.
> —*Bill Clinton, Remarks to the*
> *Democratic National Committee, January 21, 1995*

What ultimately makes possible the inclusive *we* with which Ingraham, Noonan, and others join themselves with Middle Americans at the unhip is the exclusive *they* it's implicitly opposed to. Those are the people that Ingraham describes as "the elites," a word that encapsulates the right's rewriting of the language of populism. When C. Wright Mills wrote *The Power Elite* in 1956, the title referred to the interlocking leadership of politics, business, and the military: "They are in command of the major hierarchies and organizations of modern society. They rule the big corporations. They run the machinery of the state and claim its prerogatives. They direct the military establishment. They occupy the strategic command posts of the social structure."

That was then. Now, few of the denizens of those command posts would qualify for the *elite* label in American political conversation. As the right uses the word, it applies only to inhabitants of the power elite's outer boroughs—the celebrities, academics, journalists, and others whom Mills described as "part of the immediate scene in which the drama of the elite is enacted." References to the media elite or the Hollywood elite are more common than references to the business elite or financial elite not just on Fox News but on CNN. The fact that in British papers the proportions are reversed is a telling sign of how far American usage of *elite* has departed from the original meaning of the word.

The Republican attacks on "the elite" began in the 1960s. In "The Speech" which Ronald Reagan gave numerous times on behalf of Barry Goldwater and which made his early political reputation, he charged liberals with believing that "an intellectual elite in a far-distant capital can plan our lives for us better than we can plan them ourselves." And in his second State of the Union address in 1971, Richard Nixon challenged "the idea that a bureaucratic elite in Washington knows best what is best for people everywhere." But more than anyone else, it was Spiro Agnew again who gave the word its modern cast, shifting it from a political to a cultural category with repeated attacks on the media as a "small unelected elite."

The right's reinterpretation of the word got a further lift in 1992, when Vice President Dan Quayle sparked a national controversy by denouncing Candace Bergen's TV character Murphy Brown for having a child out of wedlock, using the occasion to attack a supposed "cultural elite" that was undermining traditional American values (he also suggested that the show bore some of the responsibility for the Rodney King riots in Los Angeles). "We have two cultures," Quayle said, "the cultural elite and the rest of us." Asked afterward to define the "cultural elite," Quayle responded coyly: "They know who they are." But others were more explicit: *Newsweek* published a list of one hundred members of the cultural elite that included not just poster-child liberals like Woody Allen, Bill Moyers, Ted Turner, Spike Lee, Gloria Steinem, Oprah, and Susan Sontag, but also William Bennett, George F. Will, Lynne Cheney, Rupert Murdoch, Arnold Schwarzenegger, and William F. Buckley, not to mention Quayle himself ("smart enough to put the elite on the national agenda," the magazine observed).

By any standard of power or influence, it was hard to argue with those calls. But when people on the right talk about "the elite" nowadays, you can be sure they're not thinking of William F. Buckley or William Bennett.

Elite always presupposes the modifier "liberal," whether it's actually pro-nounced or not. As Michael Kinsley noted in *Time* in 1995:

> House Speaker Newt Gingrich uses the term *elite* as an all-purpose epi-thet, meaning little more than someone or something he doesn't like. Just since the election he has applied the term to directors of art museums ("self-selected elites using your tax money and my tax money to pay off their friends"), to the Bipartisan Entitlement Reform Commission ("driven by elite values"), to people who send E-mail messages supportive of President Clinton ("urbanites make up the Internet elite," according to a Gingrich spokesman) and, of course, time and again, to the "elite me-dia" or "media elite."

The conservative legal scholar Robert Bork talks about "the 'elite' classes that despise conservatism and its culture, and are thus well to the left of the general public," presumably exempting the industrialists who fund right-wing think tanks and the corporate CEO's who contribute disproportionately to Republican campaigns. Peggy Noonan decries the opposition to the Iraq war among "America's elite," whom she identifies as "the politicians, wise men, think-tank experts, academics, magazine and editorial-page editors, big-city columnists, TV commentators." Those would be Democratic politicians and network TV commentators, of course—Fox News broadcasters are non-elite by definition, since, as Fox's Bill O'Reilly likes to say, "We're looking out for *you*."

For Laura Ingraham, in fact, being "an elite" is chiefly a matter of atti-tudes: "Essentially, elites are defined not so much by class or wealth or position as they are by a *general outlook*. Their core belief—embraced with a fervor that does not allow for rational debate—is that they are su-perior to We the People. They know better . . . Their brilliance is to be presumed." That enables Ingraham to identify as "elites" any group whose political views depart from those of "We the People"—not just ivory-tower academics, one-worlders, teachers' unions, journalists, Euro-peans, and Hollywood actors, but also pro-choice Republicans and "mavericks" like Senator John McCain (whose offenses against the People were to vote to reduce the Bush tax cuts and to say in a campaign speech,

"We are the party of Abraham Lincoln, not Bob Jones"). Even some corporate CEOs can be elites, Ingraham says, not because of their power or political influence but because they refuse to open their annual shareholder meetings by reciting the Pledge of Allegiance on behalf of the corporation.

What makes all those people "elites," as the right tells it, is not simply their left-wing sympathies but their smug superiority, which puts them "out of touch" with the lives of ordinary people and normal Americans.* As the right-wing commentator Linda Chavez put it just after the 2004 election:

> The real loser in Tuesday's election wasn't Democrat John Kerry, but the liberal media and intellectual elite who demonstrated, once again, how out-of-touch they are with the American public. . . . I have some advice for these learned souls. If they want to understand the American electorate, maybe they should spend less time at Starbucks sipping double lattes over the Sunday *Times* and more time at church or the local high school football game or in line at a Wal-Mart. They might actually learn something about the values that drive most Americans . . .

That's the cant that comes with the right-wing system disk, with its picture of a left-wing elite separated from "real Americans" by its corrosive values and its seditious taste in beverages. As the right uses the word, *elite* transfers suspicion from the genuinely powerful to the people who used to be regarded merely as their clerks and factotums, and in the process suppresses real disparities of wealth and power. There are only the people who shop at Wal-Mart and people who don't, with the people who own the operation presumably away for the weekend. *Elite* rephrases class conflicts as high-school rivalries, where the stuck-up townies look down their noses at the 4H Club hayseeds at the next cafeteria table. As Ingraham puts it, in exactly the right high-school tone, "They think we're stupid."

---

*Over the past ten years, major newspapers have run 250 stories in which *elite* appears within ten words of "out of touch."

If the bluster about "elites" were confined to the language of the right, most Americans would probably take it with a grain of salt. The public is relatively shrewd about discounting blatant polemical bombast, whichever side it comes from. But like a lot of the right's new vocabulary, the new usage of *elite* has been picked up by the mainstream media and the general public, as well. It isn't just that those media are more likely to describe journalists as elite than business leaders; they also associate the word specifically with liberals. It's not surprising to find that references to the "liberal elite" outnumber references to the "conservative elite" on Fox News by better than 30-to-1. But even on CNN and in the *New York Times*, the ratio is better than 3-to-1, and on the Web it's 8-to-1. The association of *elite* and *liberal*, that is, has pretty much entered the language, like the exclusive association of liberals with the middle class.

The shifting use of *elite* has its complement in the new uses of *populist*. That word has come a long way since it was first applied to the early twentieth-century radicals who advocated an eight-hour day, restrictions on corporate power, and a graduated income tax—proposals frightening enough to lead their critics to describe them as "wild-eyed, rattle-brained fanatics." By mid-century, *populist* sounded quaint and outmoded, but it gained a new lease on life with the electoral realignments of the Nixon years, conveniently stripped of the awkward connotations of class struggle that alarmed the establishment a century earlier. In the 1980s, as Michael Kazin notes, "populism became something of a fashion statement," as people started using the word for everything from computer printers to Banana Republic's "populist pants." Today *populist* can refer not just to those who speak for the downtrodden and the down-at-heel but to anyone or anything whose appeal seems down-home, down-to-earth, or down-market. In recent years, the media have used the word to describe Steven Spielberg, Arnold Schwarzenegger, Fox News, Burger King, Donald Trump, the Google initial public stock offering and Oscar de la Renta's new mid-price fashion line. (By the modern definition, the Populist hero William Jennings Bryan almost certainly wouldn't qualify as a populist, not with all those long sentences full of allusions to Napoleon, Cicero, and Peter the Hermit.)

The effect of all this is to turn the distinction between "the people" and "the elite" into a matter of style rather than substance. Often the difference comes down to nothing more than what mode of locomotion you favor. During the 2004 presidential campaign, *National Review*'s Jay Nordlinger praised President Bush for engaging in "populist campaigning" when he visited Indiana and Michigan on a bus tour, presumably demonstrating his empathy with those who are required to do their cross-country travel by Greyhound, while the *Daily News*'s Richard Sisk mocked John Kerry for engaging in "elitist sports like snowboarding and windsurfing." (Sisk was plainly a bit out of touch himself—windsurfing is a lot more proletarian than the sailing and motorboating that the Bush family goes in for, and the majority of America's six million snowboarders are droop-drawered adolescents with 50 Cent cranked up on their I-Pods.) And Kerry's efforts to strike a populist note by going bird hunting in Elmer Fudd–style camouflage made him seem all the more risibly out of his element, just like Michael Dukakis's misadventure when he was photographed wearing an oversized helmet while awkwardly riding in a tank.

It's that rewriting of populism that has permitted George W. Bush to become the most unlikely "man of the people" since William Henry Harrison. Bush doesn't simply exploit the new populism, he incarnates it—he's living proof that style and "authenticity" can trump the facts of economics and social class. Some people on the right have tried to impose that narrative literally on Bush's life. Peggy Noonan locates the secret of Bush's heartland appeal in an idyllic Texas childhood that somehow inured him against his privileged background:

> Mr. Bush is the triumph of the seemingly average American man. He's normal. . . . There's nothing lemonade-on-the-porch-overlooking-the-links-at-the-country-club about Mr. Bush. He isn't smooth. He actually has some of the roughness and the resentments of the self-made man. I think the reason for this is Texas. He grew up in a white T-shirt and jeans playing ball in the street with the other kids in the subdivision . . . . Until he went off to boarding school, he thought he was like everyone else.

That's a gift, to think you're just like everyone else in America. It can be the making of you.

True, not many people would credit that picture of Bush as a Harry Potter figure who discovers his special legacy only when he goes off to prep school, after the shrub is already bent. And you have the feeling that even the Republican National Committee would have second thoughts about putting Bush and "self-made" in close syntactic proximity. In fact, Noonan's story slights Bush's genuine gifts for working the political room, using a just-folks manner and accent to offset a background of obvious privilege.* But in a world in which Donald Trump can count as a populist, the facts of Bush's biography are really beside the point. What matters is the impression that Bush creates: he comes off, as David Brooks puts it, as someone "who could come to any suburban barbershop and fit right in."

The right has been skillful at using Bush's homespun appeal and tastes to caricature the "elite liberals" who find him antipathetic. When Bush was first running for the presidency in 1999, Harold W. Anderson, the former editor of the *Omaha World-Herald,* wrote that "liberal Eastern columnists are squirming at the prospect that George W. Bush might become the 43rd president of the United States. First of all, he's a Republican. And, for heaven's sake, he's a Texan who wears cowboy boots and in his drinking days reportedly preferred Lone Star beer to Chardonnay. Definitely NOKD—not our kind, dear."

That's another of the right's bizarre inversions of the American elite, where the journalists are cast as the swells and the Skull-and-Bones Yalie plays a déclassé prole—it's as if Cary Grant and James Stewart had switched roles in *The Philadelphia Story.* It's true that many liberals feel an antipathy for Bush that goes beyond their disapproval of his policies and actions, not because they consider him a proletarian rube but because he's merely playing one on TV. The contempt that American liberals have for

* Bush comes by the accent honestly, it's true, but it took a certain foresight to preserve it through his years at Andover and Yale—his brother, Jeb, has managed to lose most of his, even though he went from Andover to the University of Texas.

Bush is very unlike the attitude of the Europeans, who tend to associate him uncritically with their age-old stereotypes of American boorishness. You think of the pictures of anti–Iraq War demonstrators in London, Prague, and Copenhagen carrying signs that read "Go Home Cowboy." A fat lot they know. You'd never see signs like that at anti-war demonstrations in San Francisco or New York, where the left is much more likely to ridicule Bush as a faux-bubba poseur. ("Big hat, five cattle," as the presidential historian Douglas Brinkley has described him.) To liberals, the brush-cutting, *g*-dropping, "nucular"-challenged Bush seems to personify the larger game the right has been playing when it tricks itself out in the guise of just folks.

Looking at the way the media was throwing around the word *populist* in the 1996 election, the liberal columnist Molly Ivins was moved to protest in the name of the progenitors of the original Populist movement:

> The quadrennial assault by the media on the meaning of a noble, useful and important American political tradition is once more under way. This year, we find Steve Forbes, Pat Buchanan, Ross Perot (again) and even Phil Gramm (Lord save us) described as "populists." In the name of Sockless Jerry Simpson, I beg you to stop! Poor Dr. Charles Macune is spinning in his grave. The ghost of William Lamb is going to haunt all you careless, ignorant scribes who toss that word around like confetti.

I take Ivins's point. But as Michael Kazin points out, small-*p* populism is not simply a historical movement, but "a language whose speakers conceive of ordinary people as a noble assemblage not bounded narrowly by class, view their elite opponents as self-serving and undemocratic, and seek to mobilize the former against the latter." In that sense, the objection to the populism of the modern right is not that it's false to its linguistic and historical roots, but that it's false to the realities of power in America. In smoothing over differences of class, in defining the "elite" in terms of values and lifestyle, it creates specious solidarities, and transforms genuine anger and frustration into irrelevant or inauthentic forms of resentment.

One notable feature of the right's new rhetoric, in fact, is the way it turns the conflicts between liberals and conservatives into personal squabbles. Election maps or no, the division between the "elite" and "ordinary Americans" isn't really drawn along geographical lines, or along lines of class or income. The very ubiquity of the brands, sports, and diversions that are supposed to define the red and blue lifestyles is a reminder that the tribes are everywhere bumping elbows. Here's another version of David Brooks's image of America as a "cafeteria nation":

> Remember high school? There were nerds, jocks, punks, bikers, techies, druggies, God Squadders, drama geeks, poets, and Dungeons & Dragons weirdoes. All these cliques were part of the same school: they had different sensibilities; sometimes they knew very little about the people in the other cliques; but the jocks knew there would always be nerds, and the nerds knew there would always be jocks. And that's the way America is . . . We are not a divided nation. We are a cafeteria nation.

Brooks main object here is to deny the importance of class—"the old Marxist categories"—in Americans' pictures of the social world. And indeed, the object of the right's new populism is precisely to replace those economic divisions with social categories based on "values" and lifestyles. The right's very insistence on that theme is a sign of how far it is from being an indisputable reality of American life—if that were how everybody naturally sees the world, conservatives wouldn't have to keep going on about it.

But perhaps inadvertently, Brooks's image of high-school cliques also suggests just how immediate the divisions are: you can literally find both sorts represented in the same cafeterias, the same towns, the same malls. Despite some press reports, there's little evidence that Americans are more geographically segregated by party affiliation than they used to be—the political scientist Philip Klinker points out that the average voter lives in a county that was close to evenly divided in the 2000 election. And nowadays, even the roughly one-third of voters who live in areas that are heavily skewed toward one party or the other have exposure to other views through the media, not just in formal settings and interviews, but in the routinized political cockfights of the cable news networks and the back-and-forth of the call-in shows.

Taken together with the sharp increase in the partisanship of the political classes, that helps to explain why a majority of Americans have the impression that the country is more polarized than it used to be, even as Americans' actual political attitudes are converging. But it also affects the way people understand the quarrel between liberals and conservatives. Broadcast political discussion isn't simply a far more pervasive form of public spectacle than ever before, but a more intimate one. Pol-TV and pol-radio are populated with personalities who are as familiar to their audiences as the late-night talk show hosts and their guests. "Personalities" is the key word there. If the "cultural" differences that separate liberals and conservatives are relatively slight and superficial—any of us can wake up one morning and decide to start dressing like a Goth or a preppie, or trade in our Volvo for a Hummer—the personal differences are seen as very deep, linked to character traits that have nothing to do with economic self-interest or philosophical positions. As the right tells the story, liberals and conservatives are different kinds of people.

Not surprisingly, that tone is most marked in the language of the right-wingers who invented the new broadcast formats and still dominate them. You can hear it in the pert nickname *libs* that's favored by broadcasters like Sean Hannity and Rush Limbaugh. ("This is anathema to the libs, folks.") There's no equivalently slangy label for the other side; some liberals have tried to introduce *cons*, but it hasn't caught on. *Lib* is an oddly familiar term; it's the sort of tag you'd give to a snooty high-school clique or the pretentious assholes who live in the big house up the block. In fact, *lib* has a lot in common with *asshole*, a word we reserve for jerks who belong to our own tribe: you might call your boss an asshole, or even a familiar celebrity, but it isn't a word you'd use of Abu Musab al-Zarqawi. *Lib* and *asshole* are both words for people who make us feel indignant, and not simply angry.

That note of personal antipathy is an essential element in the rhetorical maneuver that Thomas Frank describes as "performing indignation." Listen to the right-wing radio hosts and you get a new insight into what it means to say that all politics is local. Not that the hosts and callers don't have strong antipathies for Zarqawi, criminals, illegal immigrants, the U.N., porn merchants, and the undeserving poor, but when they raise those names it's usually as a pretext for denouncing the libs who coddle or excuse them.

On right-wing talk radio and the more polemical cable news shows, virtually every story has to be given an ideological cast, however much of a stretch it is:

ALAN COLMES: I have to ask, like who are these parents to allow their kids to sleep with Michael Jackson?

SEAN HANNITY: Liberals.

Often, major stories develop sidebars that exist almost solely for the purpose of bashing liberals. During the build-up to the Iraq War, for example, conservatives seemed to be spending as much time denouncing the French as Saddam Hussein: in the months leading up to the war, France or the French were mentioned in more than half the Fox News segments that mentioned Iraq. Yet conservatives pretty much gave a free pass to the Germans, who were as adamant in opposing the war as the French were. Nobody was calling for a boycott of German products or pouring out bottles of Schloss Johannisberger into the gutter along with the bottles of Chateau d'Yquem.* But that made sense if you took the criticisms as really directed less at the French than at our own Francophile classes. As Victor Davis Hanson wrote in *National Review,* "[H]eartland Americans . . . have a clearer appreciation of the quite profound amorality in Europe than anyone in the Ivy League." That helps to explain the insistence of House Republicans that french fries should be rebaptized "freedom fries" on the menu of the House cafeteria. As an attempt to offer an actual insult to the French, the gesture was mystifying: as if the French cared whether we credit them for coming up with the idea of deep-frying sliced potatoes (particularly since it turns out to have been the Belgians). But that was just the point: the renaming was

*In Google Groups postings from this period that mentioned Iraq, the French were six times as likely to be described as "the frogs" as the Germans were to be described as "the krauts."

so patently irrelevant and absurd that everybody could understand it was really aimed at getting a rise out of the Sauterne-sipping, Roquefort-sniffing intellectuals and movie stars who took the French side when the war was being debated.

That's the ultimate goal of the right's rebranding of liberals: to turn anger over alien evils into indignation at the jerks down the street. It's the final stage in the transformation of class conflicts into cafeteria rivalries—or sometimes, into an even more intimate kind of rancor. Listening to the way the right talks about the distinction between liberals and conservatives, you might conclude that the two were distinct political genders. "You liberals!" a talk-show host will say to a guest, with the eye-rolling exasperation that calls to mind "You gals!" (As Fox's token liberal Alan Colmes puts it, "I'm going to do business cards now, and have them say, 'You Liberals.'" He's got something there—in Google Groups postings, "you liberals" outpolls "you conservatives" by better than 7-to-1.)* Ann Coulter publishes a book with the you-just-don't-understand title of *How to Talk to a Liberal*. And Senator Trent Lott makes the point in New-Agey language that would have had an old-style conservative like Robert A. Taft scratching his head: "Republicans and Democrats think with different sides of their brains, just like men and women . . . We think with our left brain . . . I like to think we are the party of Mars." That isn't just a reprise of the old stereotypes of effete liberals and manly conservatives. It suggests that conservatives and liberals are divided by indelible psychological differences, so that political disagreements are like bedside squabbles that can never be resolved rationally—it's a mistake even to try to argue with these people.

That's the picture that leads people to talk about liberals and conservatives as having different "mindsets," a term that first appeared in the late 1970s. And it's implicit in the notion that ideological differences will correlate with the intimate details of one's personal life. In 2004, for example, ABC News reported that a survey of Americans' sex lives showed that more Republicans than Democrats reported being very satisfied with

---

* In case you're curious, "we liberals" and "we conservatives" come out as pretty much a wash.

their sex lives, that Republicans were more likely to be sexually adventurous, and that Democrats were more likely to fake orgasms. As it happened, those results were statistically meaningless, since the survey hadn't taken age, race, or gender into account (since women are more likely to be Democrats, the fact that more Democrats reported faking orgasms shouldn't be surprising). That didn't stop conservatives from having fun with the survey—understandably, since it was too juicy an item to ignore. (The *Boston Herald*'s headline over its story on the poll ran, "Kerry Must Be the Only Democrat Changing Positions.") But it's a sign of the times that anyone thought to ask the questions in the first place.

that psycho-sexual conception of the liberal-conservative distinction displaces the "two nations" narrative about as far as it could possibly get from the economic and social divisions of American life. Of course, people have always known that those orientations owe a lot to individual psychology, culture, and perhaps even genes—choosing to favor liberal or conservative views isn't a purely philosophical matter like deciding whether you favor the designated-hitter rule. Long before scholars like Abraham Maslow, Harold Lasswell, Erik Erikson, and Theodor Adorno began their investigations of the relation of personality to politics, W. S. Gilbert wrote in *Iolanthe:*

> I often think it's comical
> How nature always does contrive
> That every boy and every gal,
> That's born into this world alive,
> Is either a little Liberal,
> Or else a little Conservative!

But there's always a risk of reduction here, where people take political labels as no more than shorthand for a cluster of personality traits, so that it becomes unnecessary to take someone's views seriously in their own terms. That's what the right has tried to achieve with its liberal stereotyping and its talk of the "liberal mindset"—when you hear somebody begin a sentence with "You libs!" you can usually assume that what follows will be as dismissive as if the sentence had begun with "You women" or "You Jews."

Yet these days a lot of liberals, too, like to think of political orientations as the manifestations of antithetical personality types that have their origins far from politics or economics. That helps to explain the enthusiasm for George Lakoff's *Don't Think of an Elephant*, a popularization of the views he developed in his earlier book *Moral Politics*. Some of that is a response to the alluring idea that the Democrats' problems can be addressed by better issue framing. But Lakoff also struck a deep chord by arguing that liberals and conservatives are set apart by fundamentally different worldviews, which are grounded in antithetical models of the family. In a sense, there's nothing new in this—Freudians have always tried to find the roots of political attitudes in early family attachments (where else would they have looked?). But it's fair to say that no one has come up with a version of this story that is quite as reductive or specific as Lakoff's is. And its wide appeal suggests just how consoling—but for liberals, perilous—the picture of warring mindsets can be.

Lakoff begins by asking what unifies the disparate positions associated with modern conservatism:

> In 1994, I dutifully read the "Contract with America" and found myself unable to comprehend how conservative views formed a coherent set of political positions. What, I asked myself, did opposition to abortion have to do with the flat tax? What did the flat tax have to do with opposition to environmental regulations? What did defense of gun ownership have to do with tort reform? Or tort reform with opposition to affirmative action? . . . The answer is that there are distinct conservative and progressive worldviews. The two groups simply see the world in different ways.

Lakoff arrives at those contrasting worldviews not by clinical research, surveys, or ethnographic studies, but by looking at the language that each side uses to justify its positions, all of which he sees as reflecting an underlying metaphor based on one's basic conceptions of the family.

I worked backward. I took the various positions on the conservative side and on the progressive side and I said, "Let's put them through the [family] metaphor from the opposite direction and see what comes out." I put in the two different views of the nation, and out popped two different models of the family: a strict father family and a nurturant parent family.

As Lakoff describes it, the "nurturant parent" model of the family stresses empathy and responsibility. Projected into the political realm, he says, that model shapes "traditional progressive values"—government should protect people by providing a social safety net and regulation, universal education, civil liberties and equal treatment, economic policies aimed at benefiting all citizens, and a foreign policy that promotes cooperation.

The strict father model, by contrast, assumes that "children are born bad and must be made good. The strict father is the moral authority who has to support and defend the family, tell his wife what to do, and teach his kids right from wrong. The only way to do that is through painful punishment." From that model follow all the positions of "the radical right-wing politics that has been misnamed 'conservative.'" Wealth is a measure of discipline and self-reliance and taxes are punishments that take money from good people to give to others who have not earned it. Social programs "spoil" people and keep them dependent. The goal of the government's foreign policy should be to impose its moral authority wherever it can. Environmentalism is wrong because "God has given man dominion over nature. Nature . . . [is] there to be used for human profit."

Lakoff's analysis has little in common with Coulter's and Ingraham's slash-and-burn polemics about liberal snobbery or with Brooks's satirical investigations of political lifestyles. Yet at the deepest level, he shares the most basic assumptions of the red-blue theorists of the right. Like conservatives, for example, he assumes that prototypical liberals are drawn from the urban upper-middle class. Granted, he traces the roots of the two family models back to prebiblical times and doesn't try to connect them to class, income, or lifestyle. But he describes "nurturant parents" as people who don't believe in spanking children, find work a means of realizing their contribution to their community and developing their potential, believe that both parents should share equally in child rearing, and want to protect their children from cigarettes, cars without seat belts, dangerous toys, inflammable clothing, pesticides in food, and unscrupulous businessmen. That puts the omphalos of the liberal mindset squarely among Lakoff's Berkeley neighbors—that is, the sorts of people who are apt to use words like *nurturant* in the first place.

Lakoff's depictions of conservatives are colored by similar stereotyping. Conservatives believe abortion is wrong, he says, because "pregnant teenagers have violated the commandments of the strict father" and "career women [who have abortions] challenge the power and authority of the strict father. Both should be punished by bearing the child . . . ." (The fact that such people are also "against prenatal care, postnatal care, and health care for children," he adds, shows that they are "using the idea of terminating a pregnancy as part of a cultural-war strategy to gain and maintain political power.") It's a far cry from the much more nuanced and sympathetic depictions of rank-and-file pro-lifers that emerge from the interviews and ethnographic studies reported by liberals like Thomas Frank, William Saletan, and Carolyn Maxwell. As Maxwell observes, those people are less likely to think of pregnant women seeking abortions as sinners who must be punished by carrying their children to term than as women who have been "abandoned by the men who impregnated them or by the men who employed them without options for maternity—and duped by society into believing their best, or their only option was to abort." It's a difference with important consequences for the way liberals frame their appeals to voters who hold anti-abortion views.

But what do we say about a working-class white or an African American who believes in capital punishment but opposes Social Security privatization and the war in Iraq? (Or for that matter, what about a pro-choice, environmentalist, free-market Republican?) Such people, as Lakoff tells it, are "biconceptuals" who have "mixed models" of the family, which lead to their adopting inconsistent political views: "Many blue-collar workers are strict fathers at home, but nurturant toward their coworkers." In effect, people like those are imperfect liberals, unlike the

unremittingly nurturant urban professionals who embody the liberal archetype—just as the right has been saying all along.

The political corollary of that view is that "liberal" and "conservative"
define consistent, unified sets of positions that follow from an underlying
worldview in something like the way mathematical theorems follow from
a set of basic axioms. As Lakoff tells it, the same principles that lead you
to favor the flat tax would lead you to oppose abortion and favor abstinence-only programs in the schools. That's just what conservatives have
been saying for a long time, as they try to weave a philosophy that unites
the "values" conservatives and free-market economic conservatives. One
favorite maneuver is to selectively extend the notions of "rights" and
"freedom" to some groups, like property owners, businesses, crime victims, parents, and the unborn, while giving short shrift to the rights of
consumers, employees, pregnant women, and gays. But those stories always have an after-the-fact air about them, and they can't obscure the
tensions within the movement that make it possible for pro-life social
conservatives like Pat Buchanan to win wide support for populist attacks
on programs that pro-business conservatives hold dear, like amnesty for
undocumented workers.

In the end, there's a simpler and more plausible answer to the questions
that Lakoff poses about the connections among conservatives' social and
economic views: actually, there aren't any. Support for the flat tax doesn't
have a whole lot to do with opposition to abortion, nor is a zeal for tort
reform philosophically linked to opposition to gun control or affirmative
action. If those positions happen to be found in the same shopping basket
right now, that's mostly a reflection of current political alliances and coalitions and of a political idiom that creates an illusion of coherence among
them. Over the years, after all, conservatives have gone from isolationists
to interventionists (and then back again, or so it is starting to appear), and
from believing, like Barry Goldwater, that government should stay out of
people's private lives to arguing that the state has an obligation to enforce
"traditional standards" of sexual morality. And the views that characterize
liberals have changed just as dramatically over that period. But how could
that have happened, if people's issue positions followed from their underlying worldviews or models of the family?

In fact, the majority of Americans don't have what Lakoff would consider ideologically consistent views on most of these issues. The statistically average American is pro-choice and believes large corporations have too much power, is ambivalent about gun control, and is in favor of the death penalty and making English the official language of the country. Lakoff could say, of course, that that shows how widely "mixed models" of the family are diffused, but that doesn't explain why people tend to go with one or the other model depending on the issue at stake.

None of this means that Lakoff is wrong to see connections between people's ideals of the family and their political views. As he points out, we often draw metaphorical connections between the two—we talk about the Founding Fathers (or used to, anyway), send our sons off to war, and so on. And with some issues, like capital punishment, family models may be the decisive factor in shaping people's views. But there are plenty of other metaphorical schemes that we use to talk about the nation, many of them with equally deep roots in the language and in history. The nation can be a body with a head, stomach, heart, and arms, or a person who is young, grows old and sick, and dies:

> States have degrees, as human bodies have,
> Spring, Summer, Autumn, Winter, and the Grave.

The nation can be a ship, as poet Walt Whitman portrayed it, which sails on, loses its moorings, drifts, or has to be righted. It can be a theater, where people and issues wait in the wings, take center stage, or lay an egg. It can be a house, crumbling at the foundations or built to withstand the buffeting of the winds. It can be a city, as both Ronald Reagan and Mario Cuomo described it, though with different images of what was going on in its neighborhoods. It can be a party (to which everyone must be invited). Or as David Brooks suggests, it can be a high-school cafeteria. And sometimes it's just a nation: not all the vocabulary we use to talk about national life has its conceptual origin in some other domain. (When it comes to the crunch, even the most nurturant parents have misgivings about running their households according to the principle "one man, one vote.")

All of those metaphors can be useful on various occasions, depending on the point you want to make, but none of them is determinative. In fact, people are very good at bailing out on metaphors when they perceive a clash between their literal and figurative meanings. I find it helpful to think of my computer screen as a desktop, but I'm not tempted to clean it off by tipping it on its side. Like the other kinds of practical reasoning that cognitive psychologists study, political reasoning is a much more complicated and messier business than Lakoff suggests. We make our electoral decisions on the basis of a hodgepodge of conflicting metaphors, symbols, and rules of thumb, weighing group solidarity, self-interest, and moral principles in different proportions. Philosophical consistency figures very far down on this list (except for orthodox libertarians, who manage to be philosophically consistent and politically infantile at the same time).

Ultimately, this is just another, liberal-friendly version of the right's "two nations" scenario of an America divided by incommensurable cultures or mindsets, where social values trump economic issues and class. (For Lakoff, your support for unrestrained free-market capitalism is merely an outgrowth of your views on parental discipline.)

What does this mean in practice? What liberals must do, Lakoff tells them, is to get "people in the middle . . . to use your model for politics—to activate your worldview and moral system in their political decisions. You do that by talking to people using frames based on your worldview." Lakoff is right to point out that the Democrats can't win simply by enumerating their issue positions without tying them to some deeper set of values. But the appeal to "values" in this sense can also lead liberals badly astray. Take the way Lakoff deals with the issue of tax cuts, which he makes the prototype for the way the right has managed to dictate the terms of political debate:

On the day that George W. Bush arrived in the White House, the phrase *tax relief* started coming out of the White House. . . . Think of the framing for *relief*. For there to be relief there must be an affliction, an afflicted party, and a reliever who removes the affliction and is therefore a hero. And if people try to stop the hero, those people are villains for trying to prevent relief. When the word *tax* is added to *relief,* the result is a metaphor: Taxation is an affliction. And the person who takes it away is a hero, and anyone who tries to stop him is a bad guy. . . . And soon the Democrats are using *tax relief* . . . and shooting themselves in the foot.

Well, but how should Democrats talk about taxes, then? Lakoff imagines an ad as follows:

Taxation is paying your dues, paying your membership fee in America. If you join a country club or a community center, you pay fees. Why? You did not build the swimming pool. You have to maintain it. You did not build the basketball court. Someone has to clean it. You may not use the squash court, but you still have to pay your dues.

That may accord with the values of some liberals, particularly those who can permit themselves the luxury of feeling pleased about the taxes they pay. ("Speaking for myself, I don't need a tax cut or tax relief," the *Washington Post* reported the media mogul David Geffen as saying a few years ago, a remark that most other Americans would be happy to be able to make themselves.) But it's hard to imagine an ad like that one stimulating a groundswell of support for the Democrats. The fact is that people have always regarded taxes as a burden, if not exactly an affliction. The phrase *tax relief* wasn't invented by the Bush White House; it has been used by every major Democratic figure from Al Smith to Bill Clinton. Liberal values or no, Democrats can't score political points by asking people to feel good about the taxes they pay. What they can do (and to be fair to Lakoff, he says this as well) is to make middle-income Americans realize that they are paying more than their fair share, while the rich are getting off lightly, a theme that Clinton, Gore, and others have successfully used.

This isn't simply a question of appealing to one value ("fairness") rather than another ("paying your dues"). It's a question of understanding that values themselves aren't what motivate people; instead, it's the emotions evoked by the narratives that give values flesh. As we'll see, the biggest mistake the Democrats have made is to take "values" on its face.

chapter eight

"Values" Play

Welcome to the international
language of populist resentment.
—*William Safire, 1997*

In the recent movie *Win a Date with Tad Hamilton*, Nathan Lane plays a Hollywood agent who's trying to persuade his dissolute movie-star client to dump the wholesome small-town girl he's smitten with. "Your values are different," Lane tells the actor. "For instance, she has them." The line shows how *values* can swing two ways. Sometimes it refers to mores or cultural standards, the sort of thing that can vary from one person to the next: "We should respect other people's values." And sometimes it means morals, the sort of thing that one person can have more of than another: "Kids today have no values."

You could alter Lane's line to sum up the real point that the right is making with its "two cultures" story: liberals' and conservatives' values are different; for instance, conservatives have them. The word carves both a cultural and moral boundary. It's a sign of how successful conservatives have been that pretty much everybody concedes a values edge to the red side of the cultural divide, even the so-called liberal press. As I noted earlier, in articles about domestic politics in the *New York Times*, the *Los Angeles Times*, and the *Washington Post*, *conservative values* appears about four times as often as *liberal values* does.

Things haven't always been that way. Like a great deal of the right's new language, *values* began its life as part of the jargon of the left. It first appeared in English about a hundred years ago as a translation of a term from German sociology, but it didn't really enter the general American vocabulary until the 1950s, when it was picked up in progressive circles along with other social-science terms like *alienation* and *peer group*. In those days, a sentence like "I share your values" was the sort of thing you'd expect to encounter in a Jules Feiffer cartoon or a Nichols and May skit, and the political connotations of *values* were limited to a vague association with progressive education and liberal anticommunism (that was when universities began setting up programs in "American values," where the phrase suggested only the democratic ideals that made America different from totalitarian regimes).

The politicization of "values" began in the late 1960s, when Republicans seized on the word to contrast the mores of Middle Americans with the antics of the hippies and anti-war protesters and the effete pretensions of the East Coast liberal elites. If you wanted to put a precise date on the shift of meaning, you could pick August 7, 1968, when the Republicans opened their national convention in Miami Beach with a round of inspirational songs from the preternaturally clean-cut "Up with People" chorus—"not a hippie among them," as the speaker who introduced them said—and proceeded to adopt a platform that called for the appointment of judges who "respect traditional family values and the sanctity of human life." Over the following years, the newly divisive sense of *values* was tirelessly promoted by Spiro Agnew and other Republicans. By 1988, George H.W. Bush could make *values* a literal mantra of his presidential campaign: "I represent the . . . mainstream views and the mainstream values. And they are your values, and my values, and the values of the vast majority of the American people."

Values couldn't do the work it does if it didn't cover a lot of territory. In his 1995 book *Values Matter Most*, Ben J. Wattenberg lists forty-four items that have been described as "social/values/cultural issues" over recent years. Some of these are evanescent ("bra burning," "Willie Horton," "Murphy Brown," "Troopergate"), some perennial ("infidelity," "dependency," "promiscuity," "drugs"). Some are what Wattenberg calls "social issues," which he characterizes as "important," generally agreed to be harmful to society as a whole and amenable to government action, like crime, welfare, education, and "quotas." Others are "cultural issues," which are less likely to be matters of consensus and may not permit government involvement, often for constitutional reasons—issues like abortion, the Pledge of Allegiance, school prayer, flag burning, sex and violence in the media, and pornography (he also lists the issue of gays in the military, which would now cash out as gay marriage).

In short, "values issues" are clearly a jumble, and the media usually make no effort to sort them out. A term that stands in for both opposition to abortion and the defense of "Merry Christmas" would seem to be a good candidate for meaninglessness. Yet as broad as the category seems to be, there are also some significant omissions. Wattenberg identifies values issues simply as "what are left over after economics and foreign policy have been taken off the table." But when you look at the controversies that the media tend to label as values issues, you don't find any place for corporate malfeasance, hate crimes, election reform, cronyism and corruption, domestic wiretapping, torture of prisoners, or environmental regulation, even though those aren't usually thought of as "economic" or "pocketbook" issues in the way Social Security and tax cuts are.

That's what it means to say that the right owns *values*. Since the Nixon era, the word has been shorthand for a particular collection of narratives about the decline of cultural standards concerning sexuality, religion, hard work, and patriotism—anything they can bring up that's likely to make their "Middle Americans" angry about the drift of the culture. When Joseph Lieberman boasted during the Democratic primaries in 2003 that "[the Republicans] can't say I'm weak on values," everybody understood that he was talking about his religious convictions and his campaign against sex and violence in the media, not his positions on the environment or the Iraq War. And when you run into organizations with names like the American Values Coalition or the Traditional Values Coalition, you can be confident that the values in question aren't principles like "a fair day's pay for a fair day's work" or "pick up after yourself."

that association has long been a bone in the throat of liberals, who ask what kind of "values" lead Republicans to cut funding for medical services and Head Start, to allow corporations to trash the environment, or to oppose the right of some Americans to marry. And why are maintaining Social Security and protecting the environment any less matters of "values" than school prayer or abortion are? Democrats have been trying to recapture *values* ever since the right first laid claim to the word. Back in 1984, Geraldine Ferraro made values a key theme in her vice-presidential acceptance speech: "To those concerned about the strength of American and family values, as I am, I say we are going to restore those values: love, caring, partnership." Twenty years later, the Democrats were still trying to make the same point. The Kerry-Edwards campaign styled itself "a celebration of American values"—"I will stand up for the values that have always made America great," Kerry said, "faith and family, strength and service, responsibility and opportunity for all."

After the 2004 defeat, Democrats redoubled their efforts to recapture the V-word, sparing no opportunity to remind voters that their positions on the issues are both good and godly. Senate Minority Leader Harry Reid invoked "old-fashioned moral values" in his response to Bush's 2005 State of the Union speech. New Mexico governor Bill Richardson noted that "[w]e're talking about values including better schools, access to health care, personal behavior, and I add a Western value, and that is protecting God's creation, which is land and water."

But there's no sign that the Democrats' values-talk has been particularly effective among voters, or at least among the voters who might be tempted to buy the Republicans' "values" line in the first place. In the press and the public mind, *values* still calls up issues like abortion and the Pledge of Allegiance, not child care or the environment.

The problem isn't just that the Democrat's value-talk smacks of defensive me-tooism, but that it betrays a certain semantic cluelessness. *Values* "works" for the right because it evokes the narratives that underlie its populist strategy. When conservatives present themselves as the defenders of values, they don't mean simply that their views are principled, but that they will uphold the views of "ordinary Americans" whose religious views and standards of personal morality have been mocked and traduced by out-of-touch elite liberals. *Values* is charged with the indignation and displaced class resentments that the right has been battening on for the last forty years.

By now, Republicans need merely bring up the word in a vague way to make their point. "Whenever I go home to the heartland," George Bush said in a speech to the Boy Scouts in 2000, "I am reminded of the values that build strong families, strong communities and strong character, the values that make our people unique." It required only a mention of the heartland to imply that Bush had in mind something more specific and controversial than John Kerry did when he talked about Democratic values as "responsibility, service, faith and family." Bush didn't have to spell it out any further than that.

Democrats don't really get this. They seem to assume that voters attach importance to "values" simply because they want to be reassured that a party's positions have a compelling moral basis. So they continue to talk about values as if the word could be purged of its populist connotations and restored to its old lexical purity as the bland synonym for moral principles that it was in the Eisenhower years. But if that were all there is to *values*, the word wouldn't mean much more than *excellence* does in corporate mission statements—it would come down to little more than saying that Democrats have principles, too. In the absence of an alternative populist narrative, or for that matter any compelling narrative at all, the Democrats' invocations of "values" don't have the same power to stir moral indignation the way the word does in Republican mouths, where *values* is just another word for "morals."

Often, in fact, the Democrats' efforts to reclaim *values* only confirm the right-wing assumptions that are implicit in the word. You think of Kerry's claim during the 2004 campaign that he was the real candidate of conservative values. True, it was clear what he meant, and the claim could arguably be defended if you took "conservative" and "values" on their face. But who was Kerry kidding? Not surprisingly, the remark played right into Republican hands, making Kerry an easy target of ridicule in Bush's convention acceptance speech:

My opponent recently announced that he is the candidate of "conservative values," which must have come as a surprise to a lot of his supporters.
(Laughter.) There's some problems with this claim. If you say the heart
and soul of America is found in Hollywood, I'm afraid you're not the candidate of conservative values. (Applause.) If you voted against the biparti-
san Defense of Marriage Act, which President Clinton signed, you are not
the candidate of conservative values. (Applause.)

In the end, Kerry's remark merely added to the impression of him as a
say-anything opportunist, claiming "conservative values" when he apparently wouldn't own up to having liberal ones. And it conceded the advantage to the other side: if you turn a campaign into an argument over who
best represents "conservative values," the right will win every time.

That may have been a singular misstep, but liberals make the same sort
of mistake whenever they try to play in the right's rhetorical court. Take
the way people on the left vaunt "traditional progressive values" or "traditional liberal values" to counter what they see as the right's co-opting of
traditional.* Of course, progressivism and liberalism have long and illus-
trious pedigrees, and so do the small-*v* values they stand for. But the appeal of "traditional values" isn't simply a matter of historical lineage. Like
values itself, *traditional* has acquired a specific coloring in the right's populist narratives. People didn't talk often about "traditional values" or "traditional families" in this sense until the 1970s, a few decades after they
began to talk about traditional furniture and traditional houses—all of
them meant to evoke an idyllic vision of the recent American past. Think
of a "traditional house," for example, and what comes to mind is a Colo-
nial or a Cape Cod, not a Southwest-style pueblo, even though the latter
is equally traditional in the literal sense of the word. And "traditional values" and "traditional family" evoke a small-town, middle-class world
where people believed in the rewards of hard work and loved their country and where there were no moral problems so vexed you couldn't set
them straight in a half-hour heart-to-heart with Spencer Tracy.

* I'm not talking about using *traditional* in a purely descriptive way, as in *New York's
traditional liberal values.*

When liberals or progressives talk about their "traditional values," though, they seem to be playing false to their own ideals. In fact, "traditional progressive values" has an oxymoronic sound for those who still associate *progressive* with *progress*. Whatever you take liberal values to be, the case for them has nothing to do with their being "traditional." Liberals may argue for preserving the achievements of the New Deal or for protecting civil liberties from government encroachment, but not on the grounds that that's how people have always done things.

The Democrats' focus on recapturing the word *values* is really a distraction; it misses the real significance of the right's narratives. It has become a truism to say that people tend to vote their values rather than their self-interest. But there are several ways of understanding that remark. People often take it as meaning that voters are more likely to make their decisions on the basis of symbolic issues like gay marriage or the Pledge of Allegiance than on economic issues that have a real effect on their material lives. That was the received wisdom in the press after the 2004 exit polls seemed to indicate that "moral values" were the most important single issue in the campaign. In the *New York Times*, Nicholas Kristof wrote that Kerry supporters "should be feeling wretched about the millions of farmers, factory workers, and waitresses who ended up voting—utterly against their own interests—for Republican candidates."

As it happens, that may be overstating things. Some researchers have argued that economic issues still trump social issues for all groups of white voters, and that there's little truth to the notion of an "inversion" in American politics, where the working class votes Republican and the middle class votes Democratic—the fact is, the middle class is more susceptible to "values" appeals than the working class is. But whatever the outcome of that discussion, it's clear that social values do lead large numbers of people to make electoral choices that run counter to their economic well-being and that this helps Republicans more often than it does Democrats.

People have various motivations for making those decisions, of course. Many religious conservatives are simply willing to put their antipathy to abortion and creeping secularism ahead of their economic interests, whatever the personal cost. And on the other side, wealthy liberals can afford to indulge their social ideals, even if it means that they might wind up with a higher tax bill. (A Republican lawyer friend of mine who lives in the Berkeley Hills claims that he's the only person in his entire ZIP code who votes his pocketbook.) It goes without saying that neither of those groups will be responsive to appeals to its material self-interest. If you believe that abortion is legalized murder, affordable health care is likely to take a back seat; if you're alarmed at the way Republicans are jeopardizing American civil liberties, the prospect of a capital gains cut probably won't move you to vote for them.

But for other people the choice may not be that clear-cut. They may be concerned about economic issues but believe that the Democrats can't really address their problems. Many believe—often rightly—that the government has little to offer them or that the problems that concern them, like globalization, are beyond government's ability to address. And others simply don't trust government in general, or the Democrats in particular. After conducting focus-group studies among rural voters and disaffected Bush voters in several states in 2005, the Democracy Corps's Karl Agne and Stanley Greenberg concluded that while voters see Democrats as being more on the side of the middle class and working Americans, they "only see this manifested in costly government social programs or political alliances with labor unions and minorities."

Then too—and these are by no means mutually exclusive—a lot of voters simply find cultural issues more compelling than economic ones. That isn't necessarily the same thing as being determined to vote one's social views come hell or high water: these people simply find one set of issues more stirring or infuriating than the other. Agne and Greenberg found that the voters they talked to were deeply dissatisfied about economic issues and the war in Iraq, but that "as powerful as the concern over these issues is, the introduction of cultural themes—specifically gay marriage, abortion, the importance of the traditional family unit, and the role of religion in public life—quickly renders them almost irrelevant in terms of electoral politics at the national level."

Some take that as evidence that Democrats have to redouble their efforts to go beyond economic issues and reach out to values voters.

Garance Franke-Ruta points out that self-interest doesn't end at the clasp of people's pocketbooks—it has a psychological side, as well:

> Politics has always been as much about identity and community—not to mention raw group power—as about the economy. Self-interest defined in purely economic terms is an idea that reduces the Democratic Party to little more than the human-resources department of American politics, endlessly fussing over pensions and health-care plans and whether or not you got your flu shot, rather than a party concerned with the fundamental stuff of life: who we are, how we organize our society, and what it means to be American at this particular moment in history.

It's hard to deny that, in recent years, Democrats have been conspicuously short on what George Bush père called "the vision thing." You sometimes get the feeling that liberals' impatience with people who are swayed by values issues comes down simply to complaining that working- and middle-class Americans aren't materialist enough. But Franke-Ruta's observations have a crucial corollary that Democrats often lose sight of. If "values" issues are really matters of self-interest in the broader, psychological sense of the term, it's also true that "self-interest" issues are ultimately matters of values. It's in people's nature to perceive their interests in moral terms, after all. "I deserve it" turns crass self-interest into a matter of principle that can arouse the same genuine ire and indignation that "purely symbolic" issues do.

Most wealthy people won't tell you that they favor tax cuts because they want the money, for example. They may say that tax cuts for the rich are the best way to achieve economic growth, that they provide incentives for other people to work hard, or that taxes are "punishments that take away from the good, disciplined people rewards that they have earned." That isn't really a matter of hypocrisy, which requires more cognitive dissonance than most people can sustain. These are sincere beliefs which happen to accord with wealthy people's economic self-interest and which give them grounds for indignation when the tax cuts are attacked as unfair. And similarly for middle-class Americans who are concerned about threats to Social Security: they'll tell you they feel entitled to a

secure pension because they've paid into the system, or because they believe that Social Security is a contract between American generations.

You can call some of these reasons rationalizations, but that doesn't
mean they're false or illegitimate. As the political philosopher Quentin
Skinner said: "It does not . . . follow from the fact that an agent's pro-
fessed principles may be *ex post facto* rationalizations that they have no
role to play in explaining his behavior." But they're no different in principle from the stories that people cite when they're justifying their positions on "values" issues like school prayer. In fact, saying that "values"
issues appeal to a kind of psychological self-interest of their own means
that they're often as much in need of legitimation as matters of economic
self-interest are. The point of political discourse, as anthropologist Clifford Geertz has said, is to transform sentiment into signification. People
who feel a reflexive rush of anger over the removal of the Alabama Ten
Commandments monument need to be told that they're right to be angry, with a story about liberals who are trying to drive Christianity from
American life so that they can impose their secular agenda of gay rights
and abortion. That's how Rush Limbaugh and his ilk make their living,
by providing people with rational grounds for feelings of resentment they
originally came to out of a sense of group solidarity or personal slight:
"See, let me tell you what's really wrong with that, folks." And if there's
any difference between the two kinds of issues, it's only that the "values"
issues wear their emotional content on their sleeves, whereas the economic issues are often presented in ways that make them seem remote
from "the fundamental stuff of life," as Franke-Ruta calls it.

That's where language comes in, as the means of legitimating narrow
self-interest by connecting it to a larger symbolic structure that gives it
moral and political meaning. Sometimes that can be accomplished simply by choosing the right words, if they happen to trail suitable scenarios
behind them. At the dawn of capitalism, sixteenth-century merchants
took to using *religious* to describe the punctual and conscientious performance of one's work, with the aim of suggesting that their commercial
activity wasn't simply self-seeking but itself a kind of piety. The usage
wasn't meant to be metaphorical: the point wasn't to imply that commercial activity was comparable to religious observance but that the two were

the very same thing. Nor is there anything metaphorical in the way modern companies vaunt their corporate "missions," in the hope of infusing the company's employees with the same zeal that animates the crew of the starship *Enterprise*. These are just ways of making self-interest into something nobler, so that its denial becomes an occasion for political indignation rather than simply personal irritation.

The Democrats' inability to stir voters over economic issues like health care and job security doesn't necessarily mean that those questions are intrinsically less important to voters than gay marriage or the erosion of the family, but only that the Democrats haven't been able to find the language and the narratives that make them compelling. On the basis of their focus-group studies, Agne and Greenberg conclude that voters have "no sense that Democrats have a viable alternative vision that would truly promote broad economic growth or increased prosperity for working Americans."

"Vision" is the key word there—the great economic transformations of American life have always been legitimated by symbols that invested them with a sense of higher purpose. Roosevelt realized that self-interest alone is rarely sufficient to rouse broad popular support for a cause. The New Deal was built on a scaffold of rhetoric and populist propaganda which turned it into a moral as well as an economic campaign— and which set the pattern for the pseudo-populism of the modern right forty years later. Ronald Reagan was the creation of Frank Capra and Clifford Odets.

As the labor economist Stephen Rose has pointed out, that's even truer today, when few middle-class voters are personally affected by more than one or two government programs and may not perceive the need to "trade support" with groups that need other kinds of assistance. How do you persuade a childless middle-class couple to support an increased minimum wage or funding for college loans? You can turn it into a values issue by appealing to their sense of social justice, but as Rose notes, those concerns are apt to be trumped by fiscal and security concerns or social issues. Or you can appeal to a sense of solidarity, not just by making them feel that those issues are intimately connected to their own concerns about pensions and health care costs, but by making them feel that all those issues are part of a larger struggle to provide struggling middle-class families with the stability and security enjoyed by families further up the ladder. At that point, the difference between "values" and "self-interest" doesn't simply become blurry; it disappears.

But as the failure of liberals' experiments with words like *traditional* and *values* itself makes clear, words can't always be lifted out of the narratives that give them meaning and redeployed to do new symbolic work. And merely enumerating your values by name won't help if the names don't evoke specific narratives of their own. When *Salon* asked a number of noted liberals during the 2004 campaign how John Kerry should talk about values, they tended to respond with abstract generalities. The sociologist Andrew Greeley said that the Democratic Party must demonstrate its commitment to values like "Americans have the right to honest and accountable political leadership" and "Americans should have access to financial safety nets at times of crisis in their lives." Representative Barney Frank said that the party should emphasize its concern with the poor, the elderly, and the disabled. The historian Alan Brinkley urged Kerry to talk about "honesty, hard work, tolerance, fairness, respect for other cultures and religions" (though Brinkley also suggested that given the right's aggressive use of *values*, Kerry would be better off avoiding the term). It's no wonder that Kerry's own depiction of his values was so nondescript: his talk of "faith and family" and "responsibility and opportunity" was too abstract to stir emotions.

The Democrats need a compelling narrative of their own, and in particular a populist narrative: a story about the powerless against the powerful, of dreams betrayed and righteous anger. Bill Clinton understood this perfectly. Conventional wisdom sums up his 1992 campaign as "It's the economy, stupid." But Clinton didn't make his case on economic grounds as such, but rather by focusing on the insults that Republican economic policies had visited on Americans' sense of personal security:

> For too long Washington has rigged our system for the benefit of the few, the quick buck, the gimmick, and the short run. For the first time since the twenties, 1 percent of the American people control more wealth than the bottom 90 percent. For this we were promised jobs, but instead we got

pink slips and insecurity, worries about health care and education and safe streets. We have tried it that way and now we have to change. I am tired of seeing the people who work hard and play by the rules get the shaft.

People who recount the history of that campaign often cite that phrase "people who work hard and play by the rules" approvingly, as they should; it highlights the class distinction between the middle class and the wealthy that the right has tried hard to blur. But a populist narrative requires more than just the appropriate dramatis personae—it isn't until you come to "get the shaft" that the story acquires a plot. Clinton's gift didn't stop at being able to convey that he felt people's pain; he also managed to convey that he felt their anger.

Talk of populism makes some Democrats nervous, for fear it might cost the Democrats their middle-class supporters. Al From of the centrist Democratic Leadership Council describes a populist as someone who "wants to destroy the capitalist system." And conservatives ridicule appeals for a new Democratic populism, arguing that the middle-class mistrust of Democratic cultural politics will overwhelm any sympathy they might have for the party's economic policy. As David Brooks put it a few years ago: "[M]ost Republicans would like to see the liberal populists take over the Democratic party, because they're confident the liberals would lead the Democrats to disaster at the polls."

There's a certain irony in that, given that it's the right that has made the most effective use of populist rhetoric in recent times. But even when it comes from Democrats, there's nothing in the populist style that militates against using it on behalf of the middle class. It's true that traditional populism hasn't really been the dominant Democratic language for more than half a century—the last major figure to speak it natively was Harry Truman, who was at ease with sentences like "The Republicans' rich man's tax bill sticks a knife in the back of the poor." But Democrats since then, from Carter and Cuomo to Clinton and Gore, have periodically wielded the idiom on behalf of the middle class. Immediately after the 2000 Democratic convention, Gore's evocations of "the people versus the powerful" dramatically increased his poll numbers, even among voters making between $50,000 and $75,000 a year (his undoing, in the end, had to do not with that rhetoric, but with his inability to overcome charges that he had a "character problem" and his association with Clinton). As John Judis and Ruy Teixeira have pointed out, Gore's populism didn't imply anticapitalism: "He attacked 'big tobacco, big oil, the big polluters, the pharmaceutical companies, the HMOs' for blocking consumer, environmental and health-care legislation. He was not attacking the system of profits and markets."

More recently, John Edwards pulled away from the pack in the 2004 Democratic primaries by evoking "two Americas" and other populist themes:

> [Bush] wants to see the estate tax gone; he wants to see the tax on capital gains gone; he wants to see the tax on dividends gone. . . . The president wants to shift the tax burden in America from wealth and income on wealth—people who sit at home and get their statements every month from their investments and see how much money they've made—to people like my father. . . . He wants working people to carry the tax burden.

But Edwards also managed to defuse any charge that he was anti-capitalist: "This is about a real belief in capitalism. It's a belief that our markets can do well, but in order for them to do well, we need honesty, we need truth, we need responsibility."

The moment is more propitious than ever for a new Democratic populism. Robert Reich points out that middle-class working families now have much more in common with the working poor than they have had at any time since the 1930s—both groups need a wage floor that keeps them from falling into poverty; they need affordable health care and child care, and job training, among other things. And many of the issues that split Democrats from "values" voters are no longer as prominent as they were. Welfare is off the table, and while race is certainly still an issue, it's less intensely divisive than it was a decade or two ago. True, abortion and gun control are still salient, but the first is a deep concern only to a minority of voters, and Democrats have been less confrontational about the second in recent years. And while the right has been able to make political hay by intensifying the debates over issues like gay marriage and "creeping secularism," those issues are decisive only for the religious right.

But what's important isn't that Democrats be able to go *mano a mano* with the Republicans on every one of these issues, but that they have a compelling counternarrative of their own. There's a powerful story of hope and betrayal to be told here, even more than in 1992, when Clinton spoke on behalf of "the people who work hard and play by the rules." The *Father Knows Best* world of the postwar years that's evoked by the right's talk of "traditional values" was also a world of increasing accessibility of education and home ownership, rising manufacturing wages, secure pension plans, a still-healthy labor movement, trust in government, and growing economic equality. It was also, at least through the lens of nostalgia, a time of hope and confidence for those who were able to participate in the American dream.

As late as 1977, the management theorist Peter Drucker could applaud "the achievement of U.S. business in this century: the steady narrowing of the income gap between the 'boss man' and the 'working man,'" even as he warned about a recent increase in the gap between the pay of top management and ordinary workers. At the time he was writing, the ratio of CEO compensation at top companies to the pay of an average worker was around forty. Today it's around four hundred, just one sign of the dramatic reconcentration of income and wealth in America that the *New York Times*'s Paul Krugman has described as "the new Gilded Age." Yet the rich bear a far smaller tax burden than they did thirty years ago, leaving the middle class to feel the economic squeeze and a new host of insecurities about jobs, health care, and pensions.

Turning those concerns into questions of "values" doesn't require finding the right words in advance. Words like *elite*, *values*, and *traditional* didn't work for the Republicans because they came with suitable frames already attached to them—rather, the words acquired their charged meanings in the context of the stories they were used to tell. The Democrats' task is to find stories that invest ordinary, concrete language with more specific meanings, the way Clinton did when he said that "people who work hard and play by the rules get the shaft." In the abstract, words like *fair* and *decent* can mean a lot of things, but when you talk about doing the decent thing by hard-working Americans and flesh it out with examples, it acquires a force that's missing when you simply enumerate your values as "responsibility and opportunity for all."

Indeed, some of the conservatives' words can be thrown back at them. *Elite* hasn't lost its old meaning in the course of acquiring a new one. When conservative critics of Harriet Miers's nomination to the Supreme Court complained that she hadn't attended an elite law school, the word didn't carry any implication of liberal ideology, no more than it does when people talk about elite fighting forces, and phrases like *the corporate elite* still have the power to evoke telling images in the public's mind. And there are some words, like *faith* and *freedom*, that are so deeply anchored in the vocabulary of American life that Democrats are obliged to reclaim them. But that isn't a question of merely saying the words, but of using them to tell a larger story. The important thing is to compose the tune right; the lyrics will follow.

chapter nine

On the Pavement, Thinking About the Government

If you want to raise a certain cheer in the House of
Commons make a general panegyric on economy; if you
want to invite a sure defeat, propose a particular saving.
—*Walter Bagehot,* **The English Constitution,** *1867*

One notable advantage of the right's populism is that it has low carrying costs. It isn't very expensive to implement "values" policies like restricting abortion and stem-cell research, moving funds to abstinence-only programs, appointing right-wing judges, or introducing constitutional amendments to ban flag burning and gay marriage. And often, values voters require no more than symbolic gestures aimed at secular elites or activist judges to persuade them to pick up their leaders for another season. The leaders of the cultural right would have very little incentive to try to "win" the culture wars, whatever that might mean, no more than the leaders of Oceania in Orwell's *1984* had any real interest in defeating their enemy Eurasia.

For the Democrats, though, a populist appeal is a harder row to hoe. It isn't enough for them to instill voters with a sense of indignation over the effects of Republican policies—stagnating wages, insecurity about jobs and pensions, the rising costs of health care and college, and the rest. Voters also have to believe that the government is in a position to do something substantive about these things.

That's first and foremost a question of coming up with workable and compelling programs that can address the social and economic inequities in America. But it's also a matter of persuading people that government can still be an effective agent of change. And in today's climate, that can be a tough sell. Listening to the ambient political background noise—the rhetoric from both Republicans and Democrats, the talk shows on AM radio and cable, the culty Web sites dedicated to conservative political philosophers like Friedrich Hayek and Ludwig von Mises, the Reaganesque aphorisms, the jokes about how many bureaucrats it takes to change a light bulb (1,000+ hits on Google)—it seems to be a truth universally acknowledged that government is a really terrible idea. People may be willing to rise to the defense of particular government programs, but it's hard to find anyone nowadays who will stand up for government itself as a beneficent institution.

Americans have always been ambivalent about government. It may be, as political scientist Samuel Huntington has said, that distrust of government is "as American as apple pie," but people have also looked to government to play a constructive role in their lives. The traditional debate over government took a new form in the early twentieth century, as first the Progressives and then the Democrats introduced new measures to regulate employment and commerce, and conservatives countered with attacks on centralization and growing government power. Addressing proposals to have Washington regulate the railroads in 1906, the Republican Speaker of the House "Uncle Joe" Cannon warned, "If the Federal Government continues to centralize, we will soon find that we will have a vast bureaucratic Government, which will prove inefficient if not corrupt." At the time, the word *bureaucracy* was still a word that Americans tended to associate with the undemocratic regimes of countries like Germany, Austria, and Russia. But over the following decades, it became a staple disparagement in conservative criticisms of domestic programs. "The new despotism is bureaucracy," the *Wall Street Journal* thundered in

1935, and over the course of the decade the *Journal* cited the threat of bureaucratic intrusion as its reason for opposing child labor laws, Social Security, the minimum wage, and public works like the Tennessee Valley Authority. In 1940, the Republican presidential candidate Wendell Willkie contributed "big government," which was coined as a turn on "big business." Willkie acknowledged that government intervention had been necessary to correct "abuses on the part of some American businessmen and financiers" in the 1920s. Alas, he added, the New Deal had failed to "replace this corporate tyranny with a truly liberal faith. Today it is not Big Business that we have to fear. It is big government."

Even so, public confidence in government remained strong during the New Deal era and in the postwar years, when liberalism was still riding high in the saddle. In 1964, three-fourths of the American public said they trusted Washington to do the right thing most of the time. It wasn't until the 1970s that confidence began to decline precipitously, along with the credit of liberalism itself. By 1976, the proportion of the public reporting that they trusted government had dropped to 40 percent, and in recent years it has ranged between one-fourth and one-third of the public, apart from short-lived spikes in confidence when the country rallied behind a president at times of national crisis like the seizure of the American embassy in Tehran in 1979 or the 9/11 attacks.

The declining trust in government has been a matter of endless fascination to political scientists. It has been laid to inflation and soaring property taxes, stagnating wages, Vietnam and Watergate, increasing polarization or diminishing party loyalty, the postwar rise in social expectations, a decline in community participation, media sensationalism, late-night television, and negative campaigning, among other things. And there are no fewer theories about what it means: is the dissatisfaction chiefly with politicians, with particular policies, or with government itself? How much has it contributed to the reaction against liberal social programs?

One thing is clear, though: the skepticism about government has been amplified and focused by politicians on both sides who have tried to ride the whirlwind of anti-Washington feeling, creating a new

123

antigovernment rhetoric in the process. By the 1976 election, Gerald Ford and Jimmy Carter were vying to see who could most vigorously decry big government and a bloated and unresponsive federal bureaucracy. But it was Ronald Reagan who perfected the role of the president as First Misarchist ("a person who hates or opposes government," as the *OED* defines the word). More than anyone else, Reagan transformed antigovernment rhetoric from the white-shoes laissez-faire-ism of Willkie and Eisenhower to a broader attack on the idea of government itself.

Reagan was aided in that approach by his gift for delivering one-liners like "The nine most terrifying words in the English language are: 'I'm from the government and I'm here to help.'" But the Reagan revolution also transformed the language of political debate. Over the decade ending in 1975, articles in the *New York Times* mentioned deregulation just 72 times; for the following decade that number went to over 2,800, and mentions of "getting government off people's backs" went from 3 to 130. And "big government" both tripled in frequency and shifted subtly in meaning. The real problem with government wasn't that it was too big, but that it was government in the first place. Government was not the solution to the problem, it was the problem, as Reagan famously put it— not a turn of phrase that you could have imagined coming from Willkie, Eisenhower, or even Nixon.

But that rhetoric is better suited to perorations than to specific policy proposals. People readily applaud calls for the reduction of government in the abstract: after all, the only time most of us ever deal with government as a totality is when we have to write a check to pay for it. The misgivings arise when it comes to eliminating specific programs and services: our enthusiasm for smaller government is apt to wane on the first heavy snow day.

Reagan had some appreciation for that point. After his 1981 tax cuts failed to produce the new revenue that supply-siders had predicted, he signed tax increases in the following years that offset half of the earlier reductions. A decade later, Newt Gingrich was less astute when he forced a budget showdown with Clinton that ultimately brought the whole government to a halt. When Americans realized what the Contract with America actually entailed in the way of reduction of programs, public support for Gingrich's program evaporated—it was as if someone who has built a career telling lawyer jokes suddenly announced plans to dynamite the county courthouse.

To Clinton, that seemed the right moment to try to take the big-government issue off the table once and for all, by pointing to his administration's success in reducing the deficit and discretionary spending and streamlining the bureaucracy. His declaration in his 1996 State of the Union address that "the era of big government is over" signaled a new age of Democratic political rhetoric, dominated by the themes of modesty, markets, and modernity. "There is not a program for every problem," Clinton reminded Americans, calling for "a smaller, less bureaucratic government in Washington—one that lives within its means."

Clinton's pronouncements opened the way for Democrats to embrace the rhetoric and policies of small government, rejecting the "tired liberal solutions" of the past. In his recent book *The Past and Future of America's Economy*, the Progressive Policy Institute's Robert T. Atkinson argues that the "top-heavy centralized government" of the New Deal and the Great Society reflected the outmoded old-style managerial economy of the age of mass production. Now, he says, Democrats must abandon "the old economy Keynesian, Great Society economic framework" in favor of "a fundamentally new approach to government, one that relies more on networks than hierarchy, more on civic and private sector actors than bureaucracy, and more on technology than on rule-based, bureaucratic programs."

The Third Way meets the Third Wave—the language recalls Gingrich, another technological determinist who dismissed classic liberalism as being on the wrong side of economic history. Not that the New Democrats aren't right to argue that government has a lot to learn about management from the private sector (though as Peter Drucker pointed out with uncanny prescience in 1996, the familiar business approach of indiscriminate downsizing that Republicans favor—"amputation before diagnosis," Drucker called it—is likely to "destroy performance, but without decreasing the deficit"). But the Democrats' unqualified embrace of the rhetoric of the private sector has tied their hands when it comes to defining government's unique role. As E. J. Dionne noted in

Stand Up and Fight Back, Democrats have reached the point where every policy has to be justified in market terms. "We used to call for immunizing little children against disease," he quotes one Democrat as saying. "Now we call it an investment in human capital." The result, as Dionne points out, is that it becomes hard to defend policies simply on grounds of moral rightness or to maintain that there are things that only the government can do, precisely because they have no narrowly economic justification. Democrats and liberals may believe in progressive taxation and affirmative government, Dionne says. "But they are always looking over their shoulders, fearing that the tax-and-spend charge is about to ruin their day."

The New Democrats argue that the language of modest expectations is dictated by the current zeitgeist; they cite polls showing that an increasing number of Americans prefer smaller government even if it means fewer services. "Given a choice between more government spending and some extra help paying the mortgage, saving for college, or planning for retirement," says Senator Evan Bayh, "most Americans understandably favor the latter." And so they would, when it's put to them that way. But that doesn't mean that Democrats won't have popular support when they rise to the defense of government programs like Social Security, Medicare, education spending, or domestic security.

It makes both political and rhetorical sense, of course, for Democrats to call for government that is effective and accountable, and for minimizing the tax burden of the middle class. Where they go wrong is in abandoning the language that has historically defined the party and disparaging as "tired liberal solutions" the achievements from which the party still draws its greatest strength. A recent Democracy Corps poll found that helping the poor and the neediest and expanding opportunities are still among the party's strongest positive attributes, behind only equal rights and environmental protection.

In fact, the Democrats have been deluded in thinking they could neutralize the "big-government" issue simply by adopting the Republicans' rhetoric. Like the their newfound values-talk, this is language that Democrats can never really own—as Dionne puts it, it's "talking the other guy's talk." Nor could Clinton and Gore's real achievements in streamlining government lead Republicans to modulate their attacks on "tax-and-spend" Democrats. Writing in 2000, the White House speechwriter Michael Waldman said that within a few years after Clinton announced the end of the era of big government, "the tax-cutting, government-hating strain of the GOP had lost its political potency." In retrospect, that was a little hasty. The right scarcely missed a beat after Clinton's pronouncement: they took it as a concession speech, an admission of the bankruptcy of the policies that conservatives had been attacking since the days of New Deal. The *Weekly Standard* made that clear in the heading it ran on the day after Clinton's speech: "We Win!" And rhetorically speaking, they were dead right.

Here again, the Democrats are suffering from their chronic literalism about political language: they have a hard time understanding that symbols like "big government" can't be purged overnight after decades of accumulated connotations and restored to their dictionary meanings. In the end, big government is no more an objective notion than big hair is. The problem isn't just that the notion of "government" is notoriously hard to circumscribe, or that "size" often comes down to which column you make your entries in—whether you achieve a particular goal with a direct industry subsidy or a tax credit or whether a job is performed by a federal employee or a local government worker hired with federal funds. More important, "big government" is as laced with ideological undertones as "faith-based" or "the culture of life." The phrase always implies either that the government is trying to do something that the market could do better, that it's coercing people into doing what they ought to chose freely, or that it's doing something for people that they'd be morally better off doing for themselves.

Above all, "big government" implies bad faith—when you describe a program as "big government," you're implying that it was created out of bureaucratic self-interest rather than any genuine concern about public needs. The program might be aimed at keeping voters beholden to politicians and parties (according to George Will, the Democrats' opposition to personal Social Security accounts is "rooted in reluctance to enable people to become less dependent on government"). It might be an expression of the moral arrogance that leads government to intrude in local affairs, a charge with a long history—the minority report that anti-integration Southern Democrats wrote on the party's 1960 platform plank on civil rights took issue with the belief that "big government alone, beyond any private institution or private will, has the wisdom and compassion to . . . tell people all over the land by what rules our schools should be run." Or it might be simply a result of government's inherent drive to increase its size and power. It's striking how the right is always depicting government as an animate being with a will of its own, whether in the conservative activist Grover Norquist's "starve the beast" image, Bush's calls for "restraining the spending appetite of the federal government," or in most of Reagan's antigovernment epigrams: "No government ever voluntarily reduces itself in size," and "A government bureau is the nearest thing to eternal life we'll ever see on this earth." (One reason for personifying things, John Donne said, is so that we can damn them to hell.)

The "big government" charge, in short, is mostly just prejudice tricked out as philosophy—it can't be answered simply by pointing to the reductions in the deficit you've achieved or the number of jobs or departments you've eliminated. And because the phrase is suffused with the ideology of the right, George Bush can freely invoke it to criticize the Democrats, whatever their actual positions, in the same way he can talk about "faith" and "values" with confidence that his audience will understand the phrases in a sympathetic way. "On issue after issue," Bush said during the 2004 campaign, "from Medicare without choices to schools with less accountability to higher taxes on working Americans, my opponent takes the side of more centralized control and bigger government." And Bush has tried to exploit mistrust of government to argue for moving payroll taxes into private accounts, where "the money in the account is yours, and the government can never take it away."

But for all his "big-government rhetoric," Bush also realizes that most voters actually value a lot of what government does. He eschews the hard-line rhetoric of the gangsta libertarians—following the advice of Frank Luntz, the administration has dropped its references to "deregulation" in favor of phrases like "common-sense solutions." And Bush has been amenable to creating new government programs or expanding entitlements, particularly if they promise to steal the Democrats' thunder in education or health care. Libertarian conservatives may accuse Bush of "big government conservatism," but he knows he can get away with rhetorical inconsistency here: voters will always tend to give Republicans the benefit of the doubt on big government, while the party has to prove its bona fides on "compassion." And Bush knows he can advance his own programs without having to worry that he'll compromise himself by trying to "out-Democrat the Democrats." Explaining why he was voting against Bush's prescription drug bill, the conservative Republican Jeff Flake of Arizona warned, "If voters want bigger government, they'll return to the genuine article." But there's small chance of that, so long as the Democrats are more skittish about proposing new entitlements than the Republicans are.

bush's ability to decry "big government" at the same time he's dramatically increasing both the budget and the deficit is an indication that the phrase really has less to do with contracting the actual size of government than with restricting its role as a buffer between ordinary people and corporate interests. In fact, the right's new language of government is aimed at obscuring the existence of those interests entirely. Before the 1980s, Republicans talked about government as one of several contending forces, any of which could threaten individual rights if its power was unrestrained. Dwight Eisenhower compared his proposals for limiting government with Theodore Roosevelt's campaign against monopolies: "Trust busting was a process of decentralization whereby big business was brought within reach of the people . . . Big government is in need of the same treatment." Robert A. Taft, "Mister Conservative," qualified his warnings about big government by adding that it was the business of government to protect the people against the "arbitrary excessive power" of big business. And even Barry Goldwater acknowledged that big government served as a check on big business, though he came down squarely on the side of the latter, arguing that it could accomplish what small business could not: "That is your choice: big business or a much bigger government. There is no other alternative."

Since Reagan's time, though, Republicans have been far less likely to mention big business in the same breath as big government or to suggest that government might have a legitimate role in restraining the excesses of the private sector. Nor have the media made much of an effort to remind their audience that the bigness of government and the bigness of corporations might balance each other. For the right, political life is cast as a fundamental opposition between government and "the people," with corporations and the wealthy tucked out of sight or absorbed into "the market," where agents ostensibly compete on equal terms. It's a rhetoric that exalts capitalism but ignores the existence of capitalists. (When you see the noun *capitalist* in a *Wall Street Journal* editorial or op-ed, the odds are about 4-to-1 that it's in the context of a quote from Lenin or a sarcastic comment on the language of the left—"it's the old story of nasty capitalists exploiting the Third World's picturesque poor.")

As usual, Peggy Noonan can be counted on to draw the picture in its most reductive terms:

> If government is a steamroller, and that is in good part how I see it, the individuals who work in it are the atoms in the steel. The force of forward motion carries them along. There is inevitably an unaccountability, and in time often an indifference about what the steamroller rolls over . . . .

Actually, the real steamroller here is Noonan's metaphor itself, which mows corporations and ordinary citizens down to the same helpless height, as government bears down on both with even-handed oppressiveness. That picture of things goes hand in hand with the notion of *freedom* that pervades the right's rhetoric of government. When political life is represented as an opposition between the steamroller and "the grass the steamroller flattens," as Noonan puts it, then government can only threaten an individual's freedom, not safeguard it from the encroachments of the larger stalks on either side. Government can only be the enemy of freedom, not its protector. As Reagan put it, "Runaway government threatens our economic survival, our most cherished institutions, and the very preservation of freedom itself."

Along with the trashing of the liberal label, the modern right can count the capture of the language of freedom as one of its signal linguistic triumphs. Indeed, you could argue that it's even more crucial for liberals to recapture *freedom* than to recapture their own name, and certainly more important than recapturing *values*. A word like *values* has no abiding political importance in American political discourse—it wouldn't have any political significance at all if the right hadn't pulled it off the shelf to weave into its populist narratives. It's unlikely that *values* will merit an entry in an American political lexicon fifty years from now, no more than once-potent expressions like "natural rights" or "the interests" do now. It isn't a word that's anchored in the basic myths of American identity.

But as the historian Eric Foner has written in his *History of American Freedom, freedom* is a word that is "deeply embedded in the record of our history and the language of everyday life" and is "fundamental to Americans' sense of themselves." Foner documents the way most of the major political debates in American history have been waged over dueling definitions of freedom, even as other nations often framed the very same issues in terms of notions like equality or community. Just over the last half century, redefinitions of freedom have been central in the Cold War, the civil rights struggle, feminism, the New Left, the personal liberation and self-expression movements of the 1960s and 1970s, the Reagan revolution, and the war on terror. No group or movement has been able to establish its moral authority in America without being able to claim *freedom* for its own.

As varied as they are, these debates over the notion of freedom always have the same general form: each group tries to interpret the concept of freedom that's embodied in our national myths in a way that creates new rights and entitlements or justifies or prohibits certain actions. I say "interpret" *freedom* rather than "reinterpret" or "extend" it because people always talk about freedom as if it were a single, unified concept. When you invoke the ideal of freedom to defend your opposition to the minimum wage or motor-voter laws, you have to pretend that it's exactly what George Washington's troops suffered for at Valley Forge—the same thing, not a new, metaphorical sort of freedom. That's why *freedom* is inevitably a commodious and expansive word. As the historian Daniel Rodgers noted, it's used to "bind together the confusions and discordances of American life with a single, powerfully flexible noun."

The twentieth century saw a great expansion of the notion of freedom by both liberals and conservatives. One sign of that is the gradual eclipse of the word *liberty*, which had been the dominant ideal in political discourse from the American Revolution to the time of the New Deal. The Declaration of Independence speaks of "life, liberty and the pursuit of happiness" but doesn't mention freedom at all, and it was liberty that Patrick Henry declared himself willing to die for and that the bell in Philadelphia proclaimed on July 8, 1776. During World War I, Americans bought liberty bonds and planted liberty gardens, while factories turned out liberty trucks and liberty aircraft engines.

But *liberty* is a more narrowly political concept than *freedom* is (no one would be tempted to describe *liberty* as just another word for nothing left to lose). *Freedom* seemed more appropriate as a name for the broader rights that Franklin Roosevelt wanted to set on a level with American political liberties. Of Roosevelt's Four Freedoms—of speech, of religion, from want, and from fear—only the first two might have been expressed using *liberty*. That broadening sense of *freedom* was one of the two great linguistic achievements of the New Deal era (the other being the fixing of the liberal-conservative distinction). "True individual freedom," Roosevelt said, "cannot exist without economic security and independence," as he underscored "our determination to achieve an economic freedom for the average man which will give his political freedom reality." That meaning of *freedom* was elaborated in the Economic Bill of Rights that Roosevelt championed in his 1944 State of the Union speech, which called for expanded access to health care and education, better housing, and full employment.

In the postwar period, though, Roosevelt's notion of economic freedom was largely abandoned. Truman could still use the phrase "economic freedom" in his 1950 State of the Union address when he described collective bargaining as "a fundamental economic freedom for labor." And 1950s writers like Hans Morgenthau and C. Wright Mills could argue that government had a necessary role as champion of freedom against "the unhindered growth of private power." But within a few decades, Roosevelt's Four Freedoms had become a Trivial Pursuit item, and his sense of "economic freedom" had nearly vanished from political discourse. Ronald Reagan understood the power of Roosevelt's invocations of freedom—Reagan's second Inaugural Address mentioned *freedom* fourteen times and *liberty* only once. But Reagan turned Roosevelt's meaning of the word on its head, reinterpreting "economic freedom" to mean deregulation, tax cuts, and a weakening of unions (which earlier conservatives had championed in the name of the "liberty of employers").

There's a curious split here. When we talk about "economic freedom" in our private lives, we're usually thinking about something like Roosevelt's sense of personal economic security. That's how the phrase is always used in ads for investment consultants, financial self-help courses, and franchising schemes that promise to be "your key to economic freedom." But when you run into "economic freedom" in an editorial or an op-ed article nowadays, it's almost certain to refer to freedom from government regulation rather than individual economic security—and this not just in the *Wall Street Journal*, but in the *New York Times*, where Roosevelt's sense of the term is virtually nonexistent.* In the annual "Indexes of Economic Freedom" that conservative think tanks like the Heritage Foundation and the Cato Institute compile for the countries of the world, a nation counts as "economically free" if it has no minimum wage or a very low one, few restrictions on the work week, limited unemployment benefits, and no mandatory separation pay for laid-off workers—but not, say, if workers can count on medical benefits or a guaranteed pension. And even when liberals are defending those very rights for American workers, it's striking how rarely they use the word *freedom* to make their case.

That has left the political field clear for the interpretations of *freedom* that conservatives have used to defend their view of government's role. From the late nineteenth century onward, conservatives have attacked virtually all of the reforms and regulations advocated by the Progressives and later the New Deal Democrats as encroachments on

* Out of 100 *New York Times* editorials, columns, and op-ed pieces that mentioned "economic freedom" between 1984 and 2005, ninety-nine of them used the phrase to mean freedom from government intervention in business, and only one—an op-ed written by two Iranians—used the phrase in the sense of personal economic security.

individual liberty, a theme you can trace in the *Wall Street Journal*'s editorials over the past eighty years. In the 1920s, the *Journal* warned against the threats to freedom that were implicit in minimum wage laws, the child-labor amendment to the Constitution ("an assault upon the economic independence of the family"), and laws permitting peaceful union picketing ("attacks on the Constitutional rights of the employer," the *Journal* said, adding that "peaceful picketing is a contradiction in terms"). In the 1930s, it used the same rhetoric to attack Social Security ("a vast system of socialized thrift") and public works projects like the Tennessee Valley Authority (which "threaten to engulf us in totalitarianism"). In 1943, the *Journal* warned that it would be a mistake for the government to promise full employment when the war was over: "Hitler gave full employment. Mussolini gave full employment. . . . What they took in exchange was men's freedom."

And so on. When national attention turned to women in the workforce in the 1960s, the *Journal* opined that "[t]he vision of millions of women parking their kids at subsidized [day-care] centers and rushing off to the day's grind looks less like America than Russia, where the State has done so much to disrupt family life." It denounced the fair employment and public accommodations sections of the 1964 Civil Rights Act as an "aggrandizement of the police power . . . of doubtful Constitutionality." And in 1970, it argued that pollution was first and foremost a social problem that would be easily manageable through voluntary action and education and warned that government regulation would "force a solution without waiting for the social and psychological change, sacrificing cherished traditions of personal freedom for the sake of survival."

That's still a familiar motif: whenever someone proposes a measure aimed at protecting the interests of citizens, consumers, or employees, the right opposes it as an encroachment on individual freedom, however the word has to be stretched to make the point. The only difference is that these days the "government intrusion" that the right rails at is often aimed at protecting the interests of taxpayers who are footing the bill for the products that corporations provide or the services that they fail to provide. Should the government be allowed to use its bargaining power to reduce the price of the prescription drugs it pays for under the new extensions of Medicare, the way the Veterans Administration does? Not on your life, said the pharmaceutical companies and their conservative allies. That would amount to "price controls" and would "confiscate revenue from firms, in effect seizing their property," as the Cato Institute's Doug Bandow put it (which is a bit like accusing the Pentagon of imposing price controls when it dictates how much it's willing to pay for Kevlar vests). And in *National Review*, the conservative journalist Sam Dealey argued that if government were permitted to bargain for drugs, pharmaceutical companies "would have no choice but to meet bureaucrats' hardball pricing demands," which comes down to saying that the government shouldn't be permitted to lean on its suppliers the same way Wal-Mart does.

Or, speaking of Wal-Mart, take the way conservatives reacted in early 2006 when the Maryland legislature passed a law requiring the company to spend 8 percent of its budget on employee health insurance. (Wal-Mart encourages uninsured employees to apply for state Medicaid, which is picking up the health care tab for more than one-fourth of its employees' families nationally). The U.S. Chamber of Commerce called the law "a dangerous precedent for state governments' ability to dictate how companies can operate," while Rush Limbaugh discerned the odor of creeping fascism:

> This is the government—in this case the state government—telling a private business how it must run its affairs. . . . Some might say you're getting very close to fascism here when the government starts telling everybody in business—at an increasing rate—how they have to run their business, allocate funds, and so forth.

Right-wing Web sites were rife with similar charges: the state is "using fascism to tell companies how to do their business"; "What is happening in Maryland is not merely socialist, it's totalitarian."

Listening to that, you might think nothing had changed over the last century. But while there has been no modulation in the tenor of the right's complaints about "government interference" in business, conservatives have expanded the notion of freedom itself in ways which more closely tie those objections to American political ideals, and which make it easier for them to claim that they're really speaking for the rights of all Americans, and not just corporations or the wealthy.

The process began in the New Deal era as a reaction to the expanded Rooseveltian sense of *freedom,* as the language of political liberty was extended by degrees to the capitalist economy. "Private enterprise" was replaced by "free enterprise," a phrase which had been coined by the economist Alfred Marshall in 1890, but which was rarely used until the New Deal era. Throughout the 1940s, conservatives insisted that "free enterprise" be added to the list of Roosevelt's Four Freedoms, and Harry Truman finally acceded in 1947, dropping Roosevelt's freedom from want and freedom from fear in the bargain. "Free markets" became a buzzword at around the same time—in *Wall Street Journal* editorials, the use of the term quadrupled in the postwar decade. And "free world," which Roosevelt had used to refer to the anti-Fascist democracies, was repurposed as a name for the nations not under Communist domination—whatever awkwardness people may have felt about applying the name to countries like apartheid-era South Africa, Franco's Spain, and Pinochet's Chile, those nations were soundly committed to free markets, at least.

If a single term knit those disparate senses of *free* together, it was the limitlessly flexible "freedom of choice," which broadened the older "freedom of contract." The phrase acquired a talismanic power in the postwar years. It evoked the bounteous variety of goods that capitalism made available to consumers, and advertisers made it a favorite slogan to tout the variety of their offerings (Canada Dry boasted it offered "the greatest freedom of choice in quality beverages" and Child's Restaurant advertised its table d'hôte meal under the heading "freedom of choice"). It evoked the right to choose one's employees and employer, one's co-workers, and one's professional services: conservatives invoked "freedom of choice" in opposing union shops, the proposals for "socialized medicine" that later became Medicare, and antidiscrimination laws in housing and employment, which according to a 1949 column by the *Los Angeles Times*'s political editor in 1949, "would take away the freedom thus far enjoyed by every American to choose his associates, or his co-workers, or his business partners, or his employees." And it of course suggested the rights of voters in a democratic system.

In the event those connections were lost on anyone, editorialists and advertisers made them explicit. A public service ad run by the Cities Service oil company in 1953 showed a picture of a cash register over the heading, "This is a ballot box, believe it or not!" The text continued:

> The marketplace is the symbol of economic freedom—where the consumer is free to choose this or that, or nothing at all. The polling booth is the symbol of political freedom—another kind of customer choice. Political freedom and economic freedom are Siamese twins. They thrive or suffer together.

The wedding of political and economic "freedom of choice" enables the right to cast its objections to government regulation of business in the same terms that one might use to protest abridgments of civil liberties. (Indeed, the conservative Washington Legal Foundation has opposed EPA actions against pesticides and the like as attacks on "business civil liberties," a phrase that effectively nullifies the difference between the two spheres.) But "freedom of choice" also permits conservatives to phrase those objections in ostensibly egalitarian terms, as if the interests of consumers and employees were uppermost in their minds. When you look at the way conservatives defend Wal-Mart against the charges that critics have leveled at it, you're struck by how often they make their case without ever mentioning the interests of the company itself:

> Anyone who works at Wal-Mart is free to quit that job and search for better pay or benefits somewhere else. Consumers are free to shop elsewhere. Freedom is precisely what inspires such irrational angst and loathing among Wal-Mart critics. (Alan Reynolds, Cato Institute)
>
> No one is forced to work at Wal-Mart. Every employment contract is a voluntary agreement between consenting parties . . . [Employees] are free to leave and take other jobs if the working conditions or pay at Wal-Mart are less than satisfactory. (John Semmens, *Capitalism Magazine*)

It's a free country. No one should be forced at gunpoint to shop at Wal-Mart. Or to work there. And no one is. That's what a free market is all about: the freedom to trade goods and services, to trade one's time and labor as an employee, one's dollars as a customer. (Paul Jacob, conservative commentator)

In one sense, this is nothing but the nineteenth-century argument that "liberty of contract" bars the government from interfering in the right of workers to accept whatever wages and working conditions they choose—a principle that was invoked to oppose laws limiting the work week and forbidding the payment of workers in company scrip rather than money, among other things. As no end of people have pointed out, that argument obliterates the obvious discrepancies in power between employers and employees. (As Chief Justice Charles Evans Hughes said in the famous 1937 Supreme Court decision that finally declared the minimum wage constitutional, "The Constitution does not speak of freedom of contract. It speaks of liberty . . . which requires the protection of law against the evils which menace the health, safety, morals, and welfare of the people." Workers, he noted, "are in an unequal position with respect to bargaining power, and are thus relatively defenseless against the denial of a living wage.")

The substitution of "freedom of choice" for "freedom of contract" doesn't alter the right's arguments. When it comes to the crunch, the "freedom" that conservatives champion for working Americans amounts to no more than the right to take a job or shove it. But that freedom doesn't mean a lot to working Americans whose lives are ruled by anxieties and economic insecurities. True, people aren't compelled by law to accept the jobs that Wal-Mart offers them—they're legally free to take a couple of weeks in Gstaad or go sleep under a culvert. Still, when most people are reckoning "our cherished American freedoms," they don't have in mind the absence of compulsory labor laws. Jacob gives the game away when he starts by saying, "It's a free country," a phrase we use only when political freedom is patently irrelevant to the situation. (It's what you answer when someone asks, "Can I ask your ex-girlfriend out?" not "Can a retail chain close down a store when its workers vote to unionize?")

But the new language of "freedom of choice" has several rhetorical advantages over the old language of "freedom of contract." Conservatives had always argued that the regulation of wages and benefits results in higher prices to the consumer, but now they could put the point in quasi-political terms, as if the regulations were abridgments of consumers' rights—the very same freedom of choice, indeed, that people exercise at the ballot box. And "choice" implied a degree of preference that was missing from "freedom of contract," so that conservatives could talk as if workers who accept certain terms of employment were endorsing their fairness and as if consumers were showing their solidarity with management's position when they patronize a business—what the syndicated columnist Bill Murchison is getting at when he says that Wal-Mart's critics "aren't unduly respectful of free choice, whether exercised by shoppers or workers." That move enables conservatives to mount their defense of Wal-Mart using the language of right-wing populism, as they cast themselves as the champions of workers who have freely chosen to forgo medical coverage against the meddling of elite snobs who are motivated by "fear and hatred of poor people," as Jacob contends. ("Lots of folks don't want to shop around poor people," Jacob explains, though he concedes that if Wal-Mart's prices weren't so good, he himself would prefer to shop at a place "where the employees and fellow customers are slimmer and better dressed.")

"Freedom of choice" is useful to the right in other ways—it's also a way of washing your hands of responsibility for what happens to people when the market lets them down. (Sentences that start with "It's a free country" are apt to end with ". . . people can do any damn-fool thing they like, and it's not my look-out.") Markets require human sacrifices to work their magic, after all, even in the best of circumstances. Even if Wal-Mart had dealt with its workers scrupulously and fairly, it would still have contributed to the darkening of a lot of downtown neighborhoods, thanks to its innovative use of technology and its merchandising smarts. Outfits like Costco and Target offer better wages and benefits than Wal-Mart does, but they've played no small part in the big-boxifi-cation of the American landscape, even so. Whether or not the country is better off for it, the triumph of destination retail is a textbook case of what the economist Joseph Schumpeter called "creative destruction," and most Americans are apparently willing to accept the trade-offs, even if they mourn the loss of the old downtowns. But here as elsewhere, they also expect the state to ease the blows when it comes to job loss and pro-viding vital services like health care, pensions, and education.

But free-market ideologues tend to embrace the inequities of the mar-ket, as if the body counts that capitalism exacts were proof of its moral superiority. When the Enron meltdown threw thousands of people out of work and devastated their pensions, Bush's economic adviser Lawrence Lindsay called the collapse a "tribute to American capitalism" and Trea-sury Secretary Paul O'Neill made the point even more fulsomely: "The genius of capitalism is people get to make good decisions or bad deci-sions, and they get to pay the consequence or to enjoy the fruits of their decisions. That's the way the system works."*

O'Neill caught a lot of flak for that remark, even from the business press. With creditable restraint, *Fortune* described it as "insensitive." And deservedly so, particularly since most of the people who had to "pay the consequences" for Enron management's bad decisions were the com-pany's employees and investors. (As several people remarked, Enron's rise and fall had less to do with creative destruction than creative account-ing.) But O'Neill was just reading from the same page that free-market enthusiasts always turn to when the market leaves employees or con-sumers holding the short end of the stick. That's when the right's rhetoric of "freedom" flips over to reveal its dark side.

You can hear that in the shifting inflection that conservatives give to "choice," depending on whether they're touting the privatization schemes they're proposing or defending the ones they've already enacted. Before the administration's prescription drug plan went into effect, Bush

---

* Like just about everybody else, O'Neill seems to assume that "the genius of capital-ism" is a laudatory term. But the phrase was originally based on the older sense of *genius* to mean simply "prevailing nature"—when Leon Trotsky referred to "the exploitative ge-nius of capital," he didn't intend the description in a flattering way.

was lauding it as providing "greater peace of mind by offering beneficiar-ies better health care choices than they have ever had." When the pro-gram was actually implemented in late 2005, though, "peace of mind" was the last thing that most seniors were feeling as they tried to make sense of the hundreds of competing policies offered by insurance compa-nies, each with different coverage and benefits, and with accurate infor-mation so hard to come by that even physicians and pharmacists were throwing up their hands when people asked them for advice. Tens of thousands of people were left unable to obtain their medicines; a Wall Street Journal/NBC News poll found that only 23 percent of Americans over sixty-five had a favorable impression of the plan, with three-fourths deeming it "too complicated and confusing."

The administration responded by saying that confusion and complex-ity are the inevitable effects of privatization. "We fully recognize that for some seniors, this is a daunting task," Bush said. "When you give people choice and options, it can be a situation where people say, this is some-thing I may not want to do." And Michael Leavitt, the secretary of health and human services, pointed out a bit defensively that things were tough all over: "Health care is complicated. We acknowledge that. Lots of things in life are complicated: filling out a tax return, registering your car, getting cable television." It was a damning admission, if you thought about it: Leavitt seemed to be saying that the administration's program combined the bureaucratic red tape of the IRS and the DMV with the pricing structure of the cable companies that require subscribers who want to watch HBO to pay for Spike TV in the process. But even so, the right can't resist the rhetorical allure of "choice"—if libertarian Republi-cans ever succeed in eliminating the IRS and outsourcing its collection functions to Visa and MasterCard, you can bet they'll proclaim that a victory for consumer choice, as well.

In the end, though, Republicans have had only limited success in de-fending their privatization schemes with the language of "freedom" and "choice." People might very well welcome more flexibility in the way health care and Social Security are structured, but they also value the se-curity of government programs. And whatever their qualms about the ef-ficacy of government in the abstract, these are things they'll more readily trust to the government than to the private sector. Realizing that, some on the right have been pulling in their rhetorical horns, as was evident in the semantic operetta in 2005 that surrounded the administration's efforts to win support for a program that would divert payroll taxes into privately managed equity accounts.

Just a few years ago, conservatives were describing those proposals as Social Security "privatization," but in polls that wording turned out to make a lot of people nervous. So in a brisk semantic about-face, the National Republican Congressional Committee issued a memo charging that *privatization* was a "false and misleading" term that Democrats had adopted as a scare-word. At the time, even *National Review*'s Ramesh Ponnuru described that as "brazen historical revisionism," but most proponents of privatization fell into line—the Cato Institute rebaptized its Project on Social Security Privatization as the Project on Social Security Choice, even retroactively revising documents on its Web site to reflect the new language, and much of the press went along.

But the right's newfound circumspection about "privatization" and "private accounts" has created some rhetorical awkwardness. Back in 2001, for example, Bush was saying, "I want to give younger workers the opportunity to manage some of their own money in the private markets." That reference to "people's own money" is the sort of language that comes with the Republican system disk. But the phrase sat uneasily with the administration's new assurances that people wouldn't actually have much control over their accounts. You could hear the strain in the president's remarks at the White House economic summit in December 2004: "People are not going to be allowed to take their own money for their retirement account and take it to Vegas to shoot dice." It was a sentence that tripped over its own rhetorical shoelaces: when a Republican starts a sentence by talking about "people's own money," you usually don't expect him to finish by saying what they're not allowed to do with it.

The phrase *personal account* is the Republicans' effort to square that semantic circle. Like *ownership*, *personal* suggests pride of possession without suggesting that you're getting title in the bargain, as in "Step from your stateroom onto your own personal veranda." As Frank Luntz put it, "When you personalize something, whether monogrammed towels or

Social Security, you enhance ownership by allowing the owner to leave his or her mark on it." (Luntz didn't take the analogy to its logical conclusion: the thing about personalized towels is that they're not returnable even if they turn out not to keep you dry.) In the event, though, the switch to "personal accounts" did nothing to increase support for the president's program, and ultimately even Republicans seemed happy to leave the proposals twisting in the wind.

The whole episode may have demonstrated the linguistic dexterity of the administration, but it also showed the limits of the right's rhetoric of "choice" when it came to inducing people to bail out on a government program that they largely trust, know well, and have come to think of as a guaranteed right. (As the legal scholar Cass Sunstein has said, it's likely that millions of Americans believe that Social Security is in the Constitution somewhere.)

The limits of that linguistic maneuvering were equally evident in the wake of the bungled Hurricane Katrina relief efforts, which brought the right's rhetoric of "choice" and "big government" into full and feculent flower. Conservatives looked for ways to exculpate the administration and blame the victims for the poor choices that led to their misfortunes. The *National Review* contributor T. J. Walker criticized the "moral relativism" of Bush's pledge to rebuild New Orleans, which made "no distinctions between those who bought flood insurance and those who didn't; those who choose to live in safe mountains high above sea level and those who build below sea level in flood zones predicted by every expert to be washed away." The idea, apparently, was that the people in New Orleans's Ninth Ward had nobody but themselves to blame for not having relocated to Aspen when they had the chance. David Boaz of the Cato Institute made the same argument, urging Americans to "debate right now on whether it is the responsibility of people in New York and Illinois and Colorado to pay for the education, health care, housing and business investments of people in Louisiana and Mississippi." Or in other words, let them eat beignets.

That sort of talk is what passes for "tough-mindedness" in a lot of right-wing common rooms. Conservative rhetoric has always been susceptible to a strain of macho indifference to the misfortunes of others—

its object, as the conservative writer Peter Viereck wrote disapprovingly in 1962, is to "make people ashamed of generous social impulses." But most Americans, including many conservatives, were apt to find that tone disturbingly unChristian. Once the failed relief effort had become a public relations disaster, even George Bush knew better than to imply that the victims were to blame for their misfortunes. The reason for coining "compassionate conservatism" in the first place was to try to allay the suspicion that conservatives are temperamentally hard-hearted. That may be personally unfair to most conservatives, but it's a natural reaction to their rhetoric. Epithets like "bleeding-heart" have taken their toll on liberals, but they also tend to discredit the people who use them. We may be wary of soft-hearted sentimentality, but we're also apt to be wary of people who get off on deriding it.

So most conservatives tried to displace the blame a notch. The fault wasn't with the Katrina victims themselves—they had been led down the primrose path by the liberals. It was big government that had created the culture of poverty and "so destroyed wealth and self-reliance in the people of New Orleans," as Boaz put it, "that they were unable to fend for themselves in a crisis." What the failure to deliver timely relief showed, the right argued, was only the mistake of counting on the government for help in such situations. "If big government has failed," the columnist Cal Thomas said, then it was strange to find people arguing that "what we really need is more money, and more big government. I find that to be inconsistent." And David Brooks said that Katrina showed that "government is extremely limited in what it can effectively do . . . For the brutal fact is, government tends toward bureaucracy, which means elaborate paper flow but ineffective action."

"Government is extremely limited in what it can do"—linguistically, the crucial move there was the omission of the definite article before *government*, which snuffs out the difference between the particular and the general. The Katrina relief foul-up wasn't the fault of *the* government, with its incompetence and cronyism, but of government in the abstract, and of those who were naïve enough to think it would come through for them. It's a versatile line of argument: the more egregious the failures of the Republican administration, the stronger the conservative case for reducing government. (As Gordon Lightfoot might have put it, "Everything we had is gone, that's what you get for loving me.")

The right's hope is that the government's failures will lead Americans to realize that government is essentially flawed, a wheezing Rube Goldberg contraption that can't accomplish even the most basic tasks that people entrust it with. But that's a profound misreading of American attitudes. People may report that they have little trust in government, but that doesn't mean they've lowered their expectations of what government should be able to do. Almost forty years after Apollo 11 touched down, people still start sentences with "If we can put a man on the moon" and go on to name some other, far more intractable problem that the government ought to be able to solve.

Nor are Americans eager to look elsewhere for the services that they count on government to provide. To the *Wall Street Journal*'s Daniel Henninger, the Katrina fiasco demonstrated the wisdom of outsourcing the government's functions to the private sector. Let Merck, Home Depot, and Bechtel take care of relief management, he said, and "use the bureaucracies as infantry" (maybe not the best metaphor to have picked, given the problems that our efforts at outsourcing nation building to Halliburton have run into in another part of the world). But the polls that show declining confidence in government also show declining confidence in corporations, and the public's unhappiness with the administration's privatization schemes for prescription drugs and Social Security reveal that Americans don't embrace the prospect of abandoning the security of government programs for the privilege of being put on hold with Wall Street firms and insurance companies.

i t's clearly a good moment for rethinking government's role. The Katrina debacle, the prescription-drug bill snafus, the efforts to privatize Social Security, the corporate giveaways, the environmental rollbacks, the lobbying scandals, inadequate funding of homeland security, the mess in Iraq—Democrats can't complain that the administration hasn't given them lots of material to work with. But Democrats can't make their case successfully unless they can tie it into a particular narrative about what government should be doing for people. A lot of them have realized that it's a mug's game to try to co-opt the "small-government" theme. What we should be talking about, they say, is not big or small government, but effective government.

But by itself, *effective* is one of those windy words like *opportunity* and *responsibility*: it's fine for campaign balloons, but it doesn't evoke much passion unless it's tethered to a specific story. And if the debate is merely about "good government," it's a game that both sides can play. The Jack Abramoff influence-peddling scandals may ultimately turn out to be "the largest corruption scandal since Warren Harding," as Paul Krugman suggested. But even as the papers were still full of indictments and trials of officials in Harding's administration, the nation went on to elect two Republicans of unquestionable probity, Coolidge and Hoover, before the Great Depression finally brought the Democrats to power eight years later.

History could repeat itself. After some shuffling around, congressional Republicans came down hard on the administration's bungled Katrina response, and made a show of condemning colleagues who had gotten caught up in the lobbying scandal. And they'll surely be looking for a new Coolidge or Hoover to carry their standard in 2008. Shortly after the Katrina debacle, the *Washington Post*'s David Ignatius wrote, "The new politics isn't about values; it isn't about settling scores. It's about performance . . . We have a government that can't control its borders, can't find a viable strategy for its war in Iraq, can't organize the key agencies to address the terrorism problems it has been trumpeting. The yearning in the country for something different has been palpable this year." But when it came to identifying the politician who has been "clearly articulating that vision" of performance and "thinking outside the box" about putting the country back on its feet, Ignatius settled on . . . Newt Gingrich. Left to choose a champion for a more responsive government, most Democrats would probably prefer Coolidge. But it's a sign of how versatile a garment the mantle of "effectiveness" can be if it isn't linked to any particular vision of what government is actually for. As history reminds us, neither the left nor the right has a monopoly on getting the trains to run on time.

Nor can the Democrats allow the debate to remain at an abstract level. In an article surveying the political detritus left behind by Katrina, Stephen Hill of the New America Foundation suggested mounting a public relations campaign under the heading "Government Is Good for You," featuring ads that "show the many ways that government does good things for individuals and communities." But debates about the role of government in the large always favor the antigovernment side. The real issue is the particular things that government can do better than the private sector can, with Social Security, health insurance, and education leading the list. When the argument is put in that way, people's reflexive reservations about "government" in the abstract recede. The fact is that a century of conservative warnings about the dangers of "government interference" hasn't turned Americans into laissez-faire zealots. Stanley Greenberg reports in *The Two Americas* that a substantial majority of voters, including a majority of Republicans, believe that government regulation of business and corporations is necessary to protect the public, particularly when it comes to issues like the environment, product safety, working conditions, discriminatory hiring, and failed pension funds. Americans have no illusions about the benevolence of the market's invisible hand or the altruism of large corporations. Listening to corporate spokespeople, you often have the feeling they expect the public to demonstrate the same uncritical enthusiasm for their civic-minded pronouncements that their employees dutifully accord them when they read their corporate mission statements at company gatherings. But one striking development over the last twenty years or so is that the corporations have nudged the bureaucracy aside in the public mind as the chief perpetrators of doublespeak: on the Web, references to corporate or business mumbo jumbo outnumber references to bureaucratic or government mumbo jumbo by 2-to-1. It's a remarkable shift in attitudes, particularly since government itself hasn't exactly been sleeping on the job.

E. J. Dionne has said that the most important question that progressives have to raise is "Whose side is government on?" Since the beginning of the Reagan area, the rhetoric of the right has been strenuously aimed at making that question impossible to ask, by absorbing corporations and business interests into "the people" or "the market." But simply framing the question in Dionne's way puts government back in the middle, as the protector of ordinary people's interests. Democrats who realized this have done well for themselves—think of Clinton in 1992, Gore after the 2000 Democratic National Convention (which raised his poll numbers), and John Edward's "Two Americas" theme in 2004.

Above all, it's crucial for Democrats to reclaim the language of freedom. Not that there's anything illegitimate about using "economic freedom" to talk about the need for opening up developing economies, say. But modern political language seems to have no use for the phrase when it comes to talking about the economic security of individuals. Yet the Democrats have a far better claim to describe themselves as the party of freedom than the Republicans do, not just because of their long-standing concern for civil liberties and equal opportunity, but because they are historically the ones who have championed the economic and social freedoms that matter most to ordinary Americans in the course of their daily lives: the freedom to plan for college and retirement, the freedom to take off time for family reasons, the freedom to leave a job without having to lose health insurance, the freedom from worry about unforeseen medical expenses, the freedom to buy a toy or take a pill with the assurance that it's safe.

This isn't to say that Democrats have to return to the rhetoric of the New Deal era. Nobody's about to try to pull "wage slavery" or "freedom from want" out of the lexicographical dustbin, not just because conditions are nowhere near as dire they were in Roosevelt's day but because the challenge now is to provide economic and personal security for middle-class and working Americans whose expectations were shaped in the postwar period. As Cass Sunstein has pointed out, "The United States continues to live, at least some of the time, under Roosevelt's constitutional vision." Americans believe in the right to education, to social security, to freedom from monopoly, and for many, the right to a job—things that Americans believe that everybody is entitled to as a citizen.

In fact, "economic freedom" in Roosevelt's sense is still very much part of the everyday American lexicon. The challenge facing the Democrats is to move it from ordinary conversation and the display ads for franchising schemes to the editorial pages and news broadcasts. And Democrats can fairly point out, as Roosevelt did, that the two senses of "economic freedom" complement and strengthen one another—capitalism is most successful when people have faith in the justice of the system and when they trust government to be a fair broker between the interests of business and the people whose lives it affects. Roosevelt's "economic freedom" is not an unfamiliar concept; it's merely one whose name needs rediscovering.

chapter ten

Old Bottles, New Whines

The student of politics must be on his guard
against the old words, for the words persist when
the reality behind them has changed.
        —*Aneurin Bevan*, In Place of Fear, *1952*

during the primaries leading up to the 2004 elections, Republicans were trying to depict the Democrats' criticisms of President Bush as the expressions of pathological rage. "So far all we hear is a lot of old bitterness and partisan anger," George Bush said in a speech in February 2004. The Bush campaign sent out a fund-raising letter warning that the president was under "venomous assault from rage-filled Democrats" and released an ad called "When Angry Democrats Attack." And the Republican National Committee chair Ed Gillespie said, "The kind of words we're hearing now from the Democratic candidates go beyond legitimate political discourse—this is political hate speech."

By themselves, those charges were a predictable extension of the right's campaign to depict Democrats as irrational, insecure creatures plagued by "inner doubts about their own moral position," according to Robert Bartley of the *Wall Street Journal*. But Gillespie's use of *hate speech* was a special kind of rhetorical move. It goes without saying that none of the Democratic candidates was expressing actual hatred of President Bush. The remark that got Gillespie going was Richard Gephardt's description of Bush as "a miserable failure"—hardly hate speech according to the accepted definition of the phrase, which refers to insults specifically directed at someone's race, religion, ethnicity, or sexual orientation. In fact, it's hard to imagine how Dick Gephardt could say anything about Bush that would literally count as hate speech, short of yelling "Die, whitey!"— not an easy picture to get your head around.

Even so, Republicans and conservatives pull out *hate speech* when they want to imply that negative attacks on the administration are driven by irrational—or when Hillary Clinton makes them, hormonal—rage. Conservatives may not have a lot of enthusiasm for laws or campus codes that restrict hate speech in the literal sense of the term, but they know that the phrase conjures up an image of speech that's outside the boundaries of civilized behavior. So they reinterpret it to mean simply speech that expresses hatred—or really, just remarks they consider intemperate—in the hope that the old connotations will stick to it. As with other symbols, the maneuver requires pretending the phrase is being used literally. If Gillespie had said, "the Democrats are engaging in hate speech, metaphorically speaking," the point would have been lost.

This new use of *hate speech* is not a big deal as modern political rhetoric goes, but it's a particularly clear example of "legerdemain with two senses." The maneuver wasn't invented by the modern right. You could read the whole history of American political rhetoric as a long string of puns, as old names are assigned new references without any acknowledgment that their meaning has been altered; as Alexis de Tocqueville remarked, "The last thing a political party gives up is its vocabulary." But conservatives have been particularly deft at this; most of the words they've made central to their narratives involve either blurring two senses of a word or using a word in a new way while pretending that it still has its old meaning. It's the pattern we've seen with *entrepreneur, ownership, values, freedom of choice,* and *middle-class.* In every case, a new use of a word is slipped in under the auspices of the old one, like a high-school boy who gets service at a bar by using his older brother's ID.

The art of political language is to alter and expand the meanings of symbols without letting on that anything is different, so that the symbols retain their ability to stir feelings. Once a word acquires a purely symbolic power, it can be used to create an impression of similarity between two things that are actually very different in their natures, simply because they share a name. This is the process marketers exploit when they acquire once-lustrous brands like Lancia, Godiva, Fisher Stereo, or Abercrombie and Fitch and attach them to downscale product lines in the hope that their connotations will persist. What makes this possible is that the literal meanings of symbols usually count less than their purely emotional tones—in Lippmann's terms, symbols involve "an intensification of feeling and a degradation of significance."

In recent years, the right's boldest use of this strategy has been in appropriating the language of the civil rights era. When that language first entered the received moral vocabulary, it signaled the triumph of liberal ideals of social justice in the face of conservative resistance and foot-dragging. Now the right has repurposed it to stoke resentments about race and religion, while liberals are left to thrash around for a new script.

Historically, the words that surround race and ethnicity tend to appear as symbols of progressive views, then become part of the accepted vocabulary of public life, and may finally wind up signifying retrograde attitudes as new words and notions replace them. In the early decades of the twentieth century, for example, *Negro* connoted liberal attitudes about race, and by the 1930s was widely accepted as the proper label by politicians and the mainstream media. But by the 1970s, *Negro* had acquired a condescending tone, as people replaced it with *black*, later complemented by *African American*. Lyndon Johnson was the last president to speak of "the Negro," and by now the word has virtually disappeared from public discourse, apart from its use in the names of organizations or when someone's referring to historical events.

Once a symbol becomes part of the received moral vocabulary, even those who originally avoided it try to co-opt it for their side, as the right has done with brazen audacity. Take *color-blind*. The term is associated with Justice John Marshall Harlan's 1896 affirmation that "our constitution is color-blind" in his dissent from the Supreme Court's infamous *Plessy v. Ferguson* decision, which upheld "separate but equal" facilities for blacks and whites. By the 1940s, *color-blind* had become part of the

boilerplate rhetoric of liberal opponents of segregation and racial prejudice. In 1949, for example, the *New York Times*'s Arthur Daley applauded Jackie Robinson's selection as the National League's MVP as a
victory for color-blindness, using what was becoming a familiar poly-
chromatic trope: "A champion is a champion, and a heel is a heel, and it
doesn't matter if his color is white, black, or chartreuse."

For as long as legal segregation was a contested political issue, *color-
blind* was conspicuously absent from the conservative lexicon. The
phrase never appeared in the editorials of the *Wall Street Journal*, which
was cool to the idea of court-ordered integration and civil rights protection, and repeatedly warned against trying to "force divergent cultures
into harmony." The *Journal*'s editorialists didn't warm to the virtues of
color-blindness until several tumultuous decades later, as the civil rights
debate was moving from ending legal segregation to taking steps to redress the social inequities that slavery and Jim Crow had created. The paper first used *color-blind* in a 1967 editorial reproaching civil rights
leaders for ignoring their earlier commitment to color-blind policies by
pushing for rulings that would end de facto segregation in Northern
schools. Since then, the *Journal* has used the phrase in editorials about
fifty times, every one of them expressing the paper's opposition to busing, affirmative action, racial set-asides in government contracts, equal
opportunity employment regulations, or college admissions policies that
take race into account.

Listening to conservatives talk about race, you're reminded of some-
one who discovers a collection of news clips from the 1950s and decides
to run them all in reverse video. In 1997, Newt Gingrich applauded the
Chicago Bulls for the color-blindness they showed in their win over the
Utah Jazz in the NBA playoffs by noting that in the closing moments,
Michael Jordan didn't limit himself to black teammates in looking for an
open man. "Jordan didn't look for the nearest black face," Gingrich said.
"He looked for the nearest Chicago jersey. That happened to be Steve
Kerr, who is white. This is the example for society to follow—a group of
individuals so focused on a common goal of winning that they don't have
to worry about what color the other guy is." The remark recalls Arthur
Daley's 1949 comment about Jackie Robinson or the similar lines that

were obligatory tropes of the "problem films" of the 1950s. ("I'm just pro-good doctor—black, white, or polka dot," as Sydney Poitier's medical supervisor says in Joseph Mankiewicz's 1950 movie *No Way Out*.) Except that in Gingrich's version it's the black players who offer the model for color-blindness, in one of the few fields that blacks dominate.* And in this version of the story, the implicit enemies of fairness aren't bigoted white fans or the stock racist sociopath played by Richard Widmark or Robert Ryan. They're the African Americans and their white liberal allies who have made "race consciousness" a pervasive feature of American life.

That's how conservatives have generally modified the rhetoric of the civil rights era, deploying it to defend the privileges of their strongest constituency, white male Americans. Their conversion experience to the language of civil rights came just in time to relieve them from having to change any of their positions. Read through Abigail and Stephen Thernstrom's *America in Black and White* or Dinesh D'Souza's *The End of Racism*, for example, and you find the same themes that conservatives were harping on in the 1950s and 1960s, though couched in different language. In outline, the story goes like this: blacks have made extraordinary economic and social progress and white racism is no longer a real impediment to equality. If crushing disparities between blacks and whites continue to exist, they're chiefly the result of "black failure," "black cultural pathologies," or what D'Souza calls "civilizational differences"—black culture, he says, has a "repellent underside" that liberal antiracists are blinded to by their reflexive cultural relativism. Such discrimination as exists is rational, following from the same "logic of predictive evaluation" that might lead an employer to be unwilling to hire women, "who may get pregnant and leave."

Making allowances for changing times and language, that's pretty much what conservatives were saying forty or fifty years ago—at every turn, they applauded the decline of racism and the progress blacks had made, but warned that the cultural differences between the races put

---

* Even if hockey were as big in the United States as pro basketball is, it's hard to imagine Gingrich extolling the virtues of color-blindness by noting the willingness of the Calgary Flames' white players to pass the puck to the black MVP Jarome Iginla.

integration and equality beyond the reach of government programs to achieve. After the Supreme Court's school desegregation decision in 1954, the *Wall Street Journal* suggested that the reluctance of Southerners to end segregation "is not a matter of prejudice about race itself. Rather it is a concern over a conflict of cultures, and an honest conviction on the part of Southerners that their children will be injured in many areas by submergence in a culture that has not had time fully to mature." In 1960, the *Journal* wrote that "[t]he Negro has come remarkably far," but noted that "discrimination is not just a question of skin color . . . It is a reflection of clashing cultures" and noted that "sometimes the groups against which discrimination is directed themselves intensify it."

The right's embrace of the language of color-blindness, "reverse discrimination," and the like provides ideological cover for white resentments about racial preferences that might otherwise leave people vulnerable to charges of racism and sexism. To that end, the right conveniently elides the difference between racial distinctions that redress social disparities and those that keep people in their place—what Justice John Paul Stevens was pointing to when he noted that there is a difference between a "No Trespassing" sign and a welcome mat, or between a law that makes black citizens ineligible for military service and a program aimed at recruiting black soldiers.

But then it's the function of symbols like *color-blind* to suppress gradations and distinctions, and to make unlike things the same. Conservatives like to invoke Martin Luther King's famous call for a color-blind America: "I have a dream that my four little children will one day live in a nation where they will not be judged by the color of their skin but by the content of their character." But the quotation, like conservatives' memory, is selective; conservatives rarely acknowledge that King also called for "some compensatory consideration for the handicaps [the Negro] has inherited from the past." And the fact is that conservatives don't really see the world through King's glasses or give many signs of being concerned about what King saw as an endemic racism in American life. As many conservatives tell the story, that's no longer a big problem; if the government would only stop taking race into account, nobody would notice it anymore. That was the object of the "Racial Privacy Initiative" that appeared on the 2003 California ballot, which would have prohibited the state from gathering any information about racial categories, and so "get government out of the race business," as its sponsor Ward Connerly put it. Once it becomes impossible to determine the existence of racial disparities, the idea goes, they'll no longer matter.

As it happens, though, that initiative was defeated by a 2-to-1 margin. Whatever their views on racial preferences, the vast majority of white voters acknowledge that racial discrimination is still a prevalent problem in American life—in fact, more say that now than did twenty years ago, in a paradoxical sign that racial attitudes are actually getting better. And while conservatives have scored points with their calls for "color-blind" policies, they haven't been able to make any serious inroads in the power of the counter-symbol "diversity," which most Americans accept uncritically as a social good, particularly when it's framed in terms of "outreach" and "enhanced opportunity" rather than quotas, preferences, or "special treatment." Some conservatives may attack "diversity" in the abstract, but even the Republican Party has recognized the potency of the word and uses it to provide cover for opposing some affirmative action programs. ("I strongly support diversity of all kinds, including racial diversity in higher education," Bush said, by way of prefacing his criticism of the University of Michigan's admissions program as a "quota system.") And while most white voters oppose giving "preferential treatment" to minorities and women, a large majority say they support affirmative action programs aimed at expanding opportunities. For most Americans, these debates have devolved into wonky discussions over methods, a question of means rather than ends. And though the details of the programs are still controversial, affirmative action has receded as a national political issue.

but affirmative action is really just a rhetorical target of opportunity for conservatives in a broader campaign against liberals. Conservatives' appropriation of the language of the early civil rights movement allows them to present themselves as the true inheritors of tradition represented by John and Bobby Kennedy and especially Martin Luther

King, whom the right has recast as a conservative icon. As William Bennett puts it, "If you said in 1968 that you should judge people by the content of their character, not the color of their skin, that you should be color-blind, you were a liberal. If you say it now, you are a conservative." But conservatives also credit King with other *ur*-conservative virtues. According the Heritage Foundation's Carolyn Garris, King's "core beliefs, such as the power and necessity of faith-based association and self-government based on absolute truth and moral law, are profoundly conservative," adding that "King's primary aim was not to change laws, but to change people." On King's birthday in 2006, the *Wall Street Journal* celebrated King's "commitment to non-violent social change," in the course of deploring the liberals who "do violence to the English language and the King legacy by engaging in inflammatory rhetoric."* Whatever the historical realities, many on the right have turned King into a mythic embodiment of the "good" liberalism of the early civil rights movement, before it "degenerated into a collection of political extremists, homosexual militants, Muslim activists, and anti-American Marxists," as the right-wing media watchdog group Accuracy in Media puts it.

The right's dismissal of the modern civil rights movement and its multiculturalist allies has another goal, as well. When conservatives deny that racial discrimination is still an impediment to black progress, it isn't simply to let whites off the hook and refocus attention on the social pathologies of African American culture. It also clears the field to claim the role of victim, and the language of discrimination that goes with it, for their own constituencies: whites, males, and conservative Christians.

In his tribute to the "conservative" Martin Luther King, for example, Bennett dismissed the idea that racial bigotry is still an important factor in America and then said: "There are two bigotries remaining in American life. One is the bigotry against religious people. The second is the bigotry of some people in the North and Los Angeles and other places toward the South." (Bennett didn't mention bias against males, but on

---

* The *Journal* hasn't always been so approving of King's methods. In 1967, its editorialists said that "by preaching civil disobedience over the years, Dr. King may unwittingly have helped pave the road to violence."

another occasion he probably would have added that to the list.) These days, the right's rhetoric is full of talk about "anti-Christian discrimination," and even "persecution"—the title of a recent book by the conservative columnist David Limbaugh, who argues that secular humanists "are working to scrub away Christianity from the public square and to reduce religious liberty for Christians." In the course of things, that allows conservatives to arrogate Christianity—and religion itself—for the "R" column.

When conservatives make their case for liberals' "anti-Christianity" it isn't usually in terms of the issues that actually matter most to the religious right, like abortion, sodomy laws, or stem-cell research. Instead, they turn to symbolic issues and cast their arguments in terms of civil rights or freedom of expression. For example, conservatives haven't defended Bush's judicial appointments by arguing that the judges would oppose abortion rights or vote to overturn *Roe v. Wade*. Instead, they charge Democrats who oppose the nominations with religious discrimination. When Democrats criticized Bush's district court nominee Leon Holmes for earlier statements equating pro-choice groups with Nazis and saying that "a wife is to subordinate herself to her husband," conservatives charged them with "trying to establish a religious test for federal judges" and said that their tactics were "not only bigoted, but unconstitutional" by sending message that "Catholics need not apply." The Family Research Council has equated the Democrats' threat to filibuster ultra-conservative court nominees with segregationists' opposition to racial discrimination: "The filibuster was once used to protect racial bias and now it is being used against people of faith." And when Democratic senators at John Ashcroft's 2001 confirmation hearings to be attorney general asked him whether he would be able to uphold laws that conflicted with his religious beliefs on issues like abortion, Michael Ledeen wrote with a heave of ecumenical empathy that "John Ashcroft now knows what it feels like to be a Jew."

Conservatives use the same language of civil rights entitlement to challenge corporate efforts to achieve workplace diversity. Rather than attacking the companies' policies head-on, they focus on alleged violations of the civil rights of employees who oppose them. As evidence for the secularists' "crusade to wipe Christianity from the halls of private corporations," for example, David Limbaugh cites the firing of a Kodak employee who refused to apologize for sending an e-mail to more than one thousand other co-workers that described the company's policy opposing sexual orientation discrimination as "offensive and disgusting." The episode, Limbaugh said, showed that Kodak was intolerant of the employee's Christian beliefs and encroached on his right to religious freedom. It's hard to believe that even Limbaugh thinks that corporations have a constitutional obligation to allow an employee to use the company's e-mail system to circulate attacks on its policies, or for that matter any religious or political messages, particularly when they may create a hostile work environment for co-workers. But by casting the affair in terms of "freedom of religious expression," Limbaugh turns it into a civil rights issue designed to win the sympathy of the large majority of people who wouldn't see anything "anti-Christian" in the company's diversity policies themselves.

When it comes to finding trivial contexts for its claims of anti-Christian bias, the right could go no further than the annual "war on Christmas" pageant hyped by Fox's John Gibson and Bill O'Reilly, with daily reports of nativity scenes excluded from public settings, church floats banned from local Christmas parades, and the lyrics of Christmas carols secularized by schools. Some of these incidents were the work of local officials who were overzealous in banning religious expression from public settings. But many turned out to be urban legends, some of them as ludicrous on their face as supermarket tabloid accounts of alien abduction—tales of schools forbidding students from wearing red and green during the Christmas season or banning the Declaration of Independence because it mentions God.

The silliest—yet in its way the most effective—of these charges is that militant secularists have "intimidated" stores into abandoning "Merry Christmas" in favor of "Season's Greetings" or "Happy Holidays," which O'Reilly describes as "insulting to Christian America." That's an old charge: it recalls Henry Ford's attacks on the "International Jew conspiracy" that had secularized Christmas and Easter cards and the John Birch Society's 1959 warnings that Communists were scheming to "weaken the pillar of religion in our country is the drive to take Christ out of Christmas" and that the "Godless U.N." was trying to replace religious decorations in department stores with internationalist celebrations of universal brotherhood. But Ford and the Birchers were regarded as wingnuts and didn't have the unlimited access to TV and radio that lends O'Reilly and Gibson credibility.

On the face of things, the contention that radical secularists have a "secret plan" to eradicate Christianity so they can "pass secular progressive programs like legalization of narcotics, euthanasia, abortion at will, [and] gay marriage," as O'Reilly put it, seems on a par with the black-U.N.-helicopter fantasies of the fruitcake right. But taken with the rest of the right's campaign against "anti-Christian discrimination," it has managed to convince a lot of Americans that the Democrats are hostile to religion. An August 2005 survey by the Pew Research Center found that only 29 percent of voters regard the Democratic Party as "friendly to religion," down from 40 percent just a year earlier, and the decline among independent voters was even more dramatic, from 43 to 24 percent. In fact, not even a majority of Democrats see their party as religion-friendly anymore. That's a remarkable drop over a single year, and it testifies to the efficacy of the right's stepped-up attacks on "militant secularists" over issues like the Alabama Ten Commandments monument, gay marriage, Intelligent Design, and the "war on Christmas."

One sign of the effectiveness of the right's campaign against "liberal anti-Christian bias" is the mark it has left on the language itself, which has been reconfigured to suggest a nation polarized between "secularists" on one side and "Christians" or "people of faith" on the other. *Secularist* is beginning to rival *liberal* as an epithet—in media discussions of domestic politics, it's five times as common as it was a decade ago.* For many conservatives, the word doesn't simply suggest people who believe in keeping the religious and political spheres separate, but rather those who are actively hostile to religion, a semantic sleight of hand that

---

* When people are talking about the Middle East, of course, the secularists are generally the good guys.

allows the right to use *secularist* for everyone from the ACLU to totalitarian regimes: "In every secular progressive country, they've wiped out religion," O'Reilly says, "Joseph Stalin, Adolf Hitler, Mao Zedong, Fidel Castro, all of them." Often, the word is merely a synonym for "liberal atheists"—an official of Focus on the Family carves the nation into two camps: "secularists" and "praying America." In effect, *secularist* turns "liberal believers" into an oxymoron.

The redefinition of *secularist* has its complement in the way the right uses *Christian*. As Bruce Bawer notes in his 1998 book *Stealing Jesus*, "conservative Christians, unlike liberal Christians, tend to define the word *Christian* in such a way as to exclude others—including, in most cases, a large number of their fellow conservative Christians." The exclusionary use of *Christian* is ubiquitous nowadays: when you see a Web site for "Christian singles," you can assume it's aimed at Pentecostals, evangelicals, and Protestant charismatics, not at Catholics or mainstream Presbyterians or Methodists.

That usage may be troubling to a lot of Christians who don't share either the politics or theology of Pat Robertson and Jerry Falwell, but today the media, too, often implicitly endorse the narrower meaning of the word. This isn't simply a question of adopting terms like *Christian music*, *Christian radio*, and *Christian books*, which are standard industry shorthand for products aimed at the born-again market. The media also use *Christian* by itself in an exclusionary way—and what's more disconcerting still, they sometimes use *non-Christian* in a way that seems to excommunicate the majority of Americans who would describe themselves as Christians.

A recent *New York Times* story on file sharing in the gospel music market reported that "Christian teenagers are nearly as likely to download unauthorized files as their non-Christian peers," by which the writer meant merely teenagers of any faith who prefer Coldplay or Beyoncé to Amy Grant, and a *Denver Post* article about the publicity campaign for *Narnia* warned that "Heavy marketing to Christians could turn off non-Christians," a category that it later identifies as "mainstream audiences." And when the media talk about "the Christian right," they don't have in mind the devoutly Episcopalian stockbroker from

Greenwich, Connecticut, who supports repeal of the estate tax and free trade but isn't particularly upset by the idea of gay marriage.*

t hat ambiguity allows conservatives to use *Christian* with two meanings at once, letting the narrow sense of the word stand in for the broad one. When Rush Limbaugh says that "[t]he Democrats are more fearful of Christians than they are of Al Qaeda," he conveniently lets the troops of Falwell and Robertson represent American Christians in general. And there's the same implication when brother David subtitles his book *Persecution* with "How Liberals Are Waging War Against Christianity," or when the president of the American Decency Association lambastes companies like McDonald's and Burger King for sponsoring *Queer Eye for the Straight Guy* by asking, "Where's the resistance? Where is Christian America?"

There's a similar ambiguity in *people of faith*, which first became popular about twenty-five years ago as an ostensibly inclusive way of referring to believers of all creeds and religions, about a decade after "people of color" was revived as an inclusive term for nonwhites. The phrase was actually introduced out of a New-Agey aversion to identifying with organized religions, but it soon caught on among conservative Christians who saw the advantages of comparing themselves to other oppressed groups. And *of faith*, like *of color*, was soon spun off as a suffix, so that you see references to "journalists of faith," "physicians of faith," and "Texans of faith," usually with the implication that those people are conservative Christians. In fact, unlike *religious believers* or *churchgoers*, *people of faith* implies a particular political constituency in American life. "Americans of faith" turns up over sixty-two thousand hits on Google, while phrases like "Frenchmen of faith," "Englishmen of faith," and "Mexicans of faith" turn up none at all.

Like *Christian*, *people of faith* oscillates between broad and narrow meanings. George Bush is always careful to use it in an ostentatiously

* I first heard this usage of *Christian* about twenty years ago, when an evangelical friend told me he was going out to dinner with a group of French Christians. At the time I was puzzled by the phrase, which sounded to me like talking about "a group of white Norwegians."

inclusive way—he rarely mentions "people of faith" without adding "whether they have a cross or a Star of David or a crescent on the wall." But for others on the right, *people of faith* is just an ecumenical-sounding synonym for Christians with conservative social views. On the day after the 2004 election, Jerry Falwell boasted that "25 million people of faith" had turned out at the polls, "primarily evangelicals." And in an interview a few days after the election, Karl Rove made it clear that the administration actually understands the term as covering "evangelicals and fundamentalists and Charismatics and Pentecostals" as well as conservative Catholics—in effect defining *people of faith* as "churchgoers who vote for our side." When Bush urges Congress to pass his Faith-Based Initiative program "so people of faith can know that the law will never discriminate against them again," he knows that his religious base will hear the phrase as a covert reference to their own complaints about anti-Christian bias.

Nowadays, the right talks about faith itself as a uniquely conservative attribute, the same way it does about values. Martin Luther King was a conservative, explains the Heritage Foundation's Carolyn Garris, because he "required that his followers lead moral lives, and he emphasized the importance of faith in the face of adversity," adding that "[m]odern liberalism has rebuffed this teaching, dedicating great effort to silence religion and morality." Those may be calumnies against liberals, not to mention against tens of millions of moderate Christians and other Americans who belong to other religious traditions. But to a remarkable degree, conservatives have been successful in persuading people that whether or not God is on their side, they're on His.

The success of the right's attacks on "anti-Christian secularists" has left liberals and Democrats in the awkward position of having to demonstrate that they're not hostile to religion. A lot of people have urged Democrats to cease hiding their own religiosity under a bushel. Hillary Clinton has said that Democrats should use the Bible to advance their arguments about poverty the way Republicans did with gay marriage: "Jesus had a lot more to say about how we treat the poor than most of the issues that were talked about in this election." And James Carville and Paul Begala have reminded Democrats that in the current climate, "if people don't hear a candidate referring to her faith, they presume she has none." For the scripturally challenged, Carville and Begala offer three pages of Bible passages that can be used to support Democratic positions on issues from the environment ("Hurt not the earth, neither the sea, nor the trees") to the minimum wage ("I will be a swift witness against . . . those who oppress the wage earner in his wages").

Shortly after the 2004 election, the House minority leader Nancy Pelosi illustrated that approach when she said in an interview that "[v]alues are, of course, being persons of faith and family and love of country. They also are about ministering to the needs, as it says in the Gospel of Matthew, of the least of our brethren." Not surprisingly, the right was quick to attack such Bible-talk as opportunistic. On CNN's *Crossfire*, the conservative Tucker Carlson accused Pelosi of "all but speaking in tongues." Not that he doubted Pelosi's religious beliefs, he said, but "she's never talked this way before." And the conservative columnist Kathleen Parker compared the Democrats' professions of faith to the scene in *When Harry Met Sally* where Meg Ryan fakes an orgasm, and raised the specter of "aspiring Democratic presidential candidates showing up at Promise Keepers conventions, high-fiving for Jesus, and photo-oping with little Baptist blue-hairs on their way to Wednesday-night prayer meeting."

Listening to the indignant tone of those remarks, you might imagine that Democrats had been quoting Milton Friedman rather than Jesus. But religion is not a Republican franchise, and the two successful Democratic presidential candidates over the past thirty years have both been men who are comfortable using the language of faith. Democrats with strong religious convictions are right to emphasize that their political views are grounded in their religious principles, and to call the right to account for talking about Christianity as if it were a wholly-owned subsidiary of the Republican National Committee.

Paradoxically, one tack that can help the Democrats here is to be more aggressive in defending secular values—not in the name of secularism, a notion most Americans have little understanding of, but in the name of freedom of religion. Indeed, the very fact that social conservatives have couched their attacks on "anti-Christian" Democrats in the language of civil rights and freedom of expression is a sign of some of the weaknesses of their position. On the one hand, it concedes that the right's claim to speak for all "people of faith" has to be justified by appeals to symbolic issues like school prayer, public religious displays, and the "war on Christmas," rather than issues like abortion or stem-cell research, where the right's positions don't command the allegiance of the majority of religious Americans, much less of the country as a whole. And beyond that, it's a testament to the symbolic power of the language of freedom, rights, and justice that the right has appropriated from the civil rights movement.

If it comes down to a battle over who can better protect people's freedom, after all, Democrats can give as well as they get. Take the brouhaha that erupted in the House in 2005 over the numerous complaints—the majority from Protestants—that Air Force Academy cadets had been pressured to take part in evangelical Christian prayers. When House Democrats sponsored an amendment to the defense spending bill that would ban "coercive and abusive proselytizing" at the academy, the Indiana Republican John Hostettler described it as part of "the long war on Christianity" that was being waged by "the usual suspects, Democrats . . . Like a moth to a flame, Democrats can't help themselves when it comes to denigrating and demonizing Christians." But the amendment's sponsor, Wisconsin Democrat David Obey, pointed out that the amendment was an effort to defend the religious freedom of cadets: "We have an obligation to every single cadet at the Air Force Academy that they can practice their religion without fear."

Arguments like that one play a lot better than appeals to the separation of church and state or the establishment clause, abstract ideals that don't have much symbolic resonance for most Americans. They not only speak to Americans' concerns about religious freedom and put the Democrats on the path to reclaiming the language of "freedom" and "bias" that conservatives have appropriated. They also challenge the religious right's claim to represent Christianity as a whole.

Whatever doubts Americans may have about Democrats' friendliness to religion, they also have growing qualms about the power of the religious right. The 2005 Pew survey showed that half of Americans, and a majority of independents, think that religious conservatives have too much control over the Republican Party, and that half of mainline Catholics and Protestants think conservative Christians are going too far in trying to impose their views on the rest of the country. Up to now, it's true, moderate and liberal religious groups haven't been as well organized politically as conservative Christians are. But they deeply resent the hijacking of "Christianity" by conservatives and fundamentalists—as Jim Wallis puts it in *God's Politics,* "an enormous public misrepresentation of Christianity has taken place."

But even with the most assiduous scripture quoting and spirited defenses of religious freedom, Democrats will have a way to go before they can dispel the doubts that have been raised by the right's symbolic warfare or redress the semantic imbalance the right has created between "Christians" and "liberal secularists." What's striking about the perception of the Democrats as faith-unfriendly is that it has increased sharply in the absence of any notable charges of Democratic impiety or any national party support for gay marriage, nor does it correlate with any shift in Americans' views on abortion.

In part, the Democrats' religion problems have less to do with their failure to convey their religiosity than their failure to convey a broader concern about personal morality—to persuade voters that they understand social evils like crime, drugs, illegitimacy, and teen suicide as moral problems and not just policy issues. But to a large extent, Democrats are simply the victims of culture war stereotypes: when only 1-in-6 Americans sees Hollywood, the media, and university professors as being friendly to religion, Democrats are bound to catch some of the fallout, however personally religious they are. And those perceptions themselves testify to the right's success in wielding the charge of bias—another conservative adaptation from the symbolic language of civil rights—to discredit any groups and institutions that aren't actively sympathetic to conservative views.

The War on "Truth"

Ah, sir—a distinct universe walks about under your hat and
under mine—all things in nature are different to each—the
woman we look at has not the same features, the dish we eat
from has not the same taste to the one and the other.

William Makepeace Thackeray, The History of Pendennis

When people make a point of touting their credibility, it's a good
sign that their line of work is regarded with some suspicion. A
used-car dealer might bill himself as Honest Angus, but that maneuver
would be counterproductive for a CPA. So when the newly launched Fox
News Network adopted the slogan "Fair and Balanced" in 1996, everybody understood it as a pointed allusion to the charge that the mainstream media were less than evenhanded in their news coverage. It isn't
likely that Fox thought that anyone would take the slogan at face value,
but that didn't matter, so long as its viewers saw it as the sort of thing that
would drive liberals crazy.*

---

* That's probably why Fox News CEO Roger Ailes refuses to admit that Fox is conservative in its coverage. In a 2003 *New Yorker* profile by Ken Auletta, Ailes said that
"there hasn't even been a story where we've been accused of tipping some big story to the
right in seven years"—a claim so patently false that it could only have been made to in-
furiate the network's liberal critics (Ken Auletta, "How Roger Ailes and Fox News Are
Changing Cable News," *New Yorker*, May 26, 2003).

Like a lot of the right's rhetoric, complaints about the liberal bias of the media first became prominent in the Nixon era, when Spiro Agnew led the administration's campaign against the "small unelected elite" who were tilting the news in a liberal direction. In a speech in 1969 that became an instant sensation, Agnew charged that the networks were selective in their news coverage and invariably emphasized bad news over good and gave excessive attention to black extremists and anti-war demonstrators. And living in the "unrepresentative communities" of Washington, D.C., and New York, they were out of touch with the American people: "perhaps it is time that the networks were made more responsive to the views of the nation." Over the following years, the Nixon administration continued its campaign against the media; in 1972, Pat Buchanan, then a Nixon speechwriter, threatened that the administration would consider bringing anti-trust charges against the networks if they continued to "freeze out opposing points of view and opposing information."

The right's campaign against liberal media bias continued unabated for the next twenty years, but it wasn't until Bill Clinton's election in 1992 that it went into high gear, spearheaded by well-funded think tanks and policy groups like the American Enterprise Institute, the Media Research Center, and Accuracy in Media. By then, the media themselves were giving the charges wide coverage. Over the first four years of the Clinton presidency, major newspapers mentioned media bias four times as often as they had during the presidency of George H.W. Bush. Even more striking, 95 percent of those referred to liberal bias rather than conservative bias.

There's a paradox in those proportions. After all, it isn't as if people on the left haven't been complaining for a long time about what they see as a conservative bias in the media, without getting very much attention. Yet if the media really were as liberal as the right claims they are, why would they give so much more coverage to what was being said about them in *National Review* than in the *Nation*? Indeed, the more disproportionately the media talk about their own liberal bias, the less plausible it is that they could actually have one.

But for most people, the lopsided coverage given to the charges of liberal bias confirmed its existence—on that matter, at least, people are willing to take the "liberal media" at their word. As the media's reports of the conservative charges increased, so did the proportion of Americans who believed the media had a liberal bias—from 12 percent in 1988 to 43 percent in 1996. By 2003, a Pew survey showed more than one-half of Americans agreeing that the media have a liberal bias, against only one-fourth who saw a conservative bias. And research showed that those increases were direct responses to the increasing coverage of the topic of liberal media bias in the media. By now, people pronounce "liberal media bias" as if it were a single word.

The charges of liberal bias have been so widely and insistently repeated that conservatives have been able to allude to them as a truth that requires no defending. In 2002, a *Wall Street Journal* editorial described the media's liberal tilt as one of the "facts of life so long obvious they would seem to be beyond dispute." *National Review*'s Jonah Goldberg writes that "[e]verybody knows that the major news networks lean to the left. Everybody knows that mainstream journalists see conservatives as 'biased,' 'ideological,' or 'agenda-driven.'" And in his 2002 bestseller *Bias*, former CBS producer Bernard Goldberg said that "the old argument that the networks and other 'media elites' have a liberal bias is so blatantly true that it's hardly worth discussing anymore," though he nonetheless managed to soldier on about the subject for two hundred petulant pages.

According to Bernard Goldberg, the widespread belief that the media have a liberal bias is proof enough that the claim is true: "Let's suppose that I'm dead wrong in my book, that there is no liberal bias in the media," he said in a letter to the *New Republic*. "Then I can be easily dismissed. But what about the millions and millions of Americans—including many liberals—who think I'm right. Are they all stupid? Are they under some kind of mass hypnosis?" It's easy to write that off as a pure non sequitur—after all, there's no shortage of things that millions of Americans are convinced of that have no basis in fact, like Saddam Hussein's responsibility for 9/11 and the living Elvis. But that populist theme keeps cropping up in the right's campaign against the media. "There is a perception on the part of millions of Americans that the network news is liberal," Bill O'Reilly says, with the implication that to deny the point is to reveal yourself as an elitist who's out of touch with what ordinary people are thinking. And to prove the point, conservatives cite the drift away from network news—Fox CEO Roger Ailes, explaining the success of Fox News, says that "[t]he American people felt they weren't getting the whole story on some issues."

One immediate goal of the right's attacks on liberal bias is purely tactical. As Eric Alterman puts it in his book *What Liberal Media?* it's "a useful, but unsupportable, myth about the SCLM [so-called liberal media]," through which "the media . . . have been cowed by conservatives into repeating their nonsensical nostrums virtually nonstop." Rich Bond, the Republican National Committee chairman, admitted as much in an unguarded moment during the 1992 election: "If you watch any great coach, what they do is 'work the refs.' Maybe the ref will cut you a little slack on the next one."

There's no question the strategy has worked. Alterman, David Brock, Trudy Lieberman, and others have documented at length the way the media routinely pull their punches on or even spike stories that might be construed as supporting a liberal point of view on an issue, or make a point of balancing them with reports that suggest a more upbeat view of the administration. And as we saw, that intimidation is evident in the way the media pick up on conservative catchphrases, as they shift from "estate tax" to "death tax" and from "private accounts" to "personal accounts" to accommodate right-wing pressures.

You could see that timidity in the way American media talked about what took place at Abu Ghraib prison. When the early photos were released, the British press had no qualms about describing what had gone on as torture—not just the left-wing *Guardian* ("Torture at Abu Ghraib"), but the right-wing *Express* ("Outrage at U.S. Torture of Prisoners") and even Rupert Murdoch's *Times* ("Inside Baghdad's Torture Jail"). And whatever their politics, the French, German, and Italian press all spoke of torture from the outset.

But for several weeks, the American media stuck almost universally with vaguer terms such as "abuse" and "mistreatment," mindful of how Defense Secretary Donald Rumsfeld responded to a question about torture in the prison: "What has been charged so far is abuse, which is different from torture. I'm not going to address the 'torture' word." It wasn't until more details and photos came out that the newspapers began to use "the 'torture' word," which evoked predictable charges that they were equating Abu Ghraib with the brutalities of Saddam's regime. *National Review*'s John Derbyshire wrote that "the Abu Ghraib horseplay does not rise to the level of 'torture,' and the stupendous fuss raised by the media and congressional bedwetters is at least as big a scandal as the prisoner abuses themselves." It was left to Secretary of State Colin Powell to note that this was not a place for face-saving distinctions. "Torture is torture is torture," he said in an interview on *Fox News Sunday* shortly after the photos were released—a point that it took the American media quite a while to grasp.

It's true that few conservatives would complain if all the American media took on the ideological coloration of Fox News and the *Washington Times*.* But the right's attacks on "liberal bias" are something more than a cynical effort to influence media coverage, and they're not likely to abate, however much soul-searching mainstream journalists do. The goal here isn't to reform the mainstream media but to discredit them.

In fact, most of the critics of liberal media bias don't show much interest in any of the serious questions that have been raised about the contemporary media. They have nothing to say about the media's "showbizification," as Dan Rather called it, or the increasingly superficial coverage that television news gives to important stories. They seem unconcerned about the emphasis on crime, scandal, celebrities, and personal health at the expense of hard news. They don't worry about the tendency to cover stories about issues like taxes or Social Security as political chess games rather than analyzing their substantive implications, or to reduce every political story to he-said-she-said "balance" without

* I say "few" because there are some right-wing media critics who have doubts about Fox's orthodoxy, as well. The conservative watchdog site Accuracy in Media, for example, has complained that the network has been "drifting to the left," citing appearances by Robert Kennedy Jr. and Bernie Sanders (see, e.g., Cliff Kincaid, "Fox News and Conservatives," *Accuracy in Media*, January 25, 2006, http://www.aim.org/media_monitor/4292_0_2_0_C/).

evaluating the rival claims. For that matter, they don't seem very much concerned about the scant coverage that the media give to subjects like religion, which could genuinely be said to reflect the parochialism of many journalists.

Nor are the critics very discriminating when it comes to clarifying the notion of bias itself. They discern bias whenever the media report anything that might cast Republicans or conservatives in a less-than-ideal light, or when they think the media fail to give conservative-friendly news sufficient prominence. And they make no distinction among news reports and opinion columns, or among the things said by reporters and columnists, anchors and interviewees, or journalists and late-night comedians. It's proof of bias when the *Washington Post's* fashion writer Robin Givhan makes fun of the haircut of John Bolton, Bush's nominee to be U.N. ambassador; when Peter Jennings reports that President Bush did not say the word "Iraq" in his inaugural address; or when Reuters leads a January 2006 report on housing prices by reporting that sales declined in the previous month, but waits for the second paragraph to report that sales in 2005 had set a record. It's proof of bias when *NBC News* leads its evening report with a story that Dick Cheney consumed a beer before the accidental shooting of a hunting partner, and when the *New York Times* "buries" on page eighteen its story on the arraignment of an Islamic student at the University of North Carolina who ran his truck into a crowd. And it's proof of bias when David Letterman does a bit on "Top Ten Surprises in the Dick Cheney Interview" ("Number 1: "Stunning admission: 'The gun was loaded and so was I'").

The indiscriminate breadth of those charges brings to mind Richard Hofstadter's famous 1964 article on the persistence of the "paranoid style" in American politics—"the sense of heated exaggeration, suspiciousness, and conspiratorial fantasy" that has marked political movements since the eighteenth-century panic over the influence of the Masons. By "paranoid style," Hofstadter made it clear, he wasn't speaking of a pathology that applied only to "men with profoundly disturbed minds," but rather to "the use of paranoid modes of expression by more or less normal people." Indeed, that frame of mind is perfectly acceptable in certain situations, like when we go to a baseball game ready to blame the umpire for any call that goes against our side. If team loyalty doesn't trump fair-mindedness, you're not a true fan.

But in the right's complaints about media bias, the style is in dead earnest. There's the deafness to humor, satire, and metaphor that puts a Letterman gag on the same level as a *New York Times* report.* There's the way the way the right talks about "the media" as a monolithic entity, an undifferentiated "they," effacing the differences between sources and formats. And there's the classic paranoid tendency to read an ominous pattern into ordinary and unexceptional facts: true, CBS showed footage of Jesse Jackson arriving in Florida to argue for reinserting Terri Schiavo's feeding tube, but did you notice how they didn't actually air a quote from him?

This is not a game the mainstream media can win. Those aren't charges that you would offer if you were trying to make a serious case for bias to a neutral observer—in fact, they're not really charges that you can have a conversation about at all. They're aimed at providing the converted with a way of reading the media where even the most innocuous acts turn out to reveal a bias that you already know exists. Once you understand that the media are biased, you see evidence of it everywhere.

People have been talking about media bias since journalists first began to take "objectivity" seriously in the nineteenth century. Back in 1894, the newly formed United Press boasted that it provided news that was accurate and "absolutely without bias or coloring"—a popular phrase of the era, and a useful selling point for news agencies that were offering their services to an editorially diverse clientele. But until the 1960s, people generally talked about press bias as a deliberate partiality, usually motivated by personal interest. Back in the 1940s, Harold Ickes, FDR's disputatious secretary of the interior, spearheaded a campaign against what he saw as conservative bias in the press, which he blamed on publishers' dependence on advertisers and their ties to other commercial

* You could argue, of course, that conservatives are right to spread their net so widely, given that increasing numbers of people get their news from *The Daily Show*. On the other hand, it's not clear how you would define the "mainstream media" to include Comedy Central but not Fox News.

interests. Despite an absence of government regulation, he said, the American press was not free: "It is not—because of its own financial and economic tie-ups—what it should be, a free servant of a free democracy." Ickes cited the persistent opposition to government ownership of public utilities by the Gannett newspapers, which were partly owned by the power companies, and the press's disinclination to report elevator accidents in department stores, since retailers were major advertisers.

That's still the theme you hear in the left's critiques of media bias, which tend to focus on the patterns of media ownership and the way they influence journalists' decisions about which stories to cover and how. From that point of view, it's absurd on the face of things to imagine that the corporations that own the mainstream media would permit their news outlets to be dominated by a subversive or anticorporate point of view. Harold Ickes would have been mystified by the Media Research Center's charge that NBC's Tom Brokaw let his (liberal) "personal views become the agenda of his newscast," for example. After all, NBC's parent company is General Electric, which has extensive interests in nuclear power, financial services, and defense, and which has been a major contributor to Republican campaigns.

Conservatives sometimes try to explain that discrepancy by saying that the media owners are simply too busy to monitor the day-to-day operations of their properties—what you could think of as the Enron defense. That's pretty obviously a stretch, though, particularly when you're talking about well-run companies like GE and Viacom ("Shocked, shocked, to find that there's bias going on!"). And anyway, conservatives have another, more versatile tale to tell about the way bias works, where it's beyond the power of management to do anything about it.

The new picture of bias had its roots in the psychological theories of "group perception" and "groupthink." In a famous 1954 experiment, the psychologists Albert Hastorf and Hadley Cantril found that Dartmouth and Princeton fans had different perceptions about who had initiated the rough play at a controversial 1951 football game between the schools, even after they were shown films of the game.

In the 1960s, that understanding of bias had begun to work its way into the popular consciousness, largely through the civil rights movement. In the 1950s, people had been concerned about "prejudice," a more-or-less superficial mental trait that could be alleviated by scrupulous mental housecleaning. Now they were more likely to use words like "racism," which suggested a much deeper predisposition that one could acknowledge but never completely purge. Announcing "I'm not a racist" or "I'm not biased" came to sound suspect, something like "I don't have any homosexual anxiety"—how could you be sure?

By the Nixon era, press critics were adopting that sense of *bias* to explain the alleged leftward tilt of the media. A 1969 editorial in the *Wall Street Journal* discounted Vice President Spiro Agnew's charges that a clique of newspaper owners and broadcasters was out to discredit the administration. The real problem, the *Journal* said, was the "unconscious slant" introduced by the "prevailing liberal tendencies of the national media."

For the right, that account of bias neatly explains the disparities between the political views of the media's owners and the left-wing bias of their journalists. If bias is an "unconscious slant," there's nothing that GE could do to keep Brokaw's views from influencing his coverage, and more important, nothing that Brokaw could do, either. As Brent Bozell of the Media Research Center argues, "Liberal bias in the news media is . . . not the result of a vast left-wing conspiracy; journalists do not meet secretly to plot how to slant their news reports." Rather, biased reporting simply follows from the fact that journalists tend to have a liberal point of view that inevitably works its way into their coverage, however they may try to be objective. As Bozell puts it:

[M]embers of the media argued that while personally liberal, they are professionally neutral. They argued their opinions do not matter because as professional journalists, they report what they observe without letting their opinions affect their judgment. But being a journalist is not like being a surveillance camera at an ATM, faithfully recording every scene for future playback. Journalists make subjective decisions every minute of their professional lives. They choose what to cover and what not to cover, which sources are credible and which are not, which quotes to use in a story and which to toss out.

Or as the journalist Michael Kelley put the point, journalists cannot hope to achieve "the godlike ability to perceive and present the 'objective' truth on all matters that come before us. Because we are, in fact, not unique among humans." Hence the liberal bias of the media, Kelley said, is simply "a matter of logic."

True, that readiness to toss the idea of journalistic objectivity over the side creates some philosophical awkwardness for conservatives, who in other contexts are always ridiculing postmodernists and left-wing academics for their rejections of objectivity and absolute truth. ("The idea that 'there is no such thing as objectivity or disinterestedness' is rubbish, of course," the conservative cultural critic Roger Kimball writes.)* But conservatives square that circle by falling back on what you could think of as situational absolutism—upholding objective truth as a standard for academic journals while dismissing it as an impossible ideal for anything that appears on a newsstand.

The picture of bias as ubiquitous and inescapable is crucial to the conservative media critics' larger goals. For one thing, it makes the case for liberal media bias very easy to demonstrate. If journalists' personal views inevitably color the way they cover the news, then the mere fact that a majority of journalists are Democrats or liberals is statistically conclusive; you can prove the existence of liberal media bias without actually having to open a newspaper or turn on your TV. And while many of the surveys that conservatives cite exaggerate the disproportions between liberals and conservatives, there's no question that journalists for the major national media tend to have more-or-less liberal views on social issues, like other college-educated urban professionals. From that it follows that the only way to counter liberal bias is to hire other journalists from conservative ranks who will present the news from their own point of view. Not that that would eliminate bias—a hopeless task, as the right understands the

* One thing that the self-styled postmodernists and their conservative critics have in common is a tendency to end their sentences about the existence or nonexistence of objectivity with "of course," as if objectivity were as clear and commonsensical a notion as "slop bucket" ("The Death of Objectivity," *National Review Online,* May 14, 2002, http://www.nationalreview.com/comment/comment-kimball051402.asp).

notion—but at least then the news would be slanted in both directions in perfectly equal proportions.

If all reporting is biased, moreover, the only difference between openly partisan commentary and ostensibly objective reporting is that the former is up front about its point of view, while the latter conceals its slant behind a facade of "objectivity." That's what allows conservatives to claim that the right-wing domination of AM talk radio is merely a way of "balancing" the liberal domination of network news, for example. As the conservative writer Thomas Sowell puts it: "Anyone listening to Rush Limbaugh knows that what he is saying is his own opinion. But people who listen to the news on ABC, CBS, or NBC may imagine that they are getting the facts, not just those facts which fit the ideology of the media, with the media's spin." And the *Wall Street Journal*'s Robert Bartley made the same point when he said, "I think we're coming to the end of the era of 'objectivity' that has dominated journalism over this time. We need to define a new ethic that lends legitimacy to opinion, honestly disclosed and disciplined by some sense of propriety."

As that makes clear, the right's attacks on media bias aren't simply a criticism of the way the mainstream media cover political stories: they're also aimed at undercutting the difference between reporting and commentary, and with it the notions of trust, neutrality, and even truth that have stood as the ideals of responsible journalism over the past century. The fact is, the right's disquisitions on the impossibility of true objectivity are a pure distraction here. It may or may not be possible to arrive at "objectivity" in the austere philosophical sense of the term—"the view from nowhere in particular," as the philosopher Thomas Nagel describes it. But that concept is only incidentally related to what "objectivity" means in journalism, where it stands in for a collection of attitudes, ethical principles, stylistic guidelines, and professional practices that are always bumping awkwardly into one another as the canons of the profession evolve. In his history of the development of the concept of journalistic objectivity, David Mindich identifies its components as "detachment," "nonpartisanship," "balance," attention to facts, and the inverted pyramid form of writing, though no doubt others would carve it up differently. That assortment is varied enough to make it clear that "journalistic objectivity" doesn't really say a lot more than "good journalism" does. It certainly doesn't imply the absence of perspective or what used to be called "coloring." But it does imply a commitment to getting at the truth of the matter—and to there being a truth of the matter to get at. And when journalists come up short, there are standards you can hold them to.

Those assumptions are the real target of conservatives' attacks on liberal media bias, and one way they get there is by subtly altering the meaning of *bias* itself. Nowadays, *bias* really means "hidden bias"—you're only biased if you won't own up to having an ax to grind. That's why CBS or the *New York Times* is far more likely to be described as biased than Rush Limbaugh or Bill O'Reilly—or for that matter, than Al Franken or Michael Moore. That would have puzzled Harold Ickes, who reserved his most caustic attacks on press bias for partisan columnists like Westbrook Pegler. But these days, "bias" is a failing that only the mainstream media could logically be susceptible to—there isn't any bias if there's no effort to be objective in the first place. The implication is that the "problem" of bias would disappear if everyone announced his or her point of view at the outset and let readers or viewers come to their own conclusions.

That's deeply disingenuous. A media universe that consisted of nothing but openly partisan broadcasts, columns, and blogs would be one in which everyone had license to report selectively, without feeling bound by the tiresome rules of sourcing, balance, and checking that mainstream journalists try to conform to. The real object of the attacks on "bias" is to give people permission to follow only the sources that agree with their own point of view and discount anything else on the grounds that it's colored by a "hidden agenda" (as it happens, an expression that entered the language around the same time the attacks on "media bias" began their recent tear).

In all the recent talk about bias—and this is true of both sides—people tend to focus only on the way journalists slant their stories, not on the way readers interpret them. But audiences aren't simply collections of passive souls. Bias is a way of reading, as well, a habit of refusing to accept inconvenient facts. Like a lot of San Franciscans, for example, I consider it my duty as a Giants fan to be in denial about the allegations that Barry Bonds may have—I say *may have*—used steroids. I usually skip the articles about those charges when they run in the *San Francisco Chronicle* and I'm not about to read the new book about his steroid use. I'd no doubt do that even if I didn't have a sense that the sportswriters have it in for Barry, but that suspicion makes it even easier to ignore the whole business.

That's the same habit of mind that the right is encouraging in its attacks on the mainstream media. If you open the *New York Times* or turn on CNN already certain that they have a liberal bias, you're free to discount anything you read or see about the deficit or sectarian violence in Iraq, the same way I feel free to discount what I see in the *San Francisco Chronicle* about Barry Bonds's steroid use. In both cases, in fact, discounting what those sources report counts as a badge of team spirit.

For example, a 2003 study by the University of Maryland's Program on International Policy Attitudes found that viewers of Fox News were three times as likely as people who rely on CBS for their news to hold a false belief about the war in Iraq—that Saddam Hussein was linked to the September 11 attacks or that weapons of mass destruction had been located in Iraq, for example—and ten times as likely as NPR listeners. Those misperceptions had something to do with the way Fox covered the story, but they also testified to its viewers' eagerness to accept the versions of events that make their side look good. And as people tend increasingly to choose news sources that accord with their own points of view, whether on cable news or in the blogosphere, they come more and more to inhabit parallel universes, each with its distinct bookmarks and channel presets.

The most striking example of that tendency is the way the right has politicized the kind of scientific findings that used to be outside the pale of partisan controversy. Writers like Chris Mooney, John Judis, and Michael Specter have amply documented what Mooney calls "the Republican war on science," as the administration systematically ignores, suppresses, or distorts scientific findings that it finds inconvenient and stacks its scientific agencies and advisory committees with appointees who are willing to toe the Republican line on everything from the effects of excessive sugar intake to the causes of global warming. What's striking is that a lot of conservatives consider themselves bound by principle to accept the administration's views on those questions even when they run counter to the overwhelming scientific consensus. It's one thing to reject the scientific evidence for evolution out of a personal faith in biblical inerrancy. It's another to deny the existence of global warning simply because you're a loyal conservative, or to see bias when the press fails to "balance" its reporting on the issue. Thirty-five years ago, not even Spiro Agnew would have thought to look for evidence of liberal bias on the *New York Times*'s science pages.

It's a natural tendency to believe things that accord with our sympathies—"confirmation bias," psychologists call it. And certainly people on the left are capable of selective listening, and not just when it comes to politics. Chris Mooney points out, for example, that "many who preach the human 'dangers' of genetically modified foods have clothed their moral or policy objections in scientific attire." But unlike the conservatives who deny global warning, people don't come to those views on genetic modification out of partisan loyalty—it's just pure environmentalist zeal. Whereas if the Republicans and their industry friends hadn't made an issue of global warming, most conservatives wouldn't care about it one way or the other.

That's the irony of the right's attacks on "bias"—not just in the media, but in universities and other institutions that stand for impartial inquiry. These attacks aren't aimed at eliminating or correcting bias but at making it respectable in the name of "honest opinion." That's implicit in the double meaning of Fox News's other slogan, "We Report, You Decide." In another age, that might have been a pledge to limit themselves to presenting the bare facts "without bias or color," as journalists used to say. But anyone who watches the network understands it differently: "We tell you stories, you believe the ones you want to."

In making their case for unconscious liberal bias, conservatives inevitably turn to the way the media use language—not just in choosing loaded words to describe news events, but in tending to use words that disparage or marginalize the right. The quintessential example of that claim was Bernard Goldberg's charge that during his days as a producer at CBS, broadcasters "pointedly identified conservative politicians as conservatives" but "didn't bother to identify liberals as liberals." The implication, he said, is that "conservatives are out of the mainstream and have to be identified. Liberals, on the other hand, are the mainstream and don't have to be identified."

The story is nicely crafted to illustrate the right's picture of the way journalists' political orientations color their coverage, whatever efforts they make to suppress them. If bias is evident in such an ordinary and pervasive practice as partisan labeling, it must be endemic and unavoidable. But Goldberg didn't actually bother to document his claims, short of recounting an anecdote about the way Peter Jennings identified senators entering the Clinton impeachment hearings.

The claim isn't that implausible on the face of things—not because of the media's liberal bias, but because the word *liberal* itself has become an embarrassment to so many people that it wouldn't be surprising if journalists were diffident about labeling people with it, particularly if they were reluctant to use it of themselves. But when I actually did the counts, looking at stories in major newspapers in 2002, it turned out Goldberg was dead wrong. The average liberal is more than 30 percent *more* likely to be labeled in the press than the average conservative is, even in papers like the *New York Times* and the *Washington Post*. And the same generalization holds for Supreme Court justices and other well-known figures. Contrary to what Goldberg claimed, for example, Barbra Streisand and Rob Reiner are four times more likely to be described as liberals than Tom Selleck or Bruce Willis as conservatives—this even when you screen out references to Reiner's portrayal of "Archie Bunker's liberal son-in-law."

But does that demonstrate that the media really have a conservative bias? Actually, no. When you unpack the numbers, it's apparent that journalists don't use partisan labels to inform their audiences about the ideological leanings of politicians. If that were the case, you'd expect labels to show up most often with figures who are less well known to the public. But the opposite turns out to be true: labels are much *more* likely to be attached to politicians whose views are widely known to the public.

In the counts I did in 2002, for example, Jesse Helms was labeled a conservative ten times as often as Senator Tim Hutchinson, and Ted Kennedy was labeled a liberal three times as often as Paul Sarbanes—differences that reflect the conspicuousness of those senators' national profiles, not their voting records. In other words, the media used partisan labels most often when they were least necessary—how many readers needed to be told that Ted Kennedy was a liberal or that Jesse Helms was a conservative? But if your object is to reassure the public that you share the received perspective of the political landscape, it makes more sense to label Helms and Kennedy than Hutchison and Sarbanes. You want to signal your own middle-of-the-road evenhandedness in terms of points of reference that everyone will recognize.

This example makes an important point about the way the media actually use political language. It goes without saying that the choice of language often implies a point of view, not just with politically charged catchwords, but in the incidental way we describe particular events—calling an new abortion law "harsh" obviously has different implications from calling it "strong." And it's natural that those are the usages that people notice when they're looking for signs of the way particular media slant their stories to the left or right. But the media's real slant is toward safety and conformity. That conventionalism is naturally reflected in the language they use, whether it's a question of partisan labels or any term that implies a political point of view. If we're justified in talking about "the media" as a homogeneous group, it's only with regard to the presuppositions that journalists share with everybody else.

For example, the media tend to use *regime* much more often when they're talking about governments that are unfriendly to the United States than when they're talking about U.S. allies, independent of how unstable or undemocratic the governments are. The word is far more likely to be applied to Syria, Iran, or Cuba than to Pakistan, Jordan, or Saudi Arabia, and references to the Libyan regime dropped sharply in 2003 after Libya renounced weapons of mass destruction and normalized its relations with the West. That isn't a question of official editorial policy—*regime* isn't a word that journalists give much thought to. Nor does the pattern vary much depending on whether you're looking at liberal or conservative sources—the *Washington Post* and the *Washington Times* describe Syria's government as a regime with exactly the same frequency.

That's how things work with most of the words and usages I've been talking about in this book. The fact that Americans tend to talk about the media elite more often than about the business elite reflects a picture of the organization of power and influence in America that the right has gone to great lengths to disseminate, in the same way that the media's avoidance of phrases like "working-class liberals" seems to confirm the right's picture of liberalism as a middle-class lifestyle choice. But that doesn't mean that the people who use words like that actually agree with all of those assumptions (or that they would if they stopped to think about them). They're simply using language the same way everybody else does. We're obliged to use language *as if* the world were a certain way, whatever private reservations we have. And that's nowhere so true as with the symbol-words of American political discourse, like *elite, freedom, values,* and *terrorism,* whose explicit content is suppressed in favor of purely emotional resonances. Using those words is like whistling a tune from an opera; they can't help but evoke their narrative settings.

As I've been arguing here, the real sign of the right's co-option of American political culture has been its ability to dominate that core vocabulary and make it the norm not just among its own circles, but in the larger American conversation about politics. When it comes to talking about the basic categories of American political life, the *New York Times* and CNN use pretty much the same language that Fox News and the *Washington Times* use. And for all the scorn that conservatives heap on the mainstream media for their "liberal bias," the right also counts on them to make its language sound ordinary and unexceptionable. If you encountered the phrase "unapologetic liberal" only on Fox News, you wouldn't conclude that it reflected an attitude about liberalism that everyone shares. In that sense, the mainstream media have been the right's most powerful ally in establishing its control of political language—not that they get any gratitude.

Is This a Great Country, or What?

It is impossible to conceive a more troublesome
or more garrulous patriotism; it wearies even those
who are disposed to respect it.

—*Alexis de Tocqueville,* **Democracy in America**

I t seems like a long time ago, but for a brief moment in 2001, patriotism seemed to unite America. For a few weeks or months, everybody's eyes were riveted to the same page, as Americans were drawn together in a common sense of sorrow, common rage, and fellow feeling. For that moment, at least, partisan divisions seemed small and divisive, and patriotic truisms became truths. "Right now," said the *St. Louis Post-Dispatch*, "none of us should be Democrats or Republicans, liberals or conservatives. We should be Americans," a sentiment that was repeated in more or less the same words on editorial pages across the country.

Even many of the most politically engaged realized it wasn't a moment to score partisan points. Conservatives denounced Jerry Falwell and Pat Robertson when Falwell said that the attacks were God's punishment on "the pagans, and the abortionists, and the feminists, and the gays and lesbians who are actively trying to make that an alternative lifestyle, the ACLU, People for the American Way," and Robertson said he agreed. In

National Review, Ramesh Ponnuru said that "civilized people should not let [Falwell and Robertson] into their houses," and in a moving piece called simply "Citizens," in which he described attending a vigil with his liberal Brooklyn neighbors, Rod Dreher called the two "heartless bastards."

The left also renounced its extremists. In *Mother Jones*, Todd Gitlin excoriated the reflexive "smugness, acrimony, even schadenfreude," of the "left-wing fundamentalists" who described the attacks as payback for America's crimes. And a few months later in *Dissent*, Michael Walzer rebuked leftists who greeted the attacks with "the barely concealed glee that the imperial state had finally gotten what it deserved."

Writing in the *New York Times Sunday Magazine* a few weeks after the attacks, George Packer said that "Sept. 11 made it safe for liberals to be patriots":

> Among the things destroyed with the twin towers was the notion, held by certain Americans ever since Vietnam, that to be stirred by national identity, carry a flag and feel grateful toward someone in uniform ought to be a source of embarrassment.

True, even many liberals who felt genuinely stirred by their national identity still weren't entirely comfortable displaying its symbols, but some found themselves making unfamiliar gestures. Todd Gitlin explained that he had hung a flag from the balcony of his apartment a mile from Ground Zero as "an affirmation of solidarity. It's not an affirmation that America deserves to rule the world, just that America is a community entitled to public affection." And many liberals hoped that a new, more inclusive sense of patriotism would emerge from the attacks, one that they, too, could wholeheartedly endorse. What was needed, Alan Wolfe said, was not the "love it or leave it" patriotism of the Vietnam era, but one that said, "America, stay and exemplify it."

In any event, though, September 11 didn't make patriotism "safe for liberals"; it confirmed it as the property of the right. Well before the dust had cleared, it was evident that conservatives were not going to let patriotism get away from them. In one way or another, they took the upsurge of patriotic feeling as a confirmation of liberal failures. Liberal responses to the attacks, *National Review*'s John O'Sullivan wrote in early October, revealed an "inverted jingoism"—an instinctive preference for other nations and a marked prejudice that in any conflict the enemy of America is in the right. In the *Boston Herald*, before the casualty figures were even known, the columnist Don Feder castigated liberals for failing to fly the flag with sufficient enthusiasm: "Even after an unprovoked attack on their homeland, by creatures so evil that hell would spurn them, and 5,500 of their fellow Americans dead, public-broadcast donors just can't get over their red, white and blue aversion."

Other conservatives greeted the resurgence of liberal patriotism in a spirit of "welcome aboard," as if it were a sign that liberals had finally seen the error of their ways. For David Brooks, the ubiquity of American flags was an indication that "the most reactionary liberals amongst us are capable of change." A contributor to the *Washington Times*'s Insight on the News said that "[a]s of late October, there are no liberals in America. Only conservatives and fools." In the *Weekly Standard*, Noemie Emery suggested that "[t]entatively, slowly, some [liberals] are allowing themselves now to feel warm toward their country, embarrassed though they may be by these primordial feelings."

Laced through all those remarks was the unchallenged presumption that liberals' diffidence about patriotic displays betrayed a genuine absence of patriotism. For a lot of people, "patriotic liberal" seems to be, if not exactly an oxymoron, at least a rare collocation, like "dour Italian." (On the Web, it's outnumbered by "patriotic conservative" by 40-to-1.) True, there have always been some on the left who find the very idea of patriotism uncongenial. A few cosmopolitans reject it on philosophical grounds, arguing that one's primary allegiance should be not to one's own nation but to "the worldwide community of human beings," as the philosopher Martha Nussbaum has put it—an intellectually coherent position, but one that runs counter to most people's instinctive sympathies. (It's a fine thing to feel like a citizen of the world, but most of us don't have the languages or the frequent-flyer miles to bring it off.) And another group, a little larger and noisier, make up what Gitlin has called the "one-eyed left," who reject American patriotism in particular, on the grounds that it has been a screen for colonialism, racism, and oppression. Those are the people the right describes as the "blame America first crowd," and most of them owe what prominence they have outside of radical circles almost entirely to the tireless efforts of the right to make them the poster children for the liberal worldview.*

But by any reasonable criteria for measuring patriotism—a love of one's country, a belief in its special virtues, a willingness to make sacrifices on its behalf—there is no question that the vast majority of American liberals are patriotic. If they have reservations about past and present policies, it's most often because they believe those policies fail to live up to the best American ideals, usually a sign of patriotism and optimism in itself. Unpatriotic people don't start sentences with "America of all countries . . . ."

In fact, it's odd that patriotism should ever have become an issue in America. In their survey of the American conservative movement *The Right Nation*, the British journalists John Micklethwait and Adrian Wooldridge remark that "American patriotism runs deep. No other developed country displays its flag more obsessively or sings its national anthem more frequently." It's an observation that Europeans often make—sometimes approvingly, sometimes disapprovingly, but always a bit bemusedly. (A writer in the French *Le Figaro* observes that "everyone remembers Peter Fonda in *Easy Rider* with his leather jacket with an American flag, but seeing a jacket with a flag from a European country would make you laugh.") In polls both before and after 9/11, between 83 and 90 percent of Americans described themselves as "very proud" or "extremely proud" to be an American, much higher than the figures for most other nations. And while Republicans are somewhat more likely to describe themselves as "extremely proud," a majority of Democrats describe themselves that way as well. As wedge issues go, patriotism would seem to be a nonstarter.

---

*Sometimes the connection requires only a deft segue. On the Fox News Special Report on September 24, 2001, Brit Hume announced that ABC had barred its broadcasters from wearing American-flag lapel pins, a ban which "would no doubt meet with the approval" of a University of Texas journalism professor who had compared the September 11 attacks to civilian deaths caused by U.S. policies over the years.

But since the Vietnam era, patriotism has been associated with the right, as surely—and as speciously—as "values" has. And over the years following 9/11, the right has used the word in a ruthless and divisive way. The strategy was announced with the introduction of the USA PA-TRIOT Act—a name whose unsubtlety demonstrated just how confident the Republicans felt about their ability to play the patriotism card. It came up again when Republicans pushed for establishing the Department of Homeland Security in 2002. When Democrats objected to provisions that would weaken union protections for employees, Bush charged that they were "not interested in the security of the American people," and critics charged that they were "putting politics before patriotism" and choosing to "disdain the patriotic tide sweeping the nation." And it reached an intense pitch in the buildup to the Iraq War, culminating with Bush's appearance in full flight regalia before the "Mission Accomplished" banner aboard the USS *Lincoln* in May 2003. (With the wisdom of hindsight, the organizers of that event should probably have gone with something more noncommittal, like "Way to Go.")

John Kerry's convention acceptance speech illustrated all the strategies the Democrats have tried in their efforts to neutralize the "patriotism" issue. He emphasized his own credentials as a war hero ("I'm John Kerry and I'm reporting for duty") and delivered an effusive panegyric to the American flag that had been taken from the turret of his gunship in Vietnam:

> You see that flag up there? We call her "Old Glory"—"The Stars and Stripes Forever." . . . That flag flew from the gun turret behind my head, and it was shot through and through and tattered, but it never ceased to wave in the wind . . . .

Kerry reminded the delegates that saying that "America can do better" is not a challenge to patriotism; it is the heart and soul of patriotism." And he charged the Republicans with "wrapping themselves in the flag" and "question[ing] the patriotism of Americans who offer a better direction for our country." That charge was repeated by other speakers: Wesley Clark told the delegates, "This flag is ours and nobody will take it away from us," and Howard Dean said, "We're not going to let those who disagree with us shout us down under a banner of false patriotism."

The Republicans' response to that was roughly, "My, aren't we sensitive!" According to the *Wall Street Journal's* James Taranto, "The Democratic Party has a problem with patriotism. To say that the Democrats have a problem with patriotism is not to say that they are unpatriotic. But they are awfully defensive about their patriotism." In fact, he said, the Republicans hadn't impugned the Democrats' patriotism—it was the Democrats themselves who had raised the issue of patriotism "by defensively denying that they lacked it." And *National Review's* Jonah Goldberg wrote that "liberal defensiveness sometimes undermines their case. After all, if I angrily asked, 'Are you saying I'm gay?' as often as liberals say, 'Are you questioning my patriotism?' a lot of people would think I'm hiding something."

Of course, Republicans had indeed been questioning the Democrats' patriotism all along. True, both Bush and Cheney were careful not to raise the charge in so many words. Over the course of the campaign, Cheney volunteered on at least thirty occasions that he was not challenging Kerry's patriotism, often repeating it so the point wouldn't be lost on anybody.* But the message was clear when Bush said Kerry's criticisms were "undermining troops on the ground" and when a White House spokesman said that Kerry's "second-guessing of commanders on the ground . . . sends the wrong message to our troops, our allies, and our enemies." And others were even less circumspect, and not just the Swift Boat Veterans who questioned Kerry's war record and accused him of having given "aid and comfort to the enemy" when he returned from Vietnam. After Kerry quipped during the primary season that America needed a "regime change" of its own, Mark Racicot, the chairman of the

---

* In a speech in Johnstown, Pennsylvania, October 18, 2004, Cheney said, "But the concern I have is, when I look at Senator Kerry—and I am not challenging his patriotism, I don't question his patriotism for a minute—I do challenge his judgment." He made more or less the same remark in speeches at Duluth, Minnesota; Carroll, Ohio; Cedar Rapids, Iowa; Wilmington, Ohio; Manchester, New Hampshire; Milwaukee, Wisconsin; Lake Elmo, Minnesota; Davenport, Iowa; Cincinnati, Ohio; Cleveland, Ohio; Lansing, Michigan; and Meadville, Pennsylvania, among other locations, as well as in interviews on Fox News and during the vice presidential debate with John Edwards.

Republican National Committee, said that "Senator Kerry crossed a grave line when he dared to suggest the replacement of America's commander in chief at a time when America is at war." (As Paul Krugman observed in response, "[N]ever in our nation's history has it been considered unpatriotic to oppose an incumbent's re-election.")

So long as they avoid saying the word itself, Republicans have found they can freely question the p——ism of anyone who criticizes their policies in the war on terror without any serious backlash. In November 2005, the current Republican National Committee chairman, Ken Mehlman, said that "to make politics your bottom line in this critical war on terror, in the central front in the war on terror, sends the wrong message to our troops, to the Iraqi people and to the terrorists." At around the same time, Texas senator John Cornyn charged that the Democrats' criticisms of the war are "risking undermining the public resolve, supporting our men and women who are in the battlefield as I speak, and to me that's not responsible. I think people need to be very careful about what they say and the impact it has on encouraging our enemies."

Conservative talk-show hosts and commentators have been even less restrained. "John Kerry knows he gives aid and comfort to the enemy," says Michael Reagan, and Rush Limbaugh says that "John Kerry is anti-American. This is not patriot speech . . . This is pure anti-American, anti-U.S. military and these are the mouthpieces of the Democratic Party today who are assigned the effort of saying these things: constantly slam our own country." The *American Spectator*'s R. Emmett Tyrrell Jr. says that "in rendering the war controversial, [Kerry] gave aid and comfort to our enemies." And Ann Coulter, churning desperately for running room on the right, says that "[t]here is no plausible explanation for the Democrats' behavior other than that they long to see U.S. troops shot, humiliated, and driven from the field of battle."

Those charges could have been lifted verbatim from the Vietnam era; then, too, critics of the administration's policies were charged with letting down the troops, weakening American unity, and encouraging the enemy or advocating appeasement. But the language has earlier roots in World War II and the Korean War, "just wars" fought offensively against aggressor states. It's a reminder of how much the right has at stake rhetorically in depicting the current conflicts in terms of that model. Iraq becomes "the central front in the war on terror," as Mehlman puts it: we're fighting the terrorists in Baghdad so we don't have to fight them in Boston; and loyal Americans should fall in line behind the commander-in-chief's policies until the enemy loses heart and capitulates. (Since 9/11, Fox News has been referring to the president as "the commander-in-chief" five times as frequently as it did in the first nine months of his presidency.)

Above all, it's a war being fought on behalf of "freedom"—both so that the Afghans, Iraqis, and others can have theirs and because the terrorists hate ours, as Bush keeps explaining their motive, subordinating any cultural or religious basis for the Islamic terrorism to a simple hostility toward American democratic institutions. Hence the popularity of the word *Islamo-fascists*, as if the evils of the Taliban, Zarqawi, and bin Laden weren't sufficient to the day. Even if the historical resemblances to the Nazis are pretty inexact and unhelpful, we can't go after anyone now without comparing the campaign to the "good war" against Hitler, a struggle that was incontestably fought in freedom's name. Those invocations of "freedom" put critics of the Iraq War outside the pale of legitimate dissent, and make the holding of elections in Iraq alone sufficient justification for the war, even if no WMDs were found.*

It's an inapt analogy from top to bottom, particularly as events make it clear that this is not really a war about "spreading democracy" and that terrorism has hardly been "tied down" in Iraq while American troops are fighting there, as the inhabitants of London, Madrid, Istanbul, and Bali can testify. Even the syntax of the phrase "war on terror" concedes that this is a different kind of conflict, one of those interminable campaigns against pandemic evils like poverty, drugs, and corruption. (Since 9/11, "the war on terror" has largely replaced "the war on terrorism" in White House speeches.) But so long as the right can still use that story to define the goals of the war and the scope of patriotic duty, the Democrats will

---

*In press commentaries during the build-up to the Iraq War, Saddam Hussein was compared to Hitler five times as often as during the first Gulf War in 1990–1991, not because he had grown any more monstrous in the interval, but because it cast the invasion as part of a larger campaign for democracy and American values.

be in a position of having to demonstrate their patriotic bona fides in the face of Republican attacks.

Notwithstanding the Democrats' indignation, charges like those have clearly taken their toll. But the Democrats made no headway when they tried turnabout-is-fair-play, suggesting that the administration itself was deficient in patriotism. During the primary season, Bob Graham described Bush's Iraq policy as "anti-patriotic at the core," and of putting the commercial interest of firms like Halliburton "above the patriotic interest of getting more countries involved," and Wesley Clark said that Bush's landing aboard the *Lincoln* wasn't patriotic. Kerry charged that Bush's friends in the corporate world who outsourced jobs were "unpatriotic" and "Benedict Arnold CEOs" and tried to label the Republicans as chicken-hawks: "I'm tired of Karl Rove and Dick Cheney and a bunch of people who went out of their way to avoid their chance to serve [in the military] when they had the chance."

The Republicans shrugged those charges off. As the *Wall Street Journal*'s Taranto observed: "No one seriously believes Messrs. Ashcroft, Bush, Cheney and Rove are unpatriotic. When Messrs. Clark, Dean and Kerry question their opponents' patriotism, it has some mild shock value but carries no real sting, like a child trying out a naughty word he's just learned."

Taranto is right. So long as the right owns patriotism, the Democrats will be unable to change the conversation. The exchanges over patriotism in recent years would be no different if you substituted the word "values": in either case, the Democrats have had no success in emphasizing their own or trying to impeach the other side's. The Democrats can argue that it is unpatriotic to cut taxes in wartime or to provide inadequate funding for homeland security, but the term doesn't really have any symbolic weight in that context. Even if Americans see those actions as counter to the national interest, Democrats haven't succeeded in tying them to a sense of national *mission*, which is what "patriotism" always implies. Once again, Democrats have tried to reclaim the word in its dictionary meaning while ignoring the narrative it's embedded in.

but while the rhetoric of patriotism hasn't changed in fifty years, the meaning of the word is very different now. In the literal sense of the term, in fact, patriotism is actually not an issue in modern American politics—it's as close as you can get to an empty political symbol. Despite the right's attacks on the "blame America first crowd," Americans rarely doubt one another's patriotism in a serious way. There is nothing in modern America that's remotely like the mistrust of German Americans or other immigrants during World War I, of Japanese Americans during World War II, or of Communists during the McCarthy years, when certain groups of Americans were genuinely suspected of harboring loyalties to hostile powers.*

For that matter, when people are called unpatriotic nowadays, it's almost never because of something they've actually done, the way it was when people applied the word to hoarders during World War II or to draft evaders during Vietnam. The Iraq War hasn't demanded any great material sacrifices from Americans, after all, and renewing the draft isn't really in play. You can see the difference in the changed meaning of "support the troops." During World War II, that meant buying war bonds or going on scrap drives; since Vietnam it has required only backing the administration's policy or wearing a lapel pin. Patriotism has never been as low-maintenance as it is now.

That doesn't mean that the word *patriotism* has no content, but it's not simply a question of devotion to one's nation anymore. If that were all there was to it, it wouldn't be a contested notion. What passes for "patriotism" these days is really a matter of values and style, of conveying "toughness," and of subscribing to a particularly combative view of America's role. In that sense, it's merely another aspect of the familiar cultural politics of the right.

That's why the word *patriotism* has the power to be so divisive even when the overwhelming majority of American citizens profess pride in their country. There's a curious Lake Wobegon effect to American patriotism: in polls, around 60 percent of Americans describe themselves as

---

* Some Arab Americans no doubt feel differently, but they have been the victims only of individual acts of discrimination or harassment, which aren't comparable to the internments, deportations, jailings, witch hunts, and official repressions that were visited on suspect groups in earlier periods.

more patriotic than the average American, while fewer than 10 percent consider themselves to be less patriotic—or in other words, most people think that other Americans are less patriotic than they. That's of a piece with the sense of victimization that the right has fostered, where Middle Americans are made to feel put upon by a supercilious elite, so that patriotic gestures become acts of cultural defiance. To wear an American flag in your lapel, Peggy Noonan says, is "a sign that [says] 'I support my country, and if you don't like it, that's too bad.'"

You can hear that in the explanations that conservatives give for liberals' lack of patriotism. No one suggests that liberals have divided national loyalties, like the Germans or Japanese were thought to have, or that they subscribe to subversive political doctrines, like the radicals and Communists of earlier days. It's simply a matter of snobbery, like the other elite frailties. These days, says John O'Sullivan, liberals believe that "the patriotism of ordinary people is something simplistic, vulgar, and shameful, and thus to be avoided." That's how it comes about, he says, that "feminists and multiculturalists find themselves taking the side of medieval Islamists against the common American enemy. They feel more comfortable in such superior company than alongside a hard-hat construction worker or a suburban golfer in plaid pants." The liberals' disloyalty, in other words, isn't to their nation but to the values and tastes of "regular Americans."

For many voters, what confirmed John Kerry's lack of patriotism wasn't his participation in the anti–Vietnam War protests forty years ago or his reservations about the administration's current policies—it was his association with the French. Not that anybody actually thought that he had divided political loyalties, but the connection reinforced the sense of him as an effete elitist, like other Eastern liberals—a charge that no indignant protestations of patriotism could completely dispel. Bush and Cheney didn't have to challenge his war record; it was enough to ridicule his affectations. Kerry has already switched policies on Iraq several times, Bush charged, and now he has found "a new nuance," drawing the word out to underscore its Gallic overtones." ("In Texas, we don't do nuance," he said on another occasion, drawing a red line through the dictionary.)

And when Kerry called for a "more sensitive" war on terrorism, Cheney jumped on the word: "America has been in too many wars for any of our wishes, but not a one of them was won by being sensitive." For the Democrats, "sounding tough" on terrorism and national security isn't just a matter of saying the right things about Iraq and homeland security—they have to address the wussy cultural stereotypes that the right has surrounded them with. To a large extent, people's doubts about the Democrats' patriotism and toughness are the outgrowth of the right's counterfeit populism, just another side of the "values" gap.

That new conception of patriotism didn't emerge fully until the Reagan years, when the bitter divisions over the Vietnam War were ritualized as cultural divisions between what would come to be known as red and blue America. The assumptions were sufficiently rooted by 1984 so that Ronald Reagan could simply assume that the composer of a song called "Born in the USA" would be a like-minded Republican, never mind that the song was actually about an unemployed Vietnam veteran. "I have not got a clue about Springsteen's politics, if any," George Will wrote approvingly, "but flags get waved at his concerts."

In fact, there's little "traditional" about contemporary American patriotism; it has become matter of style and consumer preference to a degree that would have disconcerted Americans of earlier generations. The founder of the Hummer Owners Group recently described the vehicle as "a symbol of what we all hold so dearly above all else, the fact we have the freedom of choice, . . . the freedom of adventure and discovery, and the ultimate freedom of expression." Or as another Hummer owner put it, "[The troops] aren't out there in Audi A-4's."

The traditional symbols of patriotism are treated now with an offhandedness that would once have been considered more appropriate for sports emblems. In 1968, Abbie Hoffman was arrested for wearing an American-flag shirt to a hearing of the House Committee on Un-American Activities. But when pro-war demonstrators assembled in the days leading up to the Iraq War, they wore American-flag T-shirts, belt buckles, bandannas, halters, and jumpsuits. And there's little solemnity in the patriotic cry of "USA! USA!" that is heard now at political conventions and Republican campaign rallies, which had its origin at the 1980 Winter Olympic Games.*

The truly "patriotic" elements of American patriotism have never been as superficial or devalued as they are today. Being patriotic is not simply a matter of loving one's country but of being demonstrative about it. Nowadays, "patriotism" is largely no more than "values" written on a national screen, another artifact of the right's two-nations scenario, which obstructs the possibility of reaching the kind of genuine accord that looked possible for a while after 9/11. There can't be any true patriotic consensus so long as patriotic affirmations are routinely followed by "and if you don't like it. . . ."

That doesn't mean that Democrats and liberals shouldn't make a point of showing reverence for patriotic symbols and respect for the military. And indeed, liberals have learned the lessons of the Vietnam era, when the flag-burning, troop-taunting tantrums of a minority on the left were allowed to overshadow the moral case against the war. Liberals have the right and obligation to claim those symbols on behalf of all Americans and to fiercely resist the right's appropriation of them on behalf of one segment of American society.

But the Democrats' "patriotism problem" can't be addressed solely by showing the flag more ostentatiously. It has its roots in their failure to convey a sense of strength and constancy, and equally important, in their failure to offer a sense of national mission that can stir genuinely patriotic impulses, however they happen to be called.

---

* There's a sign of the shifting meaning of *patriotism* in the eclipse of the word *patriot*. If you exclude the use of *patriot* in the names of banks, sports teams, insurance companies, missiles, legislation, and the like, it's outnumbered by *patriotic* and *patriotism* by 10 to 1 in the press—a substantially bigger disproportion than in earlier times. But then being patriotic is a matter of style; being a patriot is a matter of actions.

Conclusion: Tell Me a Story

A very great part of the mischiefs that vex the world arise from words. People soon forget the meaning, but the impression and the passion remain.

—*Edmund Burke, Letter to Richard Burke, Esq., 1793*

When Edmund Burke wrote those words he was thinking not of the rhetorical fulgurations of the French Jacobins, but of the way the Irish Protestants had deformed the gentle word *ascendancy*, "so soft and melodious in its sound," to mask the harsh oppression of their three million Catholic countrymen. Nothing was more deeply inimical to Burke's conservatism than the usurpation of old words to legitimate new injustices and radical change.

What would Burke have made of the rhetoric of modern conservatives? *Patriotism, values, elite, traditional, faith, ownership*—by deforming the meanings of good old words like those, the right has radically reconfigured the political landscape, divided the country, and drawn the language itself to the right. People make the same noises, but their meanings are different, or the opposite, or sometimes wholly absent, so that only "the impression and the passion remain."

Liberals and Democrats are sensitive to some of those distortions, even if they often feel helpless to counter them. But other changes have become so much a part of the language that even liberals tend to accede to them. How many liberals take umbrage when people claim they "rediscovered" patriotism after 9/11, rather than implicitly acknowledging the right's meaning of the word? How many of them feel a sense of awkwardness when they hear someone extolling "traditional progressive values"? How many Democrats condemn "big government" in the hope it will deflect the right's "tax-and-spend" charges? Does anybody have a sense of just how far the right's capture of the language has gone? And what can be done to take it back?

What makes the Democrats' communication problems frustrating is that, with the exception of their views on Iraq—a *very* important exception, to be sure—the Democrats are actually less divided than they have been in recent memory. In an April 2006 *Washington Monthly* review of four recent books about the state of the party, Mark Schmitt observes that what is uppermost in Democrats' minds seems to be winning: "The old sectarian fights about ideology, between the Democratic Leadership Council and labor-left factions, seem to have disappeared." And in broad strokes at least, the Democrats seem to know what issues and programs they want to run on: tax fairness, the budget deficit, health care, homeland security, corruption and electoral reform, education, Social Security and pension protection, energy, corporate power, and generic Republican incompetence, not necessarily in that order. Or for that matter, in any clear order. As the party's new slogan makes clear, the Democrats haven't been able to come up with any story that weaves those themes together, save to say that they aren't Republicans. True, that's something, given the way things have gone. But it's not exactly the kind of narrative that can build permanent coalitions or suggest a larger sense of national purpose.

The solution has to include taking back the populist narrative that the Republicans have used so successfully to connect their disparate positions and policies. From taxes to "big government" to patriotism, from Social Security to affirmative action to Iraq, the right's story always comes back to the spurious conflict between "regular Americans" and the "liberal elite," played in different keys and with varying timbres. The right's capture of the basic vocabulary of politics merely testifies to the insistence and ubiquity of that theme. If nothing else, the right has demonstrated how versatile that kind of story can be in connecting the threads among programs and policies. But if the right can do this with an ersatz populism, surely the Democrats can do the same thing with a genuine one.

In their simplest form, narratives consist of characters and plots, expressed by subjects and verbs, which can be linked to some well-known archetype or genre. They're what is distilled in the movie blurbs in the newspaper's TV section: "Simple-hearted Vermont tuba player inherits a fortune and has to contend with opportunistic city slickers"; "Naive young senator fights political corruption"; "A frustrated small-town businessman learns what life would have been like if he had never existed." Usually, that's pretty much all we need to know; the genre does the rest of the work. And in the case of populist narratives, the genre is a familiar one: "With the help of the hero, ordinary hard-working people stand up to powerful bullies, who finally get their comeuppance."

That was the genre Bill Clinton was alluding to in 1992 when he said, "I'm tired of seeing the people who work hard and play by the rules get the shaft." The remark exemplifies most of the principles that David Kusnet laid out for successful Democratic populism in his 1992 book *Speaking American*, which should still be required reading for liberals. For one thing, it was framed in natural, colloquial language that echoed and reinforced the words that ordinary people might use. In another age, William Jennings Bryan could earn the respectful attention of the common people with high-flown orotundity. Nowadays, Americans expect their leaders to talk the way they do.

What's more, Clinton's remark drew the essential class distinction where Democrats have to locate it, between the people who have benefited from Republican policies and those who have been falling behind, whether they're drywall installers or retail store managers or aerospace engineers. That's vital for Democrats, who have to use vivid language to avoid the vagueness of "middle-class" (which admits billionaires so long as they drink longneck beer) and to erase the specious distinction between "middle-class" and "working-class." Democrats might address themselves to what Kusnet calls "middle-class working people," but that's neither clear nor evocative—it doesn't get at the everyday feelings that join a small subcontractor and a retail store manager when they sit down to try to put their tax information together. At various times Clinton spoke about "people who work hard and play by the rules," "the forgotten middle class," and "people who live from paycheck to paycheck," and Mario Cuomo talked about "people who work for a living because they have to." Or if you like, the people who have to go to the DMV for themselves, the people who have to make hard choices when gas prices rise, and so forth. None of those phrases is socioeconomically exact, but each of them suggests a miniature biography.

Then, too, Clinton's remark conveyed sympathy, passion, and anger over the problems of ordinary people. From Bobby Kennedy to Jimmy Carter to Mario Cuomo to Bill Clinton, the most successful Democratic politicians at the national level have been those who have been able to suggest a depth of moral concern. It's that, as much as anything else, that has enabled individual Democrats to overcome the difficulty of being on the wrong side of many of the "values" issues.

In the 1988 presidential debate, Michael Dukakis famously—and irrecoverably—branded himself a bloodless technocrat when CNN's Bernard Shaw asked him if he would favor the death penalty for a man who had raped and murdered his wife, and Dukakis answered fastidiously:

> No, I don't, Bernard, and I think you know that I've opposed the death penalty during all of my life. I don't see any evidence that it—it's a deterrent, and I think there're better and more effective ways to deal with violent crime.

Mario Cuomo defended his own opposition to the death penalty very differently. He opposed it, he said, "because it's wrong, because it's dumb, because it's counterproductive, because it's an instruction in violence, because it won't make my daughter safe. It won't make my mother safe. It never has." In 1991, when Sam Donaldson asked him the same question that Dukakis had booted, Cuomo revealed that his own daughter "was touched twice by the same man and we never caught him." Donaldson asked what Cuomo would have done if he had caught the man, and Cuomo answered that he probably "would have committed a terrible sin." When Donaldson pressed him: "Would you have killed him?" Cuomo answered, "I don't know, Sam, and I don't want to know. But the point is this. God forbid I should make laws that are only as good as me! . . . I want something much, much better than Mario Cuomo." The answer didn't simply underscore the religious basis of Cuomo's views (an approach that has worked for other anti-death penalty Democrats, like Virginia's governor Tim Kaine, a former Catholic missionary). The personal narrative left the audience in no doubt about his inner struggles over the question.

A great deal of what people perceive as the Democrats' weaknesses on "values," in fact, is simply their difficulty in conveying genuine feeling about the problems that leave many Americans feeling that the country is morally adrift—crime, drugs, teen suicide, illegitimacy, broken families, and the crassness and violence of some sectors of American popular culture. Democrats will readily wax passionate about Iraq, tax cuts for the rich, or domestic spying. But many of them are oddly diffident about expressing the same anger about the moral threats to family life, or about connecting those problems to the economic problems that also tear at the family—hence people's perception of the party as preoccupied with policies and programs rather than a larger vision, a perception which the party's official pronouncements don't do a lot to dispel. "America can do better" is well and good, but the politicians and movements that have created a sense of national purpose are the ones that have passionately insisted that America can *be* better, as well.

But like values, passion can only be conveyed, not asserted. Some politicians, like Reagan, Clinton, and Cuomo, have had obvious natural gifts for this that can't be mechanically replicated. But language itself can go part of the way to making passion palpable. That's often a question of using colloquial, vivid expressions like Clinton's "get the shaft," but simple moral terms like *fair* and *decent* can also do that work, so long as they're fleshed out in the right stories. In a famous study of working-class white Michigan voters after the 1984 election, for example, Stanley Greenberg found that the traditional Democratic themes of fairness and opportunity had been "invested with cynicism and racism." For those voters, Greenberg reported, the word *fairness* evoked only images of "racial minorities" and "some blacks kicking up a storm" or of lying politicians: "It never occurred to these voters that the Democrats were referring to the middle class." But the problem wasn't with the word *fairness* itself, but with the Democrats' narrative, at a time when they were having a lot of trouble persuading the white working class that the party had their interests at heart. In another context, *fairness* will connote doing right by "people who play by the rules," whatever race they are, in the same way it did for Harry Truman. *Decency*, *fairness*, "doing right by people." Any of those will work if they're used in the right stories. And it goes without saying, only if those stories are associated with policies that really do address middle-class concerns.

recapturing the language of politics is bound to be a difficult task, however well the Democrats manage to tell their stories. Conservatives still have a considerable advantage, and not just because they've had several decades to lay the linguistic groundwork. They can count on a discipline and organization in disseminating their messages that liberals can't hope to duplicate, not just because of their limited resources but because of a chronic incapacity to stay on a single page. And the right doesn't have to rely on politicians to diffuse its language—it can also count on channels like talk radio and cable news. One irony of the right's contention that openly partisan commentary "balances" the liberal tilt of the ostensibly objective mainstream media is that Limbaugh and the Fox News hosts are free to use vivid and colloquial partisan language in a way that CNN or NPR could never do, even if they really were as liberal as right-wing critics make them out to be.

True, a gifted individual Democrat can persuade voters of his or her strength or passion despite conservatives' control of the populist narrative and its language. But once you control a genre, you can cast whomever you like in a leading role—if Jimmy Stewart isn't available, you can use Jack Holt or Richard Dix, and let the genre take care of the rest. If you want a telling indication of the right's linguistic triumph, don't listen to George W. Bush talk about values—listen to Republican senators like Bill Frist, John Cornyn, or Sam Brownback, men of no evident charisma or passion who nonetheless manage to reach voters by pushing the preset linguistic buttons. Democrats have no language that will work for them in the same way; whenever they manage to overcome their "values" problems, it seems an individual tour de force.

True, some of this is changing, as a denser liberal infrastructure begins to emerge. There are more liberal think tanks working on "messaging," though they're not in a league with the Cato Institute or the Heritage Foundation when it comes to resources. The liberal and left-wing bloggers have created a network that makes the circulation of ideas and language very fluid, though it isn't clear how far their influence extends beyond wired middle-class liberals and progressives. And in broadcasters like Al Franken, Keith Olbermann, Jon Stewart, and others you can hear the stirrings of a new liberal tone of voice, one that aims at being wry and sardonic rather than aping the belligerence of the most prominent right-wing media stars—or for that matter, the insistently aggrieved indignation of a lot of the left-wing hosts on the Pacifica stations.* But none of these figures, not even Stewart, has anything like the reach of a Limbaugh or a Hannity, both of whom have weekly audiences ten or fifteen times greater than that of the nearest liberal talk-show host.

Liberals have an additional linguistic advantage, in the form of truth. To tell their populist story, conservatives have had to distort the economic and social realities of American life. In their version, the champions of the common people are Republicans and conservatives, the bullies are a collection of sociology professors, midlevel bureaucrats, Hollywood actors, and newspaper reporters, and the financial and corporate power is absent

---

* Of course there are amiable figures in right-wing broadcasting, like Tucker Carlson, Dennis Miller, Bill Kristol, and Joe Scarborough, but they haven't had the success of types like O'Reilly, Limbaugh, or Michael Savage, who have built their careers around being overbearing jerks—a style that Stephen Colbert has turned into a comic shtick with a life of its own. It's hard to think of any leading right-wing broadcaster whom even his most devoted fans would welcome having as a brother-in-law.

from the cast of characters. As I've shown here, those distortions have left corresponding traces on the language itself, as the meanings of words are stretched, doubled, blurred, or effaced until only impressions remain. And while words can live in those compromised states for a long time, the strain tells on them as the things they leave unsaid become too noticeable to ignore, and other, truer words are offered in their place. Auden spoke of the shadow cast by language upon truth, but things work the other way round, as well.

Appendix

A Note on the Word Counts in This Book

The availability of online databases like the Web and Nexis has made computational linguists of us all—they're an irresistible tool for journalists who want to reckon buzz. Usually, it scarcely matters whether the counts are accurate or not. When a columnist writes that "a Google search using the words 'King Kong racism' yielded 490,000 hits," you can take the number as just a cyber-age way of saying "a whole passel."

But as linguists are well aware, there are various problems in using these tools to quantify language use in a serious way. For one thing, Google's hit-count estimation algorithm in particular has various bugs that can lead to results that are wildly off in certain situations, particularly when hit-counts exceed one thousand. There are work-arounds for some of these problems, and other search engines like Yahoo!'s and MSN's may produce more reliable results, though all of them are subject to inaccuracy.* In general, it's a good idea to replicate searches on several search engines to make sure the results are in the right ballpark.

---

* The problem is that it's computationally too expensive for the search engines to compute the actual number of results for a query that would return a high number of hits, so the companies all fall back on estimation techniques. As Google's director of search quality Peter Norvig notes, most people don't really care if the hit-count algorithm is correct: "It's only reporters and computational linguists who care if it's really precise." (Carl Bialik, "Estimates for Web Search Results Are Often Wildly Off the Mark," *Wall Street Journal* online, September 15, 2005).

There are other problems in comparing the frequencies of items in databases of different sizes. The mere fact that a word is twice as frequent in *National Review* as in the *Nation* or in Nexis press stories from 2005 as in stories from 1990 tells us nothing unless we know how big the contrasting databases are. While there is generally no way to determine this directly, the ratios can be approximated by taking the frequency of certain high-frequency, general-meaning words as rough proxies for database size (e.g., by looking to see how often common words like *price*, *break*, and *result* appear in each time-slice or each publication). In cases like these, I have either corrected for the differences in database size or spoken of probabilities rather than frequencies; i.e., by saying that such-and-such a word is three times more likely to appear in one database as another, which is what really matters.

An analogous problem comes up when we're talking about the relative frequencies of various combinations of words. Saying that Antonin Scalia is labeled a conservative more often than Stephen Breyer is labeled a liberal is uninformative if we don't know how often each justice has been mentioned; again, what is relevant is the *likelihood* that either figure will be given a partisan label, rather than the absolute frequencies. (By analogy, there are more press articles that describe Barry Bonds as striking out than those that describe Edgar Alfonso as striking out, but only because there are many more articles that mention Bonds in the first place.)

Ambiguity and multiple senses (polysemy) raise other problems. Expressions like *secularist* and *liberal values* have one meaning in the American context and another when people are talking about the Middle East, for example. In some of those cases, I have used "restrictors" that limit a search to a particular context (e.g., ruling out articles that refer to Iraq or the Middle East or including only articles that refer to Democrats or Republicans, say), and then checking the results by hand. (Needless to say, the same restrictors have to be used when it comes to counting contrasting phrases, such as *conservative values*.)

Acknowledgments

Various passages of this book were adapted from pieces I wrote for *Fresh Air,* the *New York Times,* the *American Prospect,* and other publications. In the course of writing those pieces, I picked the brains of a lot of people whom I've already I thanked in my collections *The Way We Talk Now* and *Going Nucular.* But I want to thank a number of people who gave me helpful comments or information in the course of preparing this manuscript, including Leo Braudy, Peter Edidin, Chuck Fillmore, Larry Horn, Paul Kay, Kathleen Miller, Phyllis Myers, Barbara Nunberg, Joe Pickett, and the students in a class on political language that I taught at Stanford in 2003. In the course of tracking down the origins or usage of particular words, I often benefited from the detective work of the contributors to the American Dialect Society discussion list, and in particular Fred Shapiro, Jesse Sheidlower, and Ben Zimmer. And I owe special thanks to several friends and colleagues who patiently indulged me in long conversations as I tried to make sense of this material: Rachel Brownstein, Paul Duguid, Bob Newsom, Scott Parker, and Tom Wasow. Michele Wynn and Philip Hofmeister were greatly helpful in preparing the manuscript. Finally, I'd like to thank my agent, Joe Spieler, who helped me focus the idea for this book, and Clive Priddle, my editor at PublicAffairs, who helped bring it out of the egg.

This book is dedicated to my daughter, Sophie, who already understands what it means to live in a political world.

Notes

Introduction

1   "Or more accurately, a newly augmented slogan": Kerry's slogan was itself a variation on "America is a great country but it can do better," which John Kennedy used back in 1962.

1   "According to the congressional newspaper *The Hill*": Josephine Hearn, "Dems Test New Slogan," *Hill*, October 25, 2005. Hearn reported that polling on the slogan was done by Greenberg Quinlan Rosner Research, and in the *Washington Post*, Shailagh Murray and Charles Babington quoted Majority Leader Harry Reid as saying about the slogan, "We had meetings where senators offered suggestions. We had focus groups. We worked hard on that. . . . It's a long, slow, arduous process." "Democrats Struggle to Seize Opportunity: Amid GOP Troubles, No Unified Message," *Washington Post*, March 7, 2006. But an article in the Las Vegas *Sun* quoted Reid's spokesperson Tessa Hafen as saying that focus groups were not used to determine the slogan. Benjamin Grove, "Reid Floats Democrats' 2006 Slogan," *Las Vegas Sun*, October 20, 2005.

1   "The *Washington Post* reported that Democratic governors were scoffing at it": Shailagh Murray and Charles Babington, "Democrats Struggle to Seize Opportunity," *Washington Post*, March 7, 2006.

1   "'Pathetic,' said Hendrik Hertzberg in the *New Yorker*": Hendrik Hertzberg, "Disarray This," *New Yorker*, March 27, 2006; Rosa Brooks, "They Can't Even Win a War of Words," *Los Angeles Times*, March 10, 2006. "Democrats Give 2006 Their Better Shot," Wonkette.com, October 25, 2005, http://www.wonkette.com/politics/democrats/democrats-give-2006-their-better-shot–133034.php.

2 "Given the slogan's resounding vacuity": Grammatically, the problem is a bit more complicated than that. It's acceptable to say, for example, "America stands together" or "America banded together," where *together* turns the verb into a single collective action. But when *together* appears at the beginning of the sentence (as an "adjunct," as linguists call it), it suggests the distinct efforts of the members of a group, and for that reason is appropriate only with a plural noun. You can see the meaning difference when you contrast the sentences *Together, the two companies built all the bridges in the state* and *The two companies built all the bridges in the state together*—the first suggests only all the bridges were built by one or the other company; the second entails that the companies collaborated on all the projects.

3 "Or what's only slightly better": In recent years, there have been several very good ethnographic and sociological studies of the way people talk about politics, such as William A. Gamson's *Talking Politics* (Cambridge University Press, 1992), Nina Eliasoph's *Avoiding Politics: How Americans Produce Apathy in Everyday Life* (Cambridge University Press, 1998), and Katherine Kramer Walsh's *Talking About Politics: Informal Groups and Social Identity in American Life* (University of Chicago Press, 2004). These studies don't focus on political language as such, but they offer important insights into the way people absorb and make sense of media discourse about politics.

Chapter One

7 "a language that resonates with them": McAuliffe quoted in April Hunt, "Democrats to Explore Changing Dates of State Primaries," *Orlando Sentinel*, December 10, 2004.

7 "restore the language of values": David S. Broder, "Need to Connect with Religious, Rural Voters Noted," *Washington Post*, November 4, 2004.

7 "the entire moral vocabulary": Ellen Goodman, "Winning Back Values Voters," *Washington Post*, November 6, 2004.

10 "words starting with an 'r' or ending with an '-ity' are good": Luntz quoted in Nicholas Lemann, "The Word Lab," *New Yorker*, October 16, 2000.

11 "increased support for estate tax repeal": Larry M. Bartels, "Homer Gets a Tax Cut: Inequality and Public Policy in the American Mind," Woodrow Wilson School policy brief, December 2003.

11   "your intentions are strictly honorable." Frank Luntz, "The Environment: A Cleaner, Safer, Healthier America," unpublished report, p. 132, http://www.politicalstrategy.org/archives/001330.php.

13   "a reshuffling of tired old rhetorical clichés": Josh Green, "It Isn't the Message, Stupid," *Atlantic Monthly*, May 2005.

13   "with snazzier packaging and a new sales pitch": Ibid.

13   "neuroscientific hooey": Marc Cooper, "Thinking of Jackasses," *Atlantic Monthly*, April 2005.

13   "not what it believes, but rather how it speaks": William Galston and Elaine Kamarck, "The Politics of Polarization," Third Way report, October 2005.

14   "Republicans have mastered the art of political narrative": Robert Reich, "The Lost Art of Democrative Narrative: Story Time," *New Republic*, March 28, 2005.

15   "It's still a tale of two Americas": Robert Kuttner, "No, the Pocketbook Rules," *Boston Globe*, November 10, 2004.

15   "move away from any hope of bringing peace to irreconcilable moral disputes": Brad Carson, "Missing Message," *Blueprint Magazine*, March 16, 2005.

15   "comfortable using the language of faith": Will Marshall, "Heartland Strategy," *Blueprint Magazine*, December 13, 2004.

17   "Some of us say the Negro has made great progress": "Excerpts from Kennedy Speech on Coast," *New York Times*, October 24, 1966.

Chapter Two

21   "Before 1914, 'propaganda' belonged only to literate vocabularies": Will Irwin, *Propaganda and the News* (Whittlesey House, 1936).

22   "For quite long periods . . . people can remain undisturbed": George Orwell, "As I Please," *London Tribune*, June 2, 1944.

23   "Deconstructionist-in-Chief": Robert A. George, "Getting Away With It," *National Review* online, April 19, 2000, http://www.nationalreview.com; Timothy Noah, "Bill Clinton and the Meaning of 'Is,'" *Slate*, September 13, 1998, http://www.slate.com/id/1000162.

25   "An ordinary, everyday term X is contrasted with its euphemistic equivalent 'Y,'": If you wanted to take this back even further, you could point to the words that Tacitus put in the mouth of the British chieftain Calgacus on the eve of his battle with the Romans—"Robbery, butchery, and rapine the liars call empire; they make a desert and call it peace" ("Ubi solitudinem faciunt, pacem appelant").

26   "When you think of a concrete object": George Orwell, "Politics and the English Language," in John Carey, ed. *Essays of George Orwell* (Alfred A. Knopf, 2002) p. 965.

26   "If you're giving Advice to Writers": Actually, many linguists and psychologists would say that it isn't possible to have "wordless" perceptions of even the most concrete notions like "kick" or "ball"—language is always in the background, highlighting some features of reality and suppressing others. If you show speakers of English and speakers of Indonesian a photograph of a man's foot kicking a ball, they'll store it in memory differently, according to the particular distinctions that their languages make available. See Lera Boroditsky, Wendy Ham, and Michael Ramscar, "What Is Universal in Event Perception? Comparing English and Indonesian Speakers," in W. D. Gray and C. D. Schunn, eds., *Proceedings of the 24th Annual Meeting of the Cognitive Science Society* (2002), pp. 136–144.

27   "the label *juvenile delinquent*": Susan Seidner Adler, "Bribing Delinquents to Be Good," *Commentary*, October 1981.

28   "thicker, more rigid, and more parochial terms": Richard Rorty, "Private Irony and Liberal Hope," in *Contingency and Solidarity* (Cambridge University Press, 1989), p. 73.

30   "The question of a proper fare": Walter Lippmann, *Public Opinion* (Free Press, 1966 [1922]), p. 151.

30   "information cost-saving": Samuel Popkin, *The Reasoning Voter* (University of Chicago Press, 1994), p. 105.

31   "Words like *patriotism* and *terrorism* do not let us breathe": Roderick P. Hart, Sharon E. Jarvis, William P. Jennings, and Deborah Smith-Howell, *Political Keywords: Using Language That Uses Us* (Oxford University Press, 2004), p. 246.

32   "the originally disparaging connotations of *Whig* and *Tory*": *Whig* may have originated as a word for "bumpkin." In the early seventeenth century it referred to the Scottish Covenanter rebels and was used by Dryden simply as a synonym for "rebel." *Tory* began as a name for an Irish bandit or outlaw,

and then became a derogatory term for those who wanted the Catholic Duke of York (later James II) to succeed to the throne. By the end of the seventeenth century, both names were being used for political parties.

32   "references to the business elite are outnumbered by almost 50-to-1": On Fox News broadcasts since 1996, *elite* has occurred within two words of *media* 363 times, and within two words of *Hollywood* 44 times. The figures for *business* and *financial*, by contrast, are 6-and-0. In broadcasts, of course, a number of these mentions of the media elite came from remarks by conservative interviewees. But from the standpoint of influencing the language, the most important thing is the raw frequency of use, and it is significant that there's little corresponding use of phrases like *business elite* by liberal guests. And the proportions are pretty much the same when you look at Google Groups postings, for example, where *media elite* and *elite media* and the like outnumber the corresponding phrases with *business* by 4-to-1.

32   "elite liberal media": The overall proportions for press usage don't change much whether you look at news articles or editorials and op-eds.

32   "references to conservative values outnumber references to liberal values by almost 7-to-1": I exclude references to foreign nations, as in "bringing Western liberal values to China" and the like, where *liberal* has a broader sense.

33   "work the refs": Trudy Lieberman, *Slanting the Story: The Forces That Shape the News* (New Press, 2000); Eric Alterman, *What Liberal Media? The Truth About Bias and the News* (Basic Books, 2003); David Brock, *The Republican Noise Machine: Right-Wing Media and How It Corrupts Democracy* (Crown, 2004).

33   "'personal accounts' rather than 'private accounts'": In broadcast stories from November 2004, "personal accounts" accounted for 20 percent of the references to the accounts, with "private accounts" accounting for the rest. By March, the proportion of references to "personal accounts" had risen to 41 percent. In stories in American newspapers over the same period, references to "personal accounts" went from 23 to 39 percent of the total. On Fox News, references to "personal accounts" went from 45 to 58 percent.

34   "the patterns in the way the media uses these words": The ratio of "unabashed liberal" and "unapologetic liberal" to the corresponding expressions with "conservative" is pretty much the same whether you look at U.S. newspapers, news broadcasts, Web sites, or Google Groups—it runs about 4 to 1

in all those contexts. (It tends to be a little lower in conservative sites like nationalreview.com, presumably because conservatives still like to pretend that theirs is an embattled label, but even there the variants with "liberal" come out ahead.) Most of the other patterns I've mentioned—for example, the general disfavoring of "working-class liberals"—also fall out the same in the various electronic forums and in the press. This is not to say that the Web or the newsgroups are necessarily "representative" of American society as a whole. The average contributor to a newsgroup is probably somewhat better educated than the average American, and there's no way to know how newsgroup contributors or the people who post Web sites sort out politically or geographically. But given the similarities of pattern across the different media and between conservative and liberal papers, it's hard to believe we'd see any dramatic discrepancies if we could monitor breakfast-table discussions all over the country.

36   "I must be telling the truth. I'm too inarticulate to lie": James Carville and Paul Begala, *Take It Back: Our Party, Our Country, Our Future* (Simon and Schuster, 2006), p. 241.

36   "conservative papers were far less likely to break with 'their' administrations": Michael Tomasky, "Whispers and Screams: The Partisan Nature of Editorial Pages," Shorenstein Center Research Paper R-25, Harvard University, July 2003.

38   "Publication is partial": John Dewey, *The Public and Its Problems* (Henry Holt and Co., 1927), pp. 371–372.

Chapter Three

41   "Given the aversion this word inspires": Timothy Noah, "10 Political Words That Dare Not Speak Their Name," *New York Times*, November 19, 1986.

42   "the number of Americans willing to describe themselves as liberal": The Harris poll notes that "it is hard to think of another set of attitudinal questions that have been so extraordinarily stable."

42   "the dominant force in our political life": Richard Hofstadter, "The Pseudo-Conservative Revolt," in Daniel Bell, ed., *The Radical Right* (Criterion, 1955), p. 63.

43   "profligacy, spinelessness, malevolence": Jonathan Rieder, *Canarsie: The Jews and Italians of Brooklyn Against Liberalism* (Harvard University Press, 1985), p. 6.

43   "The masquerade is over": *Liberal* was occasionally described as "the L-word" before that, but the designation usually had to be explained. Within a few months of Reagan's speech, however, Marty Nolan could write in the Boston *Globe*, "Throughout this presidential campaign, 'Massachusetts' ranks second (after the L-word) whenever George Bush wants to, as he says, 'talk dirty,'" without feeling the need to tell his readers just what the L-word was. Campaign Watch series: "Baker's Tight Ship," *Boston Globe*, October 21, 1988.

44   "The real shift to the right has been among the Republican leadership": See Jacob S. Hacker and Paul Pierson, *Off Center: The Republican Revolution and the Erosion of American Democracy* (Yale University Press, 2005), pp. 43–44.

44   "The word itself isn't used nearly as much as it used to be": In press stories, *liberalism* is only about 60 percent as frequent relative to *conservatism* as it was in the early 1980s, though the ratio of *liberal* and *conservative* is largely unchanged.

45   "voters repudiated the left's resistance to 'progressive ideas'": This isn't to deny that there are various themes in modern conservatism that echo the concerns of early twentieth-century Progressives, for better and for worse. But that clearly isn't what Youngs is getting at—for her, "progressive" is just an adjectival form of *progress*.

45   "Seventy years is a pretty good run for a political label": *Liberal* has had a long and complicated history as a political label since it was first used in the Napoleonic period, and various of its older meanings survive in phrases such as "liberal democracy" and "liberal Western values," not to mention in the names of various European parties and movements. But its modern American sense really begins in the New Deal period, when the opposition between liberals and conservatives was established. Some conservatives like to argue that modern liberals are not "true liberals" in this or that historical sense of the term, even as liberals charge that modern conservatives are untrue to the historical sense of *their* name. This kind of essentialism has its polemical uses, but it serves no serious intellectual purpose. Talking about "the true meaning of *liberalism*" is as idle an exercise as talking about "the true meaning of *jazz*." For discussions of the development of the modern meanings of *liberal* and *liberalism*, see Ronald D.

Rotunda, *The Politics of Language: Liberalism as Word and Symbol* (University of Iowa Press, 1986), and David Green, *The Language of Politics in America* (Cornell University Press, 1987).

46   "If a man eschews extreme fads in clothing himself": "Conservative," *Wall Street Journal*, March 17, 1949.

46   "the liberal label still has its defenders": "To surrender the label 'liberal' to history," Stephen Macedo writes, "would be a profound mistake, for the great tradition of liberal thinking deserves a better fate." *Diversity and Distrust: Civic Education in a Multicultural Democracy* (Harvard University Press, 2003), p. 8.

47   "one of the most liberal leftists that we have in the House": That wording is not uncommon. A letter-writer to the *Palm Beach Post*, October 19, 2001, decried the influence of "extremely liberal leftists" in academia.

47   "a large tendency rather than a concise body of doctrine": Lionel Trilling, *The Liberal Imagination: Essays on Literature and Society* (Viking Press, 1951), p. xi.

47   "But it did give Democrats a common touchpoint": *Republicanism* plays a similar role: people have used the term since the Reagan years to refer to the political philosophy of the Republicans. But there is no corresponding word *Democratism* for the Democrats.

48   "relative to the broader political horizon": William Safire, "Iron Fist," *New York Times*, August 20, 2000. On the Web, "moderate Republican" outpolls "moderate Democrat" by 4-to-1, whereas "centrist Democrat" has a 3-to-1 edge over "centrist Republican." Many conservative Republicans dislike the implications of *moderate*. As Safire observed in 2000, "From a conservative's point of view, a moderate is the liberal's way of avoiding the pejorative tag of *liberal*. From a liberal's point of view, *moderate* is a friendly way of describing a Republican who is not a hard-core, reactionary, troglodyte kook." But Republicans aren't crazy about describing figures like Rudy Giuliani and George Pataki as "centrists," either, and the stigmatization of *liberal* has turned "liberal Republican" into a term of abuse within party circles. So even Bush's former press secretary Ari Fleischer found himself referring to "moderate Republicans" on some occasions.

Chapter Four

50   "the low and middle income whites of this country": Joseph Kraft, "The Virtues of the System," *Los Angeles Times*, August 16, 1968.

50   "tricked out as sure guides to wise policy": Joseph Kraft, "Middle America for Real," *Los Angeles Times*, January 8, 1970.

50   "the 'conservative' elements of American society": David C. Anderson, "For Nixon, Politics of Lost Confidence," *Wall Street Journal*, March 6, 1970.

51   "The phrase spiked in the press": In 1935, the *Wall Street Journal* accused FDR's brain-truster Rexford Tugwell of "preaching class warfare" when he spoke of "disestablishing the plutocracy" and warned against Republican attempts to pit workers against farmers. "Dicta of an Under-Secretary," *Wall Street Journal*, October 30, 1935. See also "Tugwell Sets 1938 to Balance Budget," *New York Times*, October 29, 1935.

51   "And the media often play along with the pretense": "Senator Breaux, one of the sort of what's become Democratic mantra is this class warfare. Do you think this is class warfare that's going on here?" Bob Schieffer on *Face the Nation*, January 12, 2003.

52   "Is it class warfare? You bet your life": Rangel quoted in Jonathan Weisman, "$350 Billion Economic Plan Is Sent to Bush; GOP Measure Lowers Taxes, Provides Fiscal Aid to States," *Washington Post*, May 25, 2003.

52   "The way to win a presidential race against the Republicans": Atwater quoted in John Aloysius Farrell, "How the 1988 Campaign Raced Through the Cold Winter of Iowa and New Hampshire to a Hot High-Tech Battleground Where the GOP Fired First, Last and Best," *Boston Globe*, November 13, 1988.

52   "smoke out the almost un-American issue of class": Robert Kuttner, "The Hidden Issue of Class," *Boston Globe*, July 21, 2004.

54   "the right's success in selling its economic programs to the public": According to the conservative columnist and former Reagan official Bruce Bartlett, for example, the widespread support for estate tax repeal is due to "the high degree of income mobility in American society"; Americans, he said, "know that they or their children might one day be rich and have to pay this tax." Actually, fewer than one-third of Americans are aware that the tax applies only to the rich, and the majority think it will apply to them at their current income levels. "Class Warfare Is Fizzling," *National Review*, October 28, 2002.

54   "the statistical misrepresentations and accounting tricks": Conservatives deny the growing economic disparities in America, for example, by pointing out that the top 1 percent of taxpayers pay a greater proportion of all federal

income taxes than they did a few decades ago—true, but only because their share of total American income has gone up far more rapidly. (If all the income went to the top 1 percent, they'd wind up paying all the taxes, but that would scarcely mean that the United States had become a more egalitarian society.) See Timothy Noah, "The 'Tax the Poor' Movement Goes Underground," *Slate,* January 2, 2003, http://slate.com/id/2076282/.

54 "When you ask Americans to volunteer a description of themselves": "'New Affluent' Households See Themselves as Middle Class," *Sacramento Business Journal*, February 8, 2005.

55 "When we talk about a *middle-class lifestyle* or *middle-class speech*": In American newspapers on Nexis, 98 percent of all references to voters by class identify them as "middle-class." Among references to accents or speech by class, by contrast, 38 percent identify them as "middle-class," against 32 percent for "upper-class" and 30 percent for "lower-class."

55 "the very rich 'seem fanatically determined to appear middle class'": http://www.forbes.com/forbes/1999/1011/6409050a_print.html.

56 "When people are asked to pick a class description": S. M. Miller, "Class Dismissed?" *American Prospect*, March 21, 1995. See also Tom W. Smith, "The Emerging 21st Century American Family," National Opinion Research Center, University of Chicago, November 24, 1999.

56 "what the grammarian H. W. Fowler described as 'legerdemain with two senses'": In the interest of grammatical accuracy, I should say Fowler's "legerdemain with two senses" isn't quite the same thing as the process I'm talking about here. He uses the term to refer to the process of "using a word twice . . . without observing that the sense required the second time is different from the sense already in possession"—roughly the same thing that classical grammarians call zeugma.

56 "The border between wealth and middle class is so fluid": http://www.ncpa.org/oped/bartlett/may2400.html.

56 "the overwhelming majority of people, when asked by pollsters, identify themselves as middle class": Abigail Thernstrom, "A Class Backwards Idea; Why Affirmative Action for the Needy Won't Work," *Washington Post*, June 11, 1995.

56 "'small business owners' includes a corporate CEO who rents out his ski condo": "Puncturing a Republican Tax Fable," from the Annenberg School of Communications' factcheck.org site; see http://www.factcheck.org/article118.html.

57 "*Entrepreneur* was pressed into service in the late nineteenth century to re-place *capitalist*": *Entrepreneur* was first borrowed into English in the 1820s to refer to "One who 'gets up' entertainments, esp. musical perform-ances," as the Oxford English Dictionary puts it, but it acquired its more general sense in the 1880s. The OED cites Richard T. Ely's 1889 *Introduc-tion to Political Economy:* "We have . . . been obliged to resort to the French language for a word to designate the person who organizes and di-rects the productive factors, and we call such a one an *entrepreneur*."

58 "It's notable that Europeans find Bush's 'ownership society' untranslat-able": The Italian daily *La Stampa* rendered the phrase as *la societá dei pro-prietari*, or "society of property owners." The German edition of the *Financial Times* used *Teilhabergesellschaft*, roughly "shareholder society." And a writer for the French business journal *Les Ecos* said that the English word *ownership* made the phrase "basically untranslatable." Many foreign-language papers simply left the phrase in English and hoped for the best.

60 "Class, conservatives insist, is not really about money or birth": Thomas Frank, *What's the Matter with Kansas?* (Metropolitan Books, 2004), pp. 113–114.

61 "reserved their moral passion for economic reform": Gary Gerstle, "The Protean Character of American Liberalism," *American Historical Review* 99 (4) (October 1994): 1043–1073.

61 "A 2005 Harris Poll showed that Americans were more likely to identify people as being liberals": For example, the poll found that 85 percent of respondents identified conservatives as opposing same-sex marriage, with 8 percent saying that conservatives support same-sex marriage and the rest unsure. By contrast, only 70 percent identified conservatives as favoring tax cuts. On the other side, just 44 percent identified liberals as opposing tax cuts, with 39 percent saying they support tax cuts, whereas 84 percent identified liberals as supporting abortion rights. See "Political Labels: Ma-jorities of U.S. Adults Have a Sense of What Conservative, Liberal, Right Wing or Left Wing Means, But Many Do Not," Harris poll, February 9, 2005, http://www.harrisinteractive.com/harris_poll/index.asp?PID=542.

Chapter Five

64 "And in the 1950s, *egghead* evoked": *Egghead* was occasionally used before the Stevenson years, but not in a political context. The word did not

appear at all in the *New York Times* over the decade of the 1940s; in the 1950s it appeared over four hundred times.

64   "made for centuries by pseudo-wholesome, 'pious' peasants": Peter Viereck, "The Revolt Against the Elite," in Bell, *The Radical Right,* p. 144.

65   "marketing terms like *upscale* and *demographics* became part of everyday conversation": *Upscale* had been around since the 1950s as advertising trade jargon, but it didn't appear in general publications like the *New Yorker* until the mid-1970s. *Demographic* is a lot older than that, of course, but usage of the noun *demographics* picked up dramatically in the 1970s. In 1960, the word appeared in *New York Times* articles just 22 times; by 1980 that figure had risen to 188.

65   "the great, ordinary, Lawrence Welkish mass of Americans": Kevin Phillips, *The Emerging Republican Majority* (Anchor Books, 1970), p. 27.

66   "And *Time* magazine described them as people whose car windows were plastered with patriotic decals": *Time*, "Man and Woman of the Year," January 5, 1970.

66   "the Volvo, white wine and cheese set": Stephanie Mansfield, "Spar Wars: The Sizzle and the Sparks of the Battling B's," *Washington Post,* July 2, 1981.

68   "You'll have noticed already that you just spent nearly $3 for a cup of coffee": David Brooks, "Welcome to the Republic of Red Line; The Subway Set That's Traded Counterculture for Counter Service," *Washington Post*, January 12, 1997.

68   "One sometimes gets the impression that the mere words 'Socialism' and 'Communism'": George Orwell, *The Road to Wigan Pier* (Harvest Books, 1973), p. 168.

69   "brie is a lot easier to find in the gourmet shops": Michael J. Weiss, "A Tale of Two Cheeses," *American Demographics*, February 1988.

70   "Phrases like *working-class liberals, Hispanic liberals,* and *black liberals* are virtually nonexistent": In *Dialog's* American papers since 1990, for example, the phrase *middle-class liberal* has appeared 93 times and *working-class liberal* just 3; the comparable figures for conservatives are 62 and 23. But *working-class Democrat* outnumbers *working-class Republican* by 146 to 17. The proportions when you replace *middle-class* and *working-class* by *white* and *black* are roughly parallel.

70   "Could this be the first election swung by the Volvo": In fact, the Europeans have tended to assume that the brand references that people are always making in American politics are really driven by the hard marketing data the parties use in their campaigning. A 2005 article in the London *Daily Mail* condemned the "sinister" use of technology to gather information about ordinary citizens in order to predict their electoral preferences: "In last year's U.S. Presidential election, it was discovered that any voter who drove a Volvo was almost certain to be a Democrat, while someone who owned both a dog and gun was virtually certain to vote Republican." And shortly after the election an article in the Italian daily *La Stampa* credited the Republicans' success to the use of sophisticated databases that allowed them to ascertain that "Volvo-owners and yoga practitioners were almost certainly Democrats, whereas anyone who owned a Lincoln or BMW was probably of the Republican faith."

70   "But then, like other Europeans, the British aren't about to be deluded": The French speak of the "caviar left" but that's analogous to "limousine liberal" rather than "Volvo liberal." They also speak, less often, of the "cassoulet right," after a traditional peasant stew—sort of like talking about the "macaroni-and-cheese right" in America.

71   "means accepting bad beer, lousy coffee, Top-40 radio, strip malls": Rob Dreher, "Birkenstocked Burkeans: Confessions of a Granola Conservative," *National Review* online, July 12, 2002, http://www.nationalreview.com/dreher/dreher071202.asp.

Chapter Six

73   "culture war . . . appeared around the same time that 'Volvo liberal' did": *Culture war* was modeled on the German *Kulturkampf*, a word coined to describe the nineteenth-century struggle between Bismarck and the church over control of education.

75   "the divide is not economic, but cultural": Michael Barone, "The 49 Percent Nation," *National Journal* 33 (23) (June 9, 2001): 1710.

75   "The divide went deeper than politics": David Broder, "Election Reveals a Divided Nation," *Washington Post*, November 8, 2000.

75   "most Americans accept the picture of a culturally polarized nation": Princeton Survey Research Associates/Newsweek poll, released June 28, 1995; quoted in Paul DiMaggio, John Evans, and Bethany Bryson, "Have

Americans' Social Attitudes Become More Polarized?" *American Journal of Sociology* 102 (3) (November 1996).

76   "Those conclusions are supported by survey data": Ibid.

76   "there is no culture war in the United States": Morris Fiorina, *Culture War: The Myth of a Polarized America* (Longman, 2004), p. 5.

76   "Just how deep can our political disagreements be": Jonathan Rauch, "Bipolar Disorder: Is America Divided?" *Atlantic Monthly*, January 2005.

77   "the self is uncommonly large": David Brooks, "One Nation, Slightly Divisible," *Atlantic Monthly*, December 2001.

78   "The distinction between Las Vegas and New York": "The Two Americas: Ironic Us, Simple Them," *New York Post*, March 13, 2001.

78   "red-state inhabitants are unpretentious, humble, courteous, reverent": Frank, *What's the Matter with Kansas?* pp. 113–114.

79   "swingy new red-state hair": Tina Brown, "America's Endless News Loop," *Washington Post*, March 31, 2005.

79   "the mass market of the post–World War II area": Michael J. Weiss, *The Clustered World* (Little, Brown, 2000), p. 24.

80   "the top-rated radio station in Nashville in 2005": Chuck Taylor, "Nashville AC Outstrips Country Radio on Its Own Turf," *Billboard Radio Monitor,* May 20, 2005.

81   "I love Texas Republicans!": George Gurley, "Coultergeist," *New York Observer*, August 26, 2002.

81   "Queens, baseball games—those are my people": Kate Zernike, "An Evening Out with Ann Coulter," *New York Times*, August 11, 2002.

81   "spectacles as improbable as those right-wing fanfares": I don't mean to suggest that all conservatives talk this way. Writers like William Safire and David Brooks readily acknowledge their own membership in the blue-state elite, which often lends their writing an ironic charm that's absent in the impostures of Coulter, Ingraham, and the like.

82   "To them, America's red states are populated by ignorant cowboys": "Happy Days," *Washington Times*, December 29, 2003.

82   "It is a large, lopsided horseshoe": William O'Rourke, "One's a Loser, the Other a Yahoo," *Chicago Sun-Times*, November 14, 2000.

83 "Southern politicians have been exploiting that 'redneck and proud of it' rhetoric": In fact *redneck* was being used as what linguists call a "reclaimed epithet" long before Jeff Foxworthy turned it into a bit of comic shtick, or indeed before Johnny Russell sang "Rednecks, White Socks and Blue Ribbon Beer" in 1969. The very first recorded use of the word was in a letter that appeared in the Pontotoc (Mississippi) *Democrat* on August 13, 1891, which called on "rednecks," "hayseeds," and "Yaller-heels," and others "who pay ten, twenty, thirty, etc. etc. per cent on borrowed money" to come out and vote for Ethelbert Barksdale. But the word was certainly in use well before then, and was probably coined by blacks during the Reconstruction era.

83 "In this they're no different from the middle-class socialists of Orwell's time": "The middle-class I.L.P.'er and the bearded fruit-juice drinker are all for a classless society so long as they see the proletariat through the wrong end of the telescope; force them into any real contact with a proletarian—let them get into a fight with a drunken fish-porter on Saturday night, for instance—and they are capable of swinging back to the most ordinary middle-class snobbishness." Orwell, *The Road to Wigan Pier,* p. 157.

Chapter Seven

85 "a word that encapsulates the right's rewriting": In the right's new lexicon, *elite* is no longer a collective noun restricted to groups—Ingraham writes things like "John Kerry sounded like an elite uncomfortable in the heartland." That usage may make some people wince—well, it makes me wince, anyway—but in fairness, I've seen this usage among writers on the left, as well. *Elite* seems to be going the way of other collective nouns, like *minority,* which nowadays can also denote an individual.

85 "few of the denizens of those command posts would qualify for the *elite* label": Nor do people talk as much about the "power structure" or "the establishment" as they did twenty or thirty years ago—nowadays, resentment is focused on cultural prominence, not mere power.

86 "References to the media elite or the Hollywood elite": On Fox News broadcasts since 1996, *elite* has occurred within two words of *media* 363 times, and within two words of *Hollywood* 44 times. The figures for *business* and *financial,* by contrast, are 6 and 0. As for British papers, in the left-wing *Observer,* the centrist *Independent,* and the right-wing *Telegraph, business elite* outnumbers *media elite* by roughly 3 to 1.

86   "We have two cultures": Quayle quoted in Andrew Rosenthal, "Quayle
      Attacks a 'Cultural Elite,' Saying It Mocks Nation's Values," *New York
      Times*, June 10, 1992.

86   "They know who they are": Quayle quoted in Christopher Connell,
      "Quayle Returns to Attack on 'Cultural Elite' over Abortion," AP
      Newswire, June 11, 1992.

86   "smart enough to put the elite on the national agenda": "The Newsweek
      100," *Newsweek*, October 5, 1992.

87   "the 'elite' classes that despise conservatism": Robert Bork, "The Soul of
      the Law: Judicial Hubris Wreaks Havoc, Both Here and Abroad," *Wall
      Street Journal*, January 25, 2003.

87   "Essentially, elites are defined not so much by class": Laura Ingraham,
      Shut Up and Sing (Regnery Publishing, 2003), pp. 1–2.

88   "That enables Ingraham to identify as 'elites'": Ibid., p. 12.

88   "The real loser in Tuesday's election wasn't Democrat John Kerry": Linda
      Chavez, "Down with the Elites," Townhall.com, November 3, 2004,
      http://www.townhall.com/print/print_story.php?sid=13547&loc=/opin-
      ion/columns/lindachavez/2004/11/03/13547.html.

89   "By mid-century, *populist* sounded quaint and outmoded": In 1972, C.
      Vann Woodward wrote an article in the *New York Times Magazine* called
      "The Ghost of Populism Walks Again," marveling at the way the label was
      turning up in "improbable and unaccustomed quarters."

89   "populism became something of a fashion statement": Michael Kazin,
      The Populist Persuasion: An American History (Cornell University Press,
      1998), p. 271.

90   "elitist sports like snowboarding and windsurfing": Richard Sisk, "Johnny
      Gets His Gun—and a Bird," *New York Daily News*, October 22, 2004.

90   "windsurfing is a lot more proletarian": David Colman, "Snowboarder
      Style Grows Up to Be Cool," *New York Times*, December 29, 2005.

91   "Mr. Bush is the triumph": "Broken Glass Democrats: Can Their Anger
      Overcome Bush's Normality?" *Wall Street Journal*, February 19, 2004.

91   "who could come to any suburban barbershop and fit right in": David
      Brooks, "The Triumph of Hope over Self-Interest," *New York Times*, Janu-
      ary 12, 2003.

92   "Big hat, five cattle": Warren Vieth, "Burnishing an Image at the USA Corral," *Los Angeles Times*, August 29, 2005.

92   "The quadrennial assault by the media": Molly Ivins, "Redeeming the Real Legacy of Populism," *Fort Worth Star-Telegram*, February 11, 1996.

92   "a language whose speakers conceive of ordinary people as a noble assemblage": Kazin, *The Populist Persuasion*, p. 1.

93   "Remember high school?": David Brooks, "One Nation, Slightly Divisible," *Atlantic Monthly*, December 2001.

93   "the average voter lives in a county that was close to evenly divided in the 2000 election": Philip A. Klinker, "Red and Blue Scare: The Continuing Diversity of the American Electoral Landscape," *Forum* (2)(2), Article 2, http://www.bepress.com/forum/vol2/iss2/art2.

95   "I have to ask, like who are these parents": *Hannity and Colmes,* February 7, 2003. Not long ago I heard Sean Hannity relate a news item about a Tennessee prostitute who was arrested when she was trying to knock off a cheese factory; he concluded the bit by saying, "Crime doesn't pay, nor does liberalism." I figure he had to be kidding on that one.

96   "'you liberals' outpolls 'you conservatives' by better than 7-to-1": On the Web itself, the proportion is 4-to-1 (I include "you libs" and "you cons" here). The disparity is probably due to the fact that Google Groups chiefly consists of discussions among members of the general public, many of which involve one-to-one exchanges over political issues.

96   "Republicans and Democrats think with different sides of their brains": Mary McGrory, "Dr. Foster and Mr. Dole," *Washington Post,* June 25, 1995.

97   "Kerry must be the only Democrat changing positions": "Race for the White House," Stephanie Schorow, *Boston Herald,* October 19, 2004.

98   "In 1994, I dutifully read the 'Contract with America'": George Lakoff, "Framing the Dems," *American Prospect*, September 1, 2003.

99   "I worked backward": George Lakoff, *Don't Think of an Elephant* (Chelsea Green Publishing, 2004), p. 6.

100   "But he describes 'nurturant parents' as people who don't": George Lakoff, *Moral Politics* (University of Chicago Press, 2002 [1996]), p. 109.

100   "using the idea of terminating a pregnancy as part of a cultural-war strategy": Lakoff puts these people in opposition to "pro-life progressives" who refuse to "use the question of ending pregnancy as a political wedge to

gain support for a broader moral and political agenda." Lakoff, *Don't Think of an Elephant*, p. 85.

100 "It's a far cry from the much more nuanced": Frank, *What's the Matter with Kansas?* See also Carol J.C. Maxwell, *Pro-Life Activists in America: Meaning, Motivation, and Direct Action* (Cambridge University Press, 2002); William Saletan, *Bearing Right: How Conservatives Won the Abortion War* (University of California Press, 2004).

100 "abandoned by the men who impregnated them": Maxwell, *Pro-Life Activists in America,* pp. 34–35.

101 "if people's issue positions followed from their underlying worldviews": For that matter, it's hard to see how to square this sort of explanation with the way people think about political orientations in other nations. You can easily identify groups in British politics that correspond to lower-case liberals and conservatives in the mid-twentieth-century sense of the term, but the differences don't spill over to issues like abortion and homosexuality. And the neat dualisms of American politics seem wholly irrelevant to nations with no history of a two-party system. For them, it makes more sense to identify political positions in terms of the old scale of left and right, which doesn't suggest anything more than the regions of a seating plan.

102 "that doesn't explain why people tend to go with one or the other model": True, Lakoff acknowledges that there are varieties of conservatism and progressivism, and that people may be more or less moderate in their views or in the means they're willing to accept to further their ends. Nonetheless, he says, "On the whole the right wing is attempting to impose a strict father ideology on America and, ultimately, the rest of the world. Although the details vary somewhat with the type of conservative, there are general tendencies." Lakoff, *Don't Think of an Elephant*, p. 82.

102 "States have degrees": Fulke Greville, "A Treaty of Warres," in *Selected Writings of Fulke Greville*, ed. Joan Rees (Athlone Press, 1973), p. 59.

104 "Speaking for myself, I don't need a tax cut": Glenn Kessler, "The Very Rich Pay Growing Tax Share," *Washington Post*, March 15, 2001.

104 "The phrase *tax relief* wasn't invented by the Bush White House": Bill Clinton: "This plan will show that you can balance the budget in seven years and . . . provide tax relief to working families" (Jerry Gray, "Battle over the Budget: The Overview," *New York Times*, January 8, 1996). Jimmy Carter: "Fundamental reform of our tax laws is essential and should begin now. Tax relief and the maintenance of a strong economy

are essential as well" (Robert A. Rosenblatt, "Carter's $25 Billion Tax Cut Plan Unveiled," *Los Angeles Times,* January 22, 1978). Lyndon Johnson: "We hope, in particular, to provide further tax relief to those in our nation who need it most" (John D. Pomfret, "President Vows Further Tax Cuts to Help the Poor," *New York Times*, June 22, 1965). John F. Kennedy: "Under this bill, every wage earner in the country will take home more money every week beginning January 1st. Every businessman will pay a lower tax rate. Low income families and small businessmen will get a special tax relief" (Radio Address on the Nuclear Test Ban Treaty, September 18, 1963). Harry Truman: "This is a rich man's tax relief, if I ever heard of one" (James Hagerty, "Truman Condemns Tax Plan of G.O.P. as Aid to Wealthy," *New York Times,* February 6, 1954). See also "Smith's Letter Exposing Needless Appropriations," *New York Times*, March 20, 1925.

Chapter Eight

105   "the international language of populist resentment": William Safire, "Call the Elite What They Are: Eggheads," *New York Times*, May 18, 1997.

105   "Kids today have no values": In that way *values* pretty much mirrors *standards*, which also does double duty for mores and morals: "They have different standards from ours," we say in a nonjudgmental way, but also, more judgmentally, "They have no standards anymore."

111   "the middle class is more susceptible to 'values' appeals than the working class is": Others disagree with that conclusion (in the end, it depends on how you define both "working class" and "values"). See Larry M. Bartels, "What's the Matter with *What's the Matter with Kansas?*" presentation at the annual meeting of the American Political Science Association, Washington, D.C., September 1–4, 2005, www.princeton.edu/~bartels/kansas.pdf; Jeffrey M. Stonecash, "Scaring the Democrats: What's the Matter with Thomas Frank's Argument?" *Forum* 3(3) (2005), www.bepress.com/forum/vol3/iss3/art4/; Thomas Frank, "Class Is Dismissed," www.tcfrank.com/dismissd.pdf; David Gopoian and Ralph Whitehead Jr., "Will the Real White Working Class Please Stand Up?" Emerging Democratic Majority weblog, October 27, 2005, http://www.emerging democraticmajorityweblog.com/donkeyrising/archives/001317.php.

112   "only see this manifested in costly government social programs": Karl Agne and Stanley Greenberg, "The Cultural Divide and the Challenge of

Winning Back Rural and Red State Voters," Democracy Corps report, August 9, 2005.

113   "Politics has always been as much about identity": Garance Franke-Ruta, "Heal Thy 'Self,'" *American Prospect*, December 6, 2004.

114   "middle-class Americans who are concerned about threats to Social Security": Historians have suggested that one reason Roosevelt decided to fund the program out of payroll taxes rather than paying for it out of general revenues was because that was the only way he could get Congress and the public to accept a tax increase. But Roosevelt himself said that the real reason for adopting an "insurance" model was that it promised recipients a dignity that was missing in the stigmatized notion of being "on relief" and that it would ensure that the program would have long-term popular support. As he put it, payroll contributions "give the contributors a legal, moral, and political right to collect their pensions . . . With those taxes in there, no damn politician can ever scrap my social security program." See Mark H. Leff, "Taxing the 'Forgotten Man': The Politics of Social Security Finance in the New Deal," *Journal of American History* 70 (2) (September 1983): 359–381.

114   "It does not . . . follow from the fact": Quentin Skinner, "Some Problems in the Analysis of Political Thought and Action," in James Tully, ed., *Meaning and Context: Quentin Skinner and His Critics* (Princeton University Press, 1988), p. 116.

114   "The point of political discourse": Clifford Geertz, *The Interpretation of Cultures* (Basic Books, 1973), p. 209.

115   "the two were the very same thing": The example is taken from Quentin Skinner, "Language and Social Change," in Tully, *Meaning and Context*, pp. 126–127.

115   "no sense that Democrats have a viable alternative vision": Agne and Greenberg, "The Cultural Divide and the Challenge of Winning Back Rural and Red State Voters."

115   "few middle-class voters are personally affected by more than one or two government programs": Stephen Rose, "Talking About Social Class: Are the Economic Interests of the Majority of Americans with the Democratic Party?" http://www.emergingdemocraticmajorityweblog.com/rose/rose.html. Rose notes that the number of prime-age people who directly benefit from activist state welfare policies is less than one-fourth of the population.

116 "Or you can appeal to a sense of solidarity": As Garance Franke-Ruta observes: "In today's society, traditional values have become aspirational . . . American voters have taken shelter under the various wings of conservative traditionalism because there has been no one on the Democratic side in recent years to defend traditional, sensible middle-class values against the onslaught of the new nihilistic, macho, libertarian lawlessness unleashed by an economy that pits every man against his fellows." See Franke-Ruta, "Remapping the Culture Debate," *American Prospect*, February 5, 2006.

117 "For too long Washington has rigged our system": Clinton address as governor, "On to the White House," Election Night Victory Speech, June 2, 1992.

117 "most Republicans would like to see": David Brooks, "The Democratic Party Gets a Brain—and Loses Its Mind," *Weekly Standard*, January 26, 1998.

118 "He attacked 'big tobacco, big oil, the big polluters'": John B. Judis and Ruy Teixeira, "Why Democrats Must Be Populists, And What Populist-Phobes Don't Understand About America," *American Prospect*, September 9, 2002.

119 "the achievement of U.S. business in this century": "Is Executive Pay Excessive?" *Wall Street Journal*, May 23, 1977.

119 "the new Gilded Age": Paul Krugman, "For Richer," *New York Times*, November 10, 2002.

Chapter Nine

122 "but people have also looked to government to play a constructive role": See Simon Szreter, "The State of Social Capital: Bringing Back in Power, Politics, and History," *Theory and Society* (31) (5) (October 2002): 573–621.

122 "the word *bureaucracy*": "Peril of the Nation as Mr. Cannon Sees It," *New York Times*, February 18, 1906. In newspaper articles from the turn of the twentieth century, *bureaucracy* and *bureaucratic* were used more than 80 percent of the time with reference to foreign governments. In recent times, the words are used about 80 percent of the time with reference to domestic politics.

123 "By 1976, the proportion of the public reporting that they trusted government": See Clem Brooks and David Cheng, "Declining Government Confidence and Policy Preferences in the U.S.," *Social Forces* (79)(4) (June 2001): 1343–1375.

123 "The declining trust in government": See Joseph S. Nye Jr., "In Government We Don't Trust," *Foreign Policy* (108) (Autumn 1997): 99–111. As Nye notes, the phenomenon of declining trust in government isn't uniquely American—there have been similar if less dramatic drops in confidence in other developed nations as well.

124 "The nine most terrifying words": Variants of the "I'm from the government" line were around for some time before Reagan made it his own—in 1976, Senator Edwin Muskie used a version that listed the three most commonly told lies as "I put your check in the mail yesterday," "I gave at the office," and "I'm from the federal government and I'm here to help you." Other versions of the second lie are more risqué: one relatively tame version has it as "I'll respect you as much in the morning." Muskie's line was reported in the Zanesville, Ohio, *Times Recorder*, March 7, 1976.

128 "big government alone . . . has the wisdom and compassion": "Text of Minority Report on the Civil Rights Plank," *New York Times*, July 13, 1960.

129 "That is your choice: big business or a much bigger government": "Goldwater Backs Big-Business Role," *New York Times*, May 9, 1961.

130 "Republicans have been far less likely to mention big business": Over the 1940s, "big business" was mentioned in about one-fourth of the *New York Times* articles that mentioned "big government." By the 1980s that figure was down to 10 percent, and in the 1990s it was 4 percent.

130 "it's the old story of nasty capitalists exploiting": I exclude *venture capitalist* and uses of *capitalist* as an adjective in phrases like "the capitalist system." There are some notable exceptions on the right to this generalization. William F. Buckley is fond of quoting the adage of the Austrian analyst Willi Schlamm to the effect that "The trouble with socialism is socialism. The trouble with capitalism is capitalists"—this by way of condemning the bloated compensation packages being paid modern CEOs, which Buckley describes as "shoddy" and "contemptible." William F. Buckley Jr., "Capitalism's Boil," *National Review*, April 20, 2005.

130 "If government is a steamroller": Peggy Noonan, "The Steamroller," *Wall Street Journal*, January 5, 2006.

130 "Runaway government threatens our economic survival": from Reagan's remarks at a rally supporting the Proposed Constitutional Amendment for a Balanced Federal Budget, July 19, 1982.

131 "bind together the confusions and discordances": Daniel T. Rogers, *Contested Truths: Keywords in American Politics Since Independence* (Basic Books, 1987), p. 215.

132 "True individual freedom": Fireside Chat, September 6, 1936. See Ronald Edsforth, *The New Deal* (Blackwell Publishers, 2000), p. 2.

132 "the unhindered growth of private power": Eric Foner, *The Story of American Freedom* (W. W. Norton, 1999), p. 269.

133 "it's striking how rarely they use the word *freedom*": As best I can tell, the only 2004 Democratic presidential candidate to use *economic freedom* in Roosevelt's sense was Dennis Kucinich. The phrase occurs just 19 times at the Web site of the *Nation*, and a number of those mentions involve quotations of conservatives. At the Web site of *National Review*, the phrase occurs 157 times.

134 "peaceful picketing is a contradiction in terms": "Unions and Liberty," *Wall Street Journal*, June 7, 1927.

134 "a vast system of socialized thrift": "What Price Jobs?" *Wall Street Journal*, October 4, 1943.

134 "Hitler gave full employment": "Paradox," *Wall Street Journal*, August 31, 1937.

134 "The vision of millions of women parking their kids": "Women Against Woman," *Wall Street Journal*, November 6, 1963.

134 "force a solution without waiting": "More Than Pollution," *Wall Street Journal*, January 23, 1970.

135 "confiscate revenue from firms, in effect seizing their property": Doug Bandow, "Demonizing Drugmakers: The Political Assault on the Pharmaceutical Industry," Cato Institute Report, May 8, 2003, http://www.cato.org/pubs/pas/pa–475es.html.

135 "Wal-Mart encourages uninsured employees to apply for state Medicaid": See Arindrajit Dube, Ken Jacobs, and Steve Wertheim, "Internal Wal-Mart Memo Validates Findings of UC Berkeley Study," October 26, 2005, http://laborcenter.berkeley.edu/lowwage/walmartmemo.pdf

135 "a dangerous precedent for state governments' ability": "U.S. Chamber Urges Maryland Lawmakers to Uphold Governor's Veto of Fair Share

Health Care Fund Act," U.S. Chamber of Commerce Press Release, January 9, 2006, http://www.uschamber.com/press/releases/2006/january/06–02.htm.

135 "This is the government": Limbaugh quoted in Media Matters for America, "Limbaugh Branded Maryland's Proposed Wal-Mart Bill as 'a Vestige of Fascism,'" May 23, 2005, http://mediamatters.org/items/200505230001.

136 "'Private enterprise' was replaced by 'free enterprise'": In the 1920s, *free enterprise* appeared in the *Wall Street Journal* just once; in the 1930s, 88 times; and in the 1940s, 733 times.

136 "Throughout the 1940s, conservatives insisted": Foner, *Story of American Freedom*, p. 262.

137 "Anyone who works at Wal-Mart is free to quit that job": Alan Reynolds, "Should Wal-Mart Hike Prices?" Cato Institute Report, November 25, 2005, http://www.cato.org/pub_display.php?pub_id=5221.

137 "No one is forced to work at Wal-Mart": John Semmens, "Wal-Mart: A Business We Can All Look Up To," *Capitalism Magazine*, April 3, 2005, http://www.capmag.com/article.asp?ID=4185.

138 "It's a free country": Paul Jacob, "The Freedom to Hate Wal-Mart," Townhill.com, November, 20, 2005, http://www.townhall.com/opinion/columns/pauljacob/2005/11/20/176217.html.

138 "this is nothing but the nineteenth-century argument": Foner, *Story of American Freedom*, p. 123.

139 "aren't unduly respectful of free choice": William Murchison, "The War on Wal-Mart," *Washington Times*, April 14, 2005.

141 "greater peace of mind": "President Discusses New Medicare Prescription Drug Benefit," White House News Release, June 16, 2005, http://www.whitehouse.gov/news/releases/2005/08/20050829–11.html.

141 "too complicated and confusing": David Wessel, "Medicare Drug-Coverage Message Is Mixed," *Wall Street Journal*, January 5, 2006.

141 "When you give people choice and options": Ricardo Alonso-Zaldivar, "Bush Admits Drug Plan Can Be Daunting," *Los Angeles Times*, December 14, 2005.

141 "Health care is complicated": Robert Pear, "Confusion Is Rife About Drug Plan as Sign-Up Nears," *New York Times*, November 13, 2005.

143 "it's likely that millions of Americans believe": Cass R. Sunstein, *The Second Bill of Rights: FDR's Unfinished Revolution and Why We Need It More Than Ever* (Basic Books, 2004), p. 5.

143 "no distinctions between those who bought flood insurance and those who didn't": T. J. Walker, "The President from New Orleans, a Scorecard," *National Review Online*, September 16, 2005, http://www.national-review.com/comment/walker200509160841.asp.

144 "make people ashamed of generous social impulses": "The Philosophical 'New Conservatism,'" in Bell, *The Radical Right*, p. 164.

144 "so destroyed wealth and self-reliance": David Boaz, "Catastrophe in Big Easy Demonstrates Big Government's Failure," Cato Institute Report, September 19, 2005, http://www.cato.org/pub_display.php?pub_id=4819.

144 "If big government has failed": Cal Thomas on *Fox News Watch,* September 17, 2005.

144 "government is extremely limited in what it can effectively do": David Brooks, "The Bursting Point," *New York Times*, September 4, 2005.

146 "the largest corruption scandal since Warren Harding": Paul Krugman, "The K Street Prescription," *New York Times*, January 20, 2006.

147 "a substantial majority of voters . . . believe that government regulation": See Stanley Greenberg, *The Two Americas* (St. Martin's Press, 2004), Appendices B, C, D.

147 "Whose side is government on?": E. J. Dionne, *Stand Up and Fight Back: Republican Toughs, Democratic Wimps, and the Politics of Revenge* (Simon and Schuster, 2004), p. 200.

148 "The United States continues to live": Cass Sunstein, *The Second Bill of Rights: FDR's Unfinished Revolution and Why We Need It More than Ever*, p. 3.

Chapter Ten

151 "So far all we hear is a lot of old bitterness and partisan anger": "Bush Takes on Critics," CNN report, February 24, 2004, http://www.cnn.com/2004/ALLPOLITICS/02/23/elec04.prez.bush/.

151 "The kind of words we're hearing now": Jennifer Harper, "The Mean of Dean," *Washington Times*, December 2, 2003.

151   "plagued by 'inner doubts about their own moral position'": "It's possible, we've witnessed, to assert moral superiority while defending the Clinton perjury, sexual escapades, vanishing billing records and last-minute pardons. But politicians, pundits and intellectuals with this record shouldn't expect much moral deference from the rest of us. Indeed, inner doubts about their own moral position is one obvious path to anger." Robert L. Bartley, "Angry Democrats: Lost Birthright," *Wall Street Journal*, September 22, 2003.

153   "In the early decades of the twentieth century": *Negro* has actually been through this process twice. It was a standard term for Americans of African descent until emancipation, when many of them rejected it (along with *black*) as part of the vocabulary of slavery, opting for *colored* instead. Its revival in the early twentieth century was championed by W.E.B. DuBois and the NAACP, who led a campaign to get newspapers to capitalize the word, a practice the *New York Times* adopted in 1930.

153   "Justice John Marshall Harlan's 1896 affirmation": Harlan didn't invent the use of *color-blind* in its racial sense—it was used as early as 1864 by the abolitionist Wendell Phillips.

154   "the *New York Times*'s Arthur Daley applauded": Arthur Daley, "Sports of the Times," *New York Times*, November 23, 1949.

154   "The phrase never appeared in the editorials of the *Wall Street Journal*": "Some Racial Facts and Fallacies," *Wall Street Journal*, March 25, 1960.

154   "The paper first used *color-blind*": In fact *color-blind* occurred a few years earlier in a 1963 editorial that quoted President Kennedy when he cited Harlan's opinion and said that "the practices of the country do not always conform to the principles of the Constitution," a remark in which the *Journal* discerned "a disturbing thread of apology," adding that "instead of castigating the American people for failure, the government might ask where is the country today which has eliminated discrimination."

154   "Since then the *Journal* has used the phrase in editorials about fifty times": Nowadays *color-blind* is used almost exclusively by conservatives; it is fifty times as likely to appear in *National Review* as in the *Nation*, and when it does appear in the latter, it's likely to be in quotes.

156   "racial preferences that might otherwise leave people vulnerable to charges of racism and sexism": Some have suggested that white resistance to affirmative action is less a consequence of residual racism than of economic factors or a growing disenchantment with the welfare state and liberal policies. But in a review of the survey literature, David Sears and his col-

leagues conclude that "symbolic racism" is by far the most significant factor in shaping white attitudes toward these programs. See David O. Sears, Colette Van Laar, Mary Carrillo, and Rick Kosterman, "Is It Really Racism?: The Origins of White Americans' Opposition to Race-Targeted Policies," *Public Opinion Quarterly* (61) (1) (Spring 1997): 16–53.

156   "What Justice John Paul Stevens was pointing to": John Paul Stevens, dissenting in *Adarand v. Peña,* 515 U.S. 200 (1995).

156   "But the quotation, like conservatives' memory, is selective": "It is impossible to create a formula for the future which does not take into account that our society has been doing something special against the Negro for hundreds of years. How then can he be absorbed into the mainstream of American life if we do not do something special for him now in order to balance the equation . . . ?" Martin Luther King, *Why We Can't Wait* (Signet, 2000 [1964]), p. 124.

157   "Whatever their views on racial preferences": A 2005 Pew study found that only 31 percent of whites said that racial discrimination was rare, fewer than said the same thing in 1987. And in recent years, there has been a decline in the number of whites who say that "we have gone too far in pushing equal rights in this country," http://people-press.org/reports/display.php3?PageID=757.

157   "And while conservatives have scored points with their calls for 'color-blind' policies": In recent years, the concept of "diversity" has been sharply attacked in books and articles by James Lynch, Roger Clegg, and Peter Wood that have been influential in conservative circles. Wood argues, for example, that "diversity" has become "a rubric for racial and ethnic quotas in college admissions and on the job . . . and for a system of ethnic favoritism that undercuts the principle of rewarding demonstrated merit and ability" and says that the emphasis on diversity promotes "a feeling that group identity is somehow more substantial and powerful than either our individuality or our common humanity." As a result, he says, the diversity movement has not simply contributed to falling educational performance, but has "undermined love of country (by elevating racial separatism); trivialized art (by emphasizing the social identity of the artist, e.g. Toni Morrison); and made certain forms of racialism respectable again." Wood is right to say that "diversity" has become a vague and elastic symbol, but he takes that as a justification for tarring all its meanings with the same brush, linking diversity programs in college admissions and corporate hiring with academic and artistic squabbles over multiculturalism and identity politics. In fact it's fair to say that most of those parochial

imbroglios would have no impact on the public if conservative critics weren't always making them into *causes célèbres*—over the past five years, Fox News programs have mentioned "multiculturalism" more often than the news shows of all three broadcast networks combined. Peter Wood, *Diversity: The Invention of a Concept* (Encounter Books, 2004).

157   "I strongly support diversity of all kinds": Ellen Nakashima and Al Kamen, "Bush Picks as Diverse as Clinton's," *Washington Post*, March 30, 2001.

157   "And while most white voters oppose giving 'preferential treatment'": In a 2003 Pew survey, 63 percent of respondents said they favored affirmative action programs designed to help blacks, women, and other minorities get better jobs and education. But opinions about these programs often swing wildly depending on how they're described. In a 2003 Pew survey, 57 percent of respondents said they favor programs that "give special preference to qualified blacks, women, and other minorities in hiring and education," whereas only 24 percent favored "giving preferential treatment" to blacks and other minorities to improve their position.

157   "And while the details of the programs are still controversial": The press talked about "racial quotas" four times as often during the George H.W. Bush presidency as during his son's first term.

158   "whom the right has recast as a conservative icon": It's notable that many of the most vociferous opponents of these programs on the right are themselves former liberals or radicals like David Horowitz and the Thernstroms. Ignazio Silone once said that the final conflict would be between the Communists and the ex-Communists, but for eschatological purposes, liberals turn out to do just as well.

158   "As William Bennett puts it": William J. Bennett, "The Conservative Virtues of Dr. Martin Luther King," Heritage Foundation Lecture, November 5, 1993, http://www.heritage.org/Research/AmericanFoundingandHistory/HL481.cfm.

158   "On King's birthday in 2006": "A Credit to Their Racism," *Opinion Journal*'s Political Diary, January 18, 2006, http://www.opinionjournal.com/politicaldiary/?id=110007896.

158   "degenerated into a collection of political extremists": "King's 'Dream' Becomes a Nightmare," Accuracy in Media Report, http://www.aim.org/aim_report/A114_0_4_0_C/sendpage/sendpage/index.php

159 "Catholics need not apply": "Right-Wing Religious McCarthyism," *People for the American Way,* September 25, 2003, http://www.pfaw.org/pfaw/general/default.aspx?oid=10838.

159 "The Family Research Council has equated": Scott Shepherd, "Religious Right in Senate Fight; GOP Leader Paints Filibuster by Democrats as Anti-Religious," *Atlanta Journal-Constitution,* April 16, 2005.

159 "John Ashcroft now knows what it feels like to be a Jew": Michael Ledeen, "The Old Dual-Loyalty Game," *National Review,* June 19, 2001.

160 "who wouldn't see anything 'anti-Christian' in the company's diversity policies themselves": In the same way, the right justifies including Intelligent Design in the school curriculum by invoking "academic freedom." As George Bush put the argument, "I felt like both sides ought to be properly taught. I think that part of education is to expose people to different schools of thought." (The media lend credence to that view of the debate when they refer to Intelligent Design or creationism as "theories"—not a description they would use for the biblical account of creation, even though all of them rely on exactly the same causal mechanism.) That approach has won broad support for teaching Intelligent Design even among those who believe in evolution. Whatever scientists and the courts may say, most people don't see Intelligent Design as an effort to impose a religious curriculum in the schools. Joe Garofoli, "Bush Pushes Very Hot Button: President's Comments Embolden Anti-Evolutionists," *San Francisco Chronicle,* August 8, 2005.

160 "banning the Declaration of Independence because it mentions God": No, said the Plano, Texas, Independent School District, we didn't bar students from wearing green and red to school during the Christmas season, as O'Reilly reported. And after Jerry Falwell denounced a Wisconsin school for changing the lyrics of "Silent Night" to "Cold in the Night," a charge repeated on Fox and MSNBC, the *Washington Post* reported that the offending carol was sung by a tree in a school play called "The Little Tree's Christmas Gift," written by the music director at Ronald Reagan's former church, which was performed along with "Angels, We Have Heard on High" and other Christmas songs. As for the school that banned the Declaration of Independence, the incident turned out to involve a teacher who had given students a handout entitled, "What Great Leaders Have Said About the Bible," which included not just a passage from the Declaration of Independence, but quotations from Jesus Christ. See "'Red and Green Clothing Ban' False Rumor," Plano Independent School District Press Release, December 12, 2005, http://www.pisd.edu/news/archive/

2005–06/oreilly.report.shtml; Neely Tucker, "Have a Holly, Jolly Holiday," *Washington Post*, December 20, 2005; and Joe Garofoli, "Battle over God in U.S. History Class," *San Francisco Chronicle*, December 8, 2005.

160   "insulting to Christian America": Dickens's characters wished each other "Season's Greetings" or "Greetings of the Season," in the absence of anyone who would hold their secularist feet to the fire.

161   "That's an old charge": See Michelle Goldberg, "How the Secular Humanist Grinch Didn't Steal Christmas," *Salon*, November 21, 2005, http://www.salon.com/news/feature/2005/11/21/christmas/index_np.html.

161   "But Ford and the Birchers were regarded as wingnuts": To their credit, some conservatives found the "Happy Holidays" brouhaha offensive to the real spirit of the season. Cal Thomas wrote, "The effort by some cable TV hosts and ministers to force commercial establishments into wishing everyone a 'Merry Christmas' might be more objectionable to the One who is the reason for the season than the 'Happy Holidays' mantra required by some store managers" ("Not So Silent Night," Townhall.com, December 13, 2005). And *National Review*'s Jonah Goldberg wrote that "[j]ust as it is counterproductive for a secular liberal to take offense at a well-intentioned 'Merry Christmas,' it doesn't help if a conservative says 'Merry Christmas' when he really means 'Eat yuletide, you atheistic bastard!' If you're putting up a Christmas tree in order to tick off the ACLU, you've really missed the point." Jonah Goldberg, "Eat Yuletide, You Atheistic Bastard!" *National Review*, December 2, 2005.

161   "An August 2005 survey by the Pew Research Center": "Religion a Strength and Weakness for Both Parties," Pew Research Center report, August 30, 2005, http://people-press.org/reports/display.php3?ReportID=254. The report showed that even among Democrats, the proportion describing their party as friendly to religion had dropped by 10 percent over the past two years. By contrast, the percentage of respondents who said that the Republicans were friendly to religion had held steady at 55 percent over the same period.

162   "Often, in fact, the word is merely a synonym for 'liberal atheists'": Jonathan Aitken, "Narnia Triumphant," *American Spectator*, February 2006; Larry Kudlow, "The Bush Exit Demo," *National Review Online*, November 16, 2000, http://www.nationalreview.com/kudlow/kudlow111600.shtml; Tom Minnery, "Our Befuddling Nation," http://www.family.org/cforum/citizenmag/departments/a0036385.cfm.

162 "As Bruce Bawer notes": Bruce Bawer, *Stealing Jesus: How Fundamentalism Betrays Christianity* (Three Rivers Press, 1998), p. 5.

162 "The exclusionary use of *Christian* is ubiquitous nowadays": Things have gotten to the point where the Catholic writer Andrew Greeley is obliged to explain in a Chicago *Sun-Times* op-ed that "I use the word 'Christian' in an extended sense and not in the sense of the Bible Christians for whom most of the rest of us who follow Jesus of Nazareth are not really Christians . . . " ("We Don't Have to Take Christmas Back—No One Took It Away," *Chicago Sun-Times,* December 31, 2004).

162 "a category that it later identifies as "mainstream audiences": John Leland, "Praise God and Pass the Music Files," *New York Times*, April 25, 2004; Colleen O'Connor, "God or Fantasy?" *Denver Post*, November 20, 2005.

163 "And when the media talk about 'the Christian right'": In this sense, *Christian* has become what linguists call an "autohyponym," a word that can refer to both a class and one of its subclasses. In its broad sense, for example, *Asian* can refer to Iranians, Pakistanis, and even Israelis, but people often use the word as a synonym for what used to be called "Orientals," as in "Asians tend to be lactose-intolerant."

163 "And there's the same implication": David Limbaugh, *Persecution, Regnery 2003*; Bill Johnson, quoted in Pete Winn, "The 'Overgaying' of America," Citizen Link (Focus on the Family Web site), http://www.family.org/cfo-rum/feature/a0027430.cfm.

163 "*people of faith,* which first became popular about twenty-five years ago": *People of faith* has been around for a long time, but until recently it was merely an orotund tribute appropriate to sermons and commencement addresses, without any strong religious force. "I salute you as people of faith, vigor, virility, and intelligence," Columbia University's president Dwight D. Eisenhower told graduates in 1950.

164 "Martin Luther King was a conservative": Carolyn Garris, "Martin Luther King's Conservative Legacy," Heritage Foundation WebMemo No. 961, http://www.heritage.org/Research/AmericanFoundingandHistory/wm961.cfm.

164 "Democrats should use the Bible to advance their arguments": Carville and Begala, *Take It Back,* p. 75; David R. Guarino, "Hill at Tufts: Use Bible to Guide Poverty Policy," *Boston Herald*, November 11, 2004.

165 "For the scripturally challenged": By way of demonstrating Democratic bona fides on religion, Democratic legislators in Alabama and Georgia recently introduced legislation that would permit optional Bible literacy courses in public schools. The problem is real—a recent Gallup poll found that fewer than half of teenagers knew that the Bible says Jesus turned water into wine at a wedding, and two-thirds couldn't explain the significance of the road to Damascus; in fact, born-again and evangelical teenagers did only slightly better than the others. But it's hard to see how school districts will come up with neutral guidelines for courses in Bible literacy when even the biology curriculum is enmeshed in cultural politics. In fact the "nonpartisan" Bible Literacy Project, which has been promoting these efforts, has close ties to the religious right.

165 "Tucker Carlson accused Pelosi of 'all but speaking in tongues'": Tucker Carlson on *Crossfire*, November 9, 2004; Kathleen Parker, "Can Liberal Democrats Fake Religion?" *Charleston Daily Mail*, November 18, 2004.

166 "Democrats can give as well as they get": The 2005 Pew poll, "Religion a Strength and Weakness for Both Parties," found that by a 52–30 percent margin, the Democratic Party is perceived as most concerned with protecting the freedom of citizens to make personal choices.

166 "the amendment's sponsor, Wisconsin Democrat David Obey": M. E. Sprengelmeyer, "A Holy War in D.C.," *Rocky Mountain News*, June 21, 2005.

167 "The 2005 Pew survey showed that half of Americans": Catholics also believe by 3-to-1 that it is improper for the church to deny communion to politicians who support abortion rights.

167 "as Jim Wallis puts it in *God's Politics*": Jim Wallis, *God's Politics* (Harper, 2005), p. 3.

167 "What's striking about the perception of the Democrats as faith-unfriendly": As Carville and Begala point out, the perception of the Democrats as faith-unfriendly is also a result of their hesitance about moving the conversation from cultural issues where they don't have wide support, like gay marriage, to those where they do, like federal legislation to ban employment discrimination against gays. A recent Gallup survey showed that 85 percent of Americans believe in equal opportunity for gay people in the workplace, up from 59 percent in 1982. "Public Polling Shows Strong Support for Employment Non-Discrimination Act," Human Rights Campaign, http://www.hrc.org/Content/NavigationMenu/HRC/ Get_Informed/Federal_Legislation/Employment_Non-Discrimina-

tion_Act/Background_Information/Public_Polls_Show_Strong_Support_for_ENDA.htm.

167 "when only 1-in-6 Americans sees Hollywood": In a 2004 Pew survey, 18 percent of respondents believed that the academics were friendly to religion, and only 16 percent said the same thing of the media and Hollywood.

Chapter 11

170 "In a speech in 1969 that became an instant sensation": Speech delivered on November 13, 1969, at "Spiro Theodore Agnew: Television News Coverage," http://www.americanrhetoric.com/speeches/spiroagnew.htm.

170 "Over the first four years of the Clinton presidency": Another, more detailed study found that complaints about media bias more than doubled between 1988 and 1996, and that the proportion of these claiming liberal bias remained around 95 percent. David Domke, Mark D. Watts, Dhavan V. Shah, and David P. Fan, "The Politics of Conservative Elites and the 'Liberal Media' Argument," *Journal of Communication* (49) (4) (Autumn 1999).

171 "As the media's reports of the conservative charges increased": Ibid. In a Rasmussen poll conducted during the 2004 campaign, more than 60 percent of voters thought the broadcast networks were biased, with about three out of four of that group saying that the coverage was aimed at helping Kerry. "Voters See All Networks with Bias," *Rasmussen Reports,* September 19, 2004, http://www.rasmussenreports.com/Broadcast%20Bias.htm.

171 "And research showed that those increases were direct responses": See Mark D. Watts, David Domke, Dhavan V. Shaw, David P. Fan, "Explaining Public Perceptions of a Liberal Press," *Communication Research* (26) (2) (1999): 144–175.

171 "The charges of liberal bias have been so widely and insistently repeated": "Bernie Non Grata," *Wall Street Journal,* January 2, 2002. Jonah Goldberg, "Goldberg Variations," *National Review Online,* December 3, 2001, http://www.nationalreview.com/goldberg/goldberg120301.shtml; Bernard Goldberg, *Bias* (Regnery Publishing, 2002), p. 213.

171 "Let's suppose that I'm dead wrong in my book": Bernard Goldberg, quoted in Eric Alterman, *What Liberal Media?* (Basic Books, 2003), p. 13.

172 "There is a perception on the part of millions of Americans that the network news is liberal": *The O'Reilly Factor,* April 12, 2001.

172 "explaining the success of Fox News, its CEO, Roger Ailes, says": Ken Auletta, "How Roger Ailes and Fox News Are Changing Cable News," *New Yorker,* May 26, 2003.

172 "Rich Bond, the Republican National Committee chairman": quoted in Alterman, *What Liberal Media?* p. 13.

173 "Alterman, David Brock, Trudy Lieberman, and others": In addition to the books by those three, see, for example, Franklin Foer, "Kid Gloves," *New Republic Online,* May 8, 2001, http://www.tnr.com/express/foer050801.html; John F. Harris, "Mr. Bush Catches a Washington Break," *Washington Post,* May 6, 2001; and numerous postings at MediaMatters.org, FAIR.org, and Bob Somersby's DailyHowler.com.

173 "I'm not going to address the 'torture' word": Defense Department Briefing, Federal News Service, May 4, 2004.

173 "the Abu Ghraib horseplay": John Derbyshire on "The Corner," *National Review Online,* January 29, 2005, http://www.nationalreview.com/thecorner/05_01_23_corner-archive.asp.

173 "Torture is torture": Interview with Colin Powell, *Fox News Sunday,* May 16, 2004.

173 "however much soul-searching mainstream journalists do to answer": Conservatives' criticisms of the media have had some postitive outcomes in the form of increased efforts to cover the religious right and the conservative movement in general. With some fanfare, in January 2004, the *New York Times* established a "conservative beat." Some conservatives found the whole business condescending—"case-closed on any question that the eds there think conservatives are an alien species," as *National Review*'s Kathryn Lopez put it—but others had praise for some of the articles. See Kathryn Lopez, posting in Crunchy Cons blog, March 11, 2004, http://crunchycon.nationalreview.com; Terry Eastland, "The Times's Conservative Problem," *Weekly Standard Online,* March 3, 2004, http://www.weeklystandard.com/Content/Public/Articles/000/000/003/785cjtka.asp?pg=1.

173 "They have nothing to say about the media's 'showbizification'": For a concise summary of these issues, see Hacker and Pierson, *Off Center,* pp. 174–181, as well as the discussions in Alterman, *What Liberal Media?* and James Fallows, *Breaking the News* (Vintage Books, 1997).

174 "They discern bias whenever the media report anything that might cast Republicans": All of these are drawn from postings by the Media Research Center at http://www.mrc.org.

174 "Hofstadter made it clear, he wasn't speaking of a pathology": Richard Hofstadter, "The Paranoid Style in American Politics," *Harper's Magazine*, November 1964.

175 "Back in 1894, the newly formed United Press": "The United Press's New Ally," *New York Times,* December 4, 1894. This was not, I believe, the direct ancestor of the United Press that later became part of UPI.

176 "the American press was not free": "Address by Secretary Ickes Before National Lawyers Guild," *New York Times*, February 11, 1939.

177 "[M]embers of the media argued that while personally liberal": Brent Bozell, "Media Bias Basics," Media Research Center, November 2004, http://www.mrc.org/inthenews/2004/news1104.asp.

178 "Or as Michael Kelley put the point": Michael Kelley, "Left Eternal," *Washington Post*, December 18, 2002.

178 "But conservatives square that circle by falling back on": Some conservative writers come down resolutely on both sides of that question. Disparaging what he sees as the wide influence of academic postmodernism, Jonah Goldberg writes sarcastically: "For lots of Americans, the idea that there are no objective standards of truth or morality is incredibly sophisticated and intelligent." But when it comes to talking about Dan Rather, Goldberg discovers a vein of skepticism: "One needn't be a postmodern relativist to understand that journalistic objectivity—the ideal of reporting the facts without prejudice or favor—is an unattainable goal." See Jonah Goldberg, "Dangerous Ideas," *National Review Online,* July 8, 2002, http://www.nationalreview.com/goldberg/goldberg070802.asp; Jonah Goldberg, "The Big I Retires: The Problem with Dan Rather," *National Review Online,* March 11, 2005, http://www.nationalreview.com/goldberg/goldberg200503110750.

178 "From that it follows that the only way to counter liberal bias": This is the same technique the right uses to prove the leftist bias of the academy, on the assumption that they can determine what's going on in the classroom simply by looking at the voter-registration rolls.

179 "As Thomas Sowell puts it": Thomas Sowell, "Media Bias on Media Bias," *Capitalism Magazine,* December 5, 2002, http://www.capmag.com/articlePrint.asp?ID=2214. The conservative blogger Hugh Hewitt makes a

similar point, arguing that the "old media" have been losing their audience because they won't come clean about their liberal bias: "The blogosphere is intensely partisan—just as old media has been. But, unlike the old media, there is truth in advertising on the Internet. This is a significant advantage going forward in the competition for credibility and trust. If old media does not develop tolerance for the majoritarian points of view in the United States, it will continue to decline in reach and authority." Hugh Hewitt, "Asymmetrical Tolerance and the Collapse of Big Media Credibility: How 2004 Brought Doom to Legacy Media," *Weekly Standard Online,* http://www.weeklystandard.com/Content/Public/Articles/000/000/005/087nhhbq.asp?pg=2.

179   "the *Wall Street Journal's* Robert Bartley made the same point": Robert Bartley, "The Press: Time for a New Era? The BBC and New York Times Scandals Show That 'Objectivity' Is Dead," *Opinion Journal,* July 28, 2003, http://www.opinionjournal.com/columnists/rbartley/?id=110003806.

179   "In his history of the development of the concept of journalistic objectivity": David Mindich, *Just the Facts* (New York University Press, 1998). What I am calling "attention to facts" is a rough paraphrase of what Mindich calls "facticity" and Michael Schudson calls "naïve empiricism"; see Michael Schudson, *Discovering the News: A Social History of American Newspapers* (Basic Books, 1978).

180   "Bias is a way of reading": The philosopher Albert Jordan defined bias a lot more elegantly a century ago as "that attribute of the mind which causes it to accept as true, on relatively slight evidence, that which agrees with its sympathies, and to reject or minimise that which is opposed to its sympathies, although the evidence be relatively strong" ("The Bias of Patriotism," *International Journal of Ethics,* October 1904).

181   "A 2003 study by the University of Maryland's Program on International Policy Attitudes": "Misperceptions, the Media and the Iraq War," PIPA/Knowledge Networks Study, October 2, 2003, http://www.worldpublicopinion.org/pipa/articles/international_security_bt/102.php?nid=&id=&pnt=102&lb=brusc.

181   "And as people tend increasingly to choose news sources": Since 2000, the audiences for Fox News and CNN have become more Republican and Democratic, respectively. "The Media: More Voices, Less Credibility," Pew Research Center report, January 25, 2005, http://people-press.org/commentary/display.php3?AnalysisID=105.

182 "Writers like Chris Mooney, John Judis, and Michael Specter": Chris Mooney, *The Republican War on Science* (Basic Books, 2005); John B. Judis, "NOAA's Flood: The Government's Junk Science," *New Republic*, February 20, 2006; Michael Specter, "Political Science: The Bush Administration's War on the Laboratory," *New Yorker*, March 13, 2006.

182 "a lot of conservatives consider themselves bound by principle": A 2005 ABC/*Washington Post* poll, for example, found a 27 percent difference between Democrats and Republicans as to whether global warming was a reality. It's true of course that Democrats are no better positioned than most Republicans to evaluate the claim, but their views merely reflect the scientific consensus—the disparity is the result of the Republicans' politicization of the issue. In fact, the views of independents tend to be much closer to those of the Democrats than those of the Republicans; for example, the proposition that global warming was underway was accepted by 69 percent of Democrats and 64 percent of independents, but by only 42 percent of Republicans. Jon Cohen and Gary Langer, "Many See No Need to Worry About Warming," *ABC News*, http://abcnews.go.com/Technology/PollVault/story?id=850438.

182 "It's another to deny the existence of global warning": Conservatives have sometimes tried to justify the administration's rejection of scientific consensus by claiming that the scientific community is subject to the same kind of bias as the press. Sally Satel, a resident scholar at the American Enterprise Institute, writes that "[i]t is common knowledge that academic experts in behavioral and public health and the environmental sciences are, on average, left-leaning. So the opportunities for conflict between a conservative administration and left-of-center academics are greater than under liberal political leadership. But that doesn't mean science is any more politicized now than before; it is just that more researchers disagree with the decisions made." Sally Satel, "Is the GOP the Elephant in the Laboratory?" *Weekly Standard*, October 31, 2005.

182 "Chris Mooney points out, for example": Mooney, *The Republican War on Science*, p. 8.

183 "Contrary to what Goldberg claimed": Details of my study can be found at "Label Whores," *American Prospect Online*, May 6, 2002, http://www.prospect.org/print/V13/8/nunberg-g.html. The other claims that the right has made about partisan labeling fare no better than Goldberg's. Sometimes they are too selective in the labels they look at. Several conservatives have charged, for example, that the networks more often label Republicans as "far right" or "hard right" than they label Democrats as

"far left" or "hard left." That's actually true, but the disparities vanish when you throw in other terms like "leftist." Or sometimes the critics seem to give no evidence of having taken Statistics 101. In one study, for example, the Media Research Center announced that on network newscasts, the conservative label was applied to Supreme Court justices twice as often as the liberal label was. What they neglected to note was that conservative Supreme Court justices were actually mentioned in broadcasts six times as often as liberals were. (That's like saying that Ray Durham hit four times as many home runs as Barry Bonds in 2005 without noting that Durham had twelve times as many plate appearances.) When you take that discrepancy into account, it turns out that the average liberal justice was actually three times *more* likely to be given a label than the average conservative was. See Geoffrey Nunberg, "Another Party Heard From," June 28, 2002, http://www-csli.stanford.edu/~nunberg/MRC.html.

184   "In the counts I did in 2002": The same pattern is reflected with other names: the Heritage Foundation is labeled conservative almost three times more often than the less well known Competitive Enterprise Institute, and Nancy Pelosi was tagged much more frequently *after* she was named House minority leader and became a national poster child for latte liberalism.

Chapter 12

187   "Right now," said the *St. Louis Post-Dispatch*": Wayne Fields, "E Pluribus Unum," *St. Louis Post-Dispatch*, September 19, 2001; Joseph Perkins, "Americans First," *San Diego Union-Tribune*, October 5, 2001; "Battle Is Joined; U.S. Must Do Everything Necessary to Win," *Columbus Dispatch*, September 13, 2001.

188   "Ramesh Ponnuru said that "civilized people": Ramesh Ponnuru, "The Uses of War," *National Review*, September 14, 2001; Rod Dreher, "Citizens," *National Review*, September 16, 2001.

188   "The left also renounced its extremists": Todd Gitlin, "Blaming America First," *Mother Jones*, January 2002; Michael Walzer, "Can There Be a Decent Left?" *Dissent*, Spring 2002.

188   "George Packer said that 'Sept. 11 made it safe for liberals to be patriots'": George Packer, "Recapturing the Flag," *New York Times Sunday Magazine*, September 20, 2001.

188   "Todd Gitlin explained that he had hung a flag": Ed Vulliamy, "Waving Not Drowning," *Observer*, September 23, 2001.

188   "What was needed, Alan Wolfe said": Alan Wolfe, "Linked at Last," *Boston Globe*, October 7, 2001.

189   "John O'Sullivan wrote in early October": John O'Sullivan, "Their Amerika," *National Review*, October 4, 2001.

189   "In the *Boston Herald*, before the casualty figures were even known": Don Feder, "Left Unfurls Cynicism at Old Glory," *Boston Herald*, October 17, 2001.

189   "For David Brooks, the ubiquity of American flags": David Brooks, "Normal, U.S.A.: Amidst the Terror, We're Turning Back to the Attitudes That Made America Great," *Daily Standard*, October 5, 2001; Tom Adkins, "Terror Attacks Against America Cast a Pall over Liberal Worldview," *Insight on the News*, October 29, 2001.

189   Noemie Emery, "Look Who's Waving the Flag Now," *Weekly Standard*, October 15, 2001.

189   "As Martha Nussbaum has put it": Martha Nussbaum, *For Love of Country* (Beacon Press, 1996), p. 4.

190   "In their survey of the American conservative movement": John Micklethwait and Adrian Wooldridge, *The Right Nation* (Penguin, 2004).

190   "A writer in the French *Le Figaro*": Jean-Christophe Buisson, "L'Amérique, a-t-elle la rage?" *Le Figaro Magazine*, March 4, 2006.

190   "In polls both before and after 9/11": "Polls on Patriotism and Military Service," American Enterprise Institute Studies in Public Opinion, June 30, 2005, http://www.aei.org/publicopinion9.

191   "When Democrats objected to provisions": "One Step Closer to a Secure U.S.," New York *Daily News*, November 19, 2002; "Pols and Politics," *Boston Herald*, November 17, 2002.

192   "According to the *Wall Street Journal*'s James Taranto": James Taranto, "The Democrats' Patriotism Problem," Opinion Journal, August 30, 2004, http://www.opinionjournal.com/pl/?id=110005545. Jonah Goldberg, "A Question of Patriotism," *National Review Online*, April 21, 2004.

192   "But the message was clear": Joshua Chaffin and James Harding, "Bush on Back Foot over Missing Iraqi Explosives," *Financial Times*, October 29, 2004; Bryan Bender, "Bush Aides Downplay Bremer View on Troops," *Boston Globe*, October 6, 2004.

192   "After Kerry quipped during the primary season that America needed a 'regime change'": Glen Johnson, "Republicans Denounce Kerry over

Remark," *Boston Globe*, April 4, 2003; Paul Krugman, "The Last Refuge," *New York Times*, April 8, 2003.

193   "the current Republican National Committee chairman Ken Mehlman said": *Meet the Press*, November 13, 2005.

193   "Texas Senator John Cornyn charged that the Democrats' criticisms": *Lou Dobbs Tonight*, CNN, October 25, 2005.

193   "Conservative talk show hosts and commentators have been even less re-strained": Reagan and Limbaugh quoted in BPhillips's C-Log, Townhall.com, December 6, 2005, http://www.townhall.com/blogs/c-log/BPhillips/story/2005/12/06/178031.html; R. Emmett Tyrrell Jr., "The Wages of Hatred," *American Spectator*, December 1, 2004; Ann Coulter, "New Idea for Abortion Party: Aid the Enemy," Townhall.com, November 24, 2005. http://www.townhall.com/opinion/columns/anncoulter/2005/11/24/176727.html.

195   "During the primary season": Graham in CNBC/WSJ Democratic Presidential Debate, September 25, 2003, http://msnbc.msn.com/id/3088203/; Clark in Richard Cohen, "Karl Rove's Nightmare," *Washington Post*, January 15, 2004; Kerry in Robert Kuttner, "The Privileged Act Worried," *Boston Globe*, January 29, 2005 and Glen Johnson, "Barbs Are Exchanged Over Military Service," *Boston Globe*, April 17, 2004.

195   "As the *Wall Street Journal*'s Taranto observed": James Taranto, "The Democrats' Patriotism Problem," *Wall Street Journal* online, August 30, 2004, http://www.opinionjournal.com/pl/?id=110005545.

196   "There's a curious Lake Wobegon effect": Karlyn H. Bowman and Bryan O'Keefe, "Polls on Patriotism and Military Service," American Enterprise Institute Report, June 28, 2005, http://www.aei.org/publications/pubID.14889/pub_detail.asp.

197   "To wear an American flag in your lapel": Peggy Noonan, "President Backbone," *Wall Street Journal*, April 7, 2003.

197   "These days, says John O'Sullivan": John O'Sullivan, "Their Amerika," *National Review*, October 1, 2001.

197   "In Texas, we don't do nuance": Richard Cohen, "Bush's War Against Nuance," *Washington Post*, February 17, 2004.

198   "And when Kerry called for a "more sensitive" war on terrorism": Dan Balz and Mark Leibovich, "GOP Assails Kerry's Call for 'Sensitive' War," *Washington Post*, August 13, 2004.

198 "I have not got a clue about Springsteen's politics": George Will, "Bruce Springsteen's Politics," *Washington Post*, September 13, 1984.

198 "The founder of the Hummer Owners Group": Danny Hakim, "In Their Hummers, Right Beside Uncle Sam," *New York Times*, April 5, 2003.

Chapter 13

202 "In an April 2006 *Washington Monthly* review": Mark Schmitt, "Backseat Strategists," *Washington Monthly*, April 2006. Review of Carville and Begala, *Take It Back*; Steve Jarding, and Dave "Mudcat" Saunders, *Foxes in the Henhouse* (Touchstone, 2006); David Sirota, *Hostile Takeover* (Crown, 2006); and Jerome Armstrong and Markos Moulitsas Zuniga, *Crashing the Gate* (Chelsea Green, 2006).

203 "in his 1992 book *Speaking American*": David Kusnet, *Speaking American: How the Democrats Can Win in the Nineties* (Thunder's Mouth Press, 1992). Kusnet distills and updates many of the points made in the book in his article, "Teaching Progressives to Speak American," in Matthew R. Kerbel, ed., *Get This Party Started* (Rowman and Littlefield, 2006), pp. 129–140.

204 "Mario Cuomo defended his own opposition": *Primetime Live*, ABC News, September 26, 1991.

205 "But like values, passion can only be conveyed, not asserted": Dukakis gave an almost equally damaging answer when he was asked in another debate if he was passionless or technocratic. He answered in part, "I'm somebody who believes deeply in genuine opportunity for every single citizen in this country and that's the kind of passion I brought to my state." It's hard to imagine that Clinton or Cuomo would have begun their answer to that question with "I'm someone who believes deeply," which gives the whole report a dispassionate third-person tone.

206 "In a famous study of working-class white Michigan voters": Quoted in Thomas Byrne Edsall with Mary D. Edsall, "Race," *Atlantic Monthly*, May 1991.

207 "But none of these figures, not even Stewart": As of fall 2005, the leading liberal talk-show hosts Al Franken, Alan Colmes, and Ed Schulz all had "cumes" (average cumulative weekly audiences) of between one and two million listeners, against over fourteen million for Limbaugh, twelve million for Sean Hannity, eight million for Michael Savage, and five million

for Laura Ingraham. Other conservative radio talkers like Bill O'Reilly, Bill Bennett, Neal Boortz, and Glenn Beck fall in the two- to four-million range ("Latest Top Host Figures," *Talkers Magazine,* October 2005). The ratings of *The Daily Show* do sometimes approach those of Fox News, but Olbermann has only a fraction of the ratings of O'Reilly.

Note on Word Counts

209 "When a columnist writes": James Pinkerton, "In its Darkness, 'Kong' Shows the Human Heart," *Newsday,* December 15, 2005.

209 "There are work-arounds for some of these problems": These issues have been discussed at length on some of the linguistics blogs. See, for example, Mark Liberman's Language Log posts "Googlinguistics: The Good, the Bad, and the Ugly," "Web Search Counts: Half Empty or Half Full of _____?" "More Arithmetic Problems at Google," and my post "When Things Don't Add Up," all of which can be found by doing a search at languagelog.com, as well as Jean Véronis's post "Google Counts Faked" and the other items it links to, at the Technologies du Langage blog, http://www.aixtal.blogspot.com/2005/01/web-googles-counts-faked.html.

Index

patriotism and (*see* patriotism)

political language, impact on, 17–18

race and civil rights, appropriation of the language of, 153–157

See also Republicans/Republican Party

consumption/consumerism the red-blue divide and, 79–80

as source for branding of liberals by conservatives, 66–71

as source for social vocabulary, 65–66

Contract with America, 11, 124–125

Cooper, Marc, 13

Cornyn, John, 193, 207

corporations
business elite, media usage of the term, 32

conservative attacks on efforts to achieve workplace diversity by, 159–160

"freedom of choice" as tool for objecting to government regulation of, 137–139

freedom reinterpreted to mean freedom from government regulation of, 133–136

public belief that government must regulate, 147

Republican efforts to restrict the role of government as buffer between ordinary people and, 129–130

Costco, 139

Coulter, Ann, 42, 81, 83, 96, 193

culture/culture wars
from battles over culture to red and blue states, 73–74

conservative claims regarding, 74–80

conservative populism based on an appeal to traditional, 49–51

conservatives and the common man regarding, 80–83

consumption patterns overriding red-blue divides, 79–80

division regarding, evidence showing lack of, 75–76

Cuomo, Mario, 102, 204–205

Daily Show, The, 175n

Daley, Arthur, 154

Davis, Gray, 45

Dealey, Sam, 135

Dean, Howard, 42, 67, 192

death tax, 9n, 10–11, 33

Defense, Department of, Total Information Awareness project, 22

Democratic Leadership Council, 44–45

Democrats/Democratic Party
big government, countering the charge of, 125–128

the liberal label and (*see* liberal label)

linguistic/messaging problems of, 1–5, 7–8

prescriptions for (*see* prescriptions for Democrats)

reframing the issues, argument supporting, 8–12

reframing the issues, skepticism regarding usefulness of, 12–14

religion friendliness of, 161, 164–167

religious discrimination by, conservative charge of, 159 (*see also* religion)

Republican references to as "Democrat Party," 31–32

sex lives of, 96–97

slogan for the 2006 midterm elections, 1–2

small government, embracing the rhetoric of, 125–127

values, attempts to recapture, 108–113

voter association with on selected issues, 43

voter belief in government as requirement for programs of, 122

voters' perceptions of, 112

See also liberals/liberalism

Derbyshire, John, 173

Dewey, John, 1, 3, 38

Dionne, E. J., 7, 125–126, 147–148

Discovery Channel, 75

Disraeli, Benjamin, 74–75

diversity, 157

Donaldson, Sam, 204–205

Donne, John, 128

Dorgan, Byron, 2

Dowd, Matthew, 74

Dowd, Maureen, 67

Dreher, Rod, 71, 188

Drucker, Peter, 119, 125

D'Souza, Dinesh, 155

Dukakis, Michael, 42, 46, 90, 204–205

economic freedom
indexes of, 133

media usage of the term, 33

revision of meaning in public discourse, 132–133

Roosevelt's sense of, 132

Roosevelt's sense of, need to reclaim, 148–149

economic policy
culture and values issues as undermining the political importance of, 59–61

Republican language regarding, 54–58

Republican selling of, 51–54

See also class, socioeconomic

Edwards, John, 36, 118, 148

egghead, 64

Eisenhower, Dwight, 124, 129
conservative reinterpretation of, 85–89

media adoption of conservative conception of, 32, 86, 89

Index

Index

Index

Index

PublicAffairs is a publishing house founded in 1997. It is a tribute to the standards, values, and flair of three persons who have served as mentors to countless reporters, writers, editors, and book people of all kinds, including me.

I.F. STONE, proprietor of *I. F. Stone's Weekly*, combined a commitment to the First Amendment with entrepreneurial zeal and reporting skill and became one of the great independent journalists in American history. At the age of eighty, Izzy published *The Trial of Socrates*, which was a national bestseller. He wrote the book after he taught himself ancient Greek.

BENJAMIN C. BRADLEE was for nearly thirty years the charismatic editorial leader of *The Washington Post*. It was Ben who gave the *Post* the range and courage to pursue such historic issues as Watergate. He supported his reporters with a tenacity that made them fearless and it is no accident that so many became authors of influential, best-selling books.

ROBERT L. BERNSTEIN, the chief executive of Random House for more than a quarter century, guided one of the nation's premier publishing houses. Bob was personally responsible for many books of political dissent and argument that challenged tyranny around the globe. He is also the founder and longtime chair of Human Rights Watch, one of the most respected human rights organizations in the world.

For fifty years, the banner of Public Affairs Press was carried by its owner Morris B. Schnapper, who published Gandhi, Nasser, Toynbee, Truman, and about 1,500 other authors. In 1983, Schnapper was described by *The Washington Post* as "a redoubtable gadfly." His legacy will endure in the books to come.

Peter Osnos, *Founder and Editor-at-Large*